Celtic's paranoia . . . all in the mind?

Celtic's paranoia . . . all in the mind?

TOM CAMPBELL

Paranoid? Us? Happy Celtic supporters in the 1950s

FORT PUBLISHING

First published in 2001 by Fort Publishing Ltd, Ayr, KA7 2RW.

Copyright © Tom Campbell, 2001.

Cover design by David Gilchrist.

Photograph on back cover, courtesy of Mirror Syndication International.

Contact from copyright owners welcomed.

Typeset in Times by S. Fairgrieve

Printed in Great Britain by Bell and Bain Ltd., Glasgow

ISBN 0-9536576-3-9

A catalogue record for this book is available from the British Library.

Contents

Paranoia: 'a mental condition characterised by delusions of persecution, unwarranted jealousy, or exaggerated self-importance, typically worked into an organised system. It may be an aspect of chronic personality disorder, of drug abuse, or of a serious condition such as schizophrenia in which the person loses touch with reality. Suspicion and mistrust of people or their actions without evidence or justification.'

The New Oxford Dictionary of English, 1998

'I was told when I joined this club about Celtic's paranoia – now I know it's true. We are hard done by religiously and politically. There are people against us ... I meet people who hate me just because I am the manager of Celtic.'

Liam Brady.

'One thinks of the mass paranoia exhibited by thousands of Rangers supporters singing in unison, "Everybody hates us, and we don't care." This, of course, is not true paranoia in the medical sense, since the essence of the illness is that the fear of persecution is unfounded while, as we all know, in reality everybody does hate Rangers.'

The Absolute Game, April 1991.

They said it ...

'I thought the SFA was like that from the age of four, because my gran told me.'

Peter Grant

'There is surely something uniquely deluded about a persecution complex suffered by supporters of a club whose silverware haul is among the biggest in the world history of the game.'

The Absolute Game

'There are certain clubs in this country who, in order to deflect talk of their own inadequate performances, blether on about supposedly 'poor' refereeing. It is drivel.'

Jim Farry

'Referee, your father would have been proud of you today.' At any rate, there was no way I could report Stein for telling me that my father, highly respected by the SFA, would have been proud of my performance.'

David Syme, *referee*

'It makes me laugh when the Old Firm argue over which gets the worse from refs when they meet. Who gives a toss? It's only four games a season. They get everything else that's going the rest of the time.'

Bill Leckie, *author and journalist*

'I am unaware of any top class referee who has been involved in refereeing games between Rangers and Celtic who is also a member of our institution. It has become trendy to describe referees as "masons in black", but there is unfortunately a degree of paranoia attached to these statements. Celtic fans will have to look for another excuse.'

Jack Ramsay,
Secretary of the Grand Orange Lodge of Scotland

'I consider myself one of the best administrators in Europe, but there has been criticism directed towards me which has abused the platform that journalists have for comment.'

Jim Farry

'I read the newspapers avidly. It is my one form of continuous fiction.'

Aneurin Bevan,
a Labour Cabinet Minister in the post-war Attlee government

'Just because you live by the sea doesn't mean you can swim.'

Kenny Dalglish,
writing about journalists in his autobiography

'High intelligence and football fanaticism seldom go together.'

Hugh Macdiarmid,
the Scottish poet, on the eve of the 1978 World Cup in Argentina

Introduction

For obvious reasons this book has been difficult to write. I have no doubt that some critics will dismiss the findings as the product of a paranoid mind, or that others will feel that I have not gone far enough in exposing the 'injustices' heaped upon Celtic. However, I felt that the book was worth doing, if only to clear up my own thinking on the subject by re-examining an issue that will simply not go away. Accordingly, this book will concentrate on the more celebrated examples of 'conspiracy' usually cited by Celtic partisans, and will attempt to evaluate each of the issues objectively.

In order to save time and effort on the part of those readers (or critics) who think it important, I should state right at the outset my own background and personal views on the topic.

I am a Celtic supporter, and have been for almost sixty years despite a career in teaching in Canada.

I am disappointed when Celtic lose, but I do not automatically blame the referee for the defeat, nor do I assume that the other side tried harder because they were playing against Celtic.

I have always been able to recognise good football, no matter who played it. I have derived genuine pleasure from watching such splendid sides as Hibernian between 1947 and 1953, and Hearts between 1955 and 1960. I have been able to admire some Rangers sides such as the one fielded between 1960 and 1963, and their recent teams. Similarly I have been impressed with the Aberdeen side coached by Alex Ferguson in the 1980s. I have enjoyed the occasional exploits in the championship of such as Dundee in 1962 and Dundee United in 1983, and of Clyde in the Scottish Cups of 1955 and 1958.

I have also enjoyed and admired genuine footballers no matter the team they played for, especially when their skills have been enhanced by exemplary sportsmanship – players such as George Young (Rangers), Willie McNaught (Raith Rovers), Willie Fernie (Celtic), Harry Haddock (Clyde), Jimmy McGowan (Partick Thistle), Gordon Smith (Hibernian), Willie Bauld (Hearts) and others. And, of course, many modern-day players.

I was born in Scotland, and consider myself Scottish; however, I am aware in a general sense that one of my grandparents (who died before I was born) came to this country from Ireland.

In human terms I deplore the situation in Northern Ireland, and would hope that some equitable solution might be forthcoming for both sides of the religious divide in that unhappy province, and I do not care who claims the credit for it. As a historian, I feel that the Irish in Scotland have had to endure difficult times and much discrimination, and I deplore that. However, I feel that such discrimination has been on the wane for decades and can no longer be used validly as an excuse to explain away failure in life or in football.

I cannot approve of the proliferation of Irish flags and emblems at Celtic Park on match days; as a supporter who travels often to away fixtures, I find myself cringing with embarrassment at the defiant and tuneless chanting of Irish and IRA anthems. I would never deny the club's proud Irish (and Catholic) traditions but I feel that excessive public manifestations (or largely drunken posturings) do not serve any useful purpose and, in fact, are counterproductive.

I am moved, on the other hand, by such anthems as *The Fields of Athenry* and *You'll Never Walk Alone*, but I cannot feel too much empathy for other more partisan Irish songs or chants.

Finally, I do not believe that any conspiracy exists to deny Celtic Football Club natural justice but I have become convinced that, over a period of time, Celtic have been dealt more than their share of harsh decisions on and off the field.

Accordingly, I feel that a realistic look at the background and consequences of some of those decisions is a worthwhile topic for research. Whether that share of unfortunate decisions is a flukish statistical blip or the result of bias or prejudice will be left for the reader to judge, but the events will be examined in detail throughout this book.

As Fate would have it, I started the actual writing of this book on 1 May 1999. The next day Rangers won the Old Firm match at Celtic Park by 3-0 to record their hundredth league victory over Celtic and to regain the championship from Celtic on the ground of their rivals.

The fixture was marred by disgraceful scenes: three players were dismissed by the referee, another eight were booked. The referee, Hugh Dallas (Motherwell) was struck by a missile, probably a coin and one of several thrown from the Jock Stein Stand by Celtic supporters incensed at some of his decisions. Mr. Dallas, as the photograph on the back cover shows, was left bleeding from a head wound and needed immediate first aid from the trainers on the pitch before continuing. He also required stitches administered by Celtic's doctor at the halftime interval.

During the commotion and the hubbub, three or four Celtic supporters attempted to storm the pitch in individual sorties, presumably to attack the referee. Fortunately, they were stopped short of their intended victim by Celtic players and, belatedly, by police and stewards.

At the end of the match, Rangers players, *en masse* and joined by their manager and coaching staff, rushed to celebrate the victory in front of their supporters – despite the stated instructions of the authorities, acting on advice from the police, that both sets of players should leave the pitch immediately at the final whistle. When the new champions did eventually leave the field, they were roundly abused by Celtic supporters some of whom spat at them and threw more missiles. The troubles did not end there: several arrests were made in the environs of Celtic Park, and at various locations throughout the city.

It was a bad day for Scottish football and for Celtic.

As I made my way home, still thinking about the match, I realised that this particular encounter would inevitably be finding its way already into the supporters' long litany of wrongs done to Celtic Football Club by referees.

My own view is quite clear: at the time, caught up in the vitriolic atmosphere at Celtic Park, I thought that the referee had a deplorable match, and that most of the key decisions had gone against Celtic. I could never condone the actions of those who had thrown missiles at him, nor those who had invaded the pitch; I was disappointed in the hysterical reactions of those Celtic players who had lost control of themselves at various points in the contest. I have seen Mr. Dallas have his off-days, but have never thought for a moment that he is a biased official, one of that select group known collectively by some Celtic followers as 'the Masons in the Black'.

However, later on, I sat down with a cup of tea and a sandwich alone in the living room and watched the recording of the match from start to finish.

What I saw made me think a bit more carefully. I saw the same match, but now from an entirely different perspective, and the events of that turbulent first half disturbed me most. I remembered having leapt to my feet in rage at several decisions which had gone Rangers' way, but what I saw on the screen convinced me that the referee had been right in **most** instances.

However, I still remain convinced that Mr. Dallas had a poor match, primarily because his handling of the players on such a fraught occasion was questionable. In the two vital instances – the ordering-off of Stephane Mahe and the later award to Rangers of a penalty kick – I felt that he was harsh to the home side and that his decisions were hasty and bordering on the vindictive.

The correctness or otherwise of the referee's decisions on this occasion would not have affected the destination of the championship trophy nor probably the outcome of this particular match. Rangers – already ahead from the fifteenth minute with a splendidly worked goal – were by far the better side, were completely in control of their emotions and were never in any danger of losing to an injury-struck Celtic side. They deserved to have won by more than their convincing three-goal margin.

The most unfortunate thing was that it provided those Celtic supporters who harbour grave suspicions about the impartiality of Scottish referees with yet more ammunition to produce as 'evidence'.

The disgraceful scenes and the controversy that arose after the completion of the fixture brought a medical-scientific word into frequent play – paranoia. It seems to be the only word from psychology in usage among football fans and writers, and this word is applied almost exclusively to followers of Celtic Football Club.

Perhaps it would be appropriate to define the word, once and for all:

> **Paranoia:** *a mental condition characterised by delusions of persecution, unwarranted jealousy, or exaggerated self-importance, typically worked into an organised system. It may be an aspect of chronic personality disorder, of drug abuse, or of a serious condition such as schizophrenia in which the person loses touch with reality. Suspicion and mistrust of people or their actions without evidence or justification. (The New Oxford Dictionary of English, 1998)*

And, as the definition introduces another psychological word and concept, let us define that:

> **Schizophrenia:** *a long-term mental disorder of a type involving a breakdown in the relation between thought, emotion, and behaviour, leading to faulty perception, inappropriate actions and feelings, withdrawal from reality and personal relationships into fantasy and delusion, and a sense of mental fragmentation. (In general use) a mentality or approach characterised by inconsistent or contradictory elements. (ibid)*

It might be facetious to point out that these definitions include aspects of behaviour common to all football fans in Scotland, and probably those in other countries. Personal observation has borne this out.

I travel to most Celtic matches on a Supporters' Bus, and frequently tickets are at a premium; accordingly, very often, along with a friend I am given tickets for the Main Stand, largely populated by supporters of the home team. The tacit understanding is that we take our places in that area, and try to avoid being mistaken for Celtic followers. Otherwise, we would be ejected from the ground regardless of our behaviour. When I returned from Canada on a permanent basis in 1990, I thought at first this threat was some sort of practical joke, but experience has taught me otherwise. I have seen some supporters of the home side anxiously scanning the places around them for 'strangers', and have seen them spend time and energy trying to 'shop' any outsiders to stewards or police instead of watching and enjoying a game of football.

What possible value can be attached to removing some isolated spectators from a football match for which they have paid, to which they have travelled some distance, and which they hope to enjoy in relative quiet? I would have to say that there are some notable exceptions to this type of xenophobia and, in particular, I would commend the supporters of Dunfermline, Raith Rovers and, to a slightly lesser extent, those of St. Johnstone, Dundee United and Aberdeen.

My normal custom is to dress in a neutral manner, and frequently a jacket and tie helps disguise us as visitors. If the home team scores, we rise – along with the surrounding supporters – and pretend to be happy; if Celtic score, we shake our heads in a display of restrained grief. I would say that our behaviour is beyond reproach, and that we have never been in any real danger of being ejected from any ground, but it is certainly not natural behaviour for followers of one team attending a sporting event. It is also pleasing to note that frequently after the match in talking with the fans in the adjoining seats in some grounds, we were immediately recognised as Celtic supporters – and that our neighbours had not been unduly worried about that fact.

However, such enforced objectivity does offer an opportunity to study the local supporters, and I would contend that most fans are paranoid for at least the ninety minutes' duration of a football match, one more reminder that the word 'fan' is derived from fanatic.

Yet, paranoia is a term almost exclusively used to define Celtic supporters. It is a term of abuse which immediately hijacks the question under discussion – whether it be the impartiality of referees, the short-sightedness of the game's administrators, or the bias of the media.

Those critics anxious to illustrate the extent of the 'paranoia' exhibited by Celtic followers inevitably point to the time when the Celtic Supporters' Association hired a private detective to investigate the background of a prominent Scottish referee. The truth is simpler – and much less sensational.

On 30 October 1990, only two days after he had refereed the Skol Cup final between Celtic and Rangers, a relatively controversy-free contest won 2–1 by Rangers in extra-time, Jim McCluskey of Stewarton was fined £25. The offence was for 'being drunk and incapable' although he claimed in his defence: 'I had been out for a night [attending a "stag" for a friend's son] with other referee friends and fell asleep waiting for a taxi. It could happen to anyone.'

The story was reported in the tabloid press, and the *Daily Record* included the 'information' that the Celtic Supporters' Association had hired a detective to investigate Mr. McCluskey's background and the incident in question. Officials of the Supporters' Association had been tipped off at the time – the previous July – that McCluskey had been arrested for 'singing sectarian songs while drunk'. Rightly concerned that, given his status as a highly rated Class 1 referee, McCluskey would almost certainly be assigned his share of future Old Firm encounters, the organisation decided to check the story.

According to Francie Hinton, the association's vice-president at the time and who remains irritated by the frequency with which this urban myth crops up, the Celtic Supporters' Association phoned an Ayrshire police station to verify the details. He denies categorically that the association hired a detective to investigate matters, but he recalls several phone calls being made to contacts in Ayrshire. When the 'story' broke in the newspapers months later, first in the *Daily Record*, the Celtic Supporters' Association should have sued for libel, he felt, but he recalls that other committee members felt more inclined to ignore it. However, the myth refuses to go away and stokes the fires of 'Celtic paranoia'.[1]

A statement from the Supporters' Association, published in *The Celtic View* within a week of the controversy backs up Hinton's claim:

> It is not the policy of the Association to investigate officials of any kind, but on receipt of many complaints from Ayrshire and indeed some press snooping concerning allegations about Mr. McCluskey, it was felt that, because of the seriousness of the allegations, an investigation should be carried out. The findings of the investigation were that the serious allegations were unfounded, and the matter was closed. If any mischief was intended, it would have been easy to do so prior to the game. At no time did the Celtic Supporters' Association approach the media on this matter and we feel we acted in a very responsible manner at all times. If the allegations had been true, the Scottish Football League would have been informed and the matter ended as far as the Celtic Supporters' Association was concerned. (11 November 1990)

In a similar way, many Celtic supporters frequently resurrect stories of 'injustice' and with time and repetition these retain a life of their own. I know one Celtic supporter who assures me and everybody else that 'Celtic were forced by the SFA to play two matches on the same day, and they did that and won both, and won the league anyway despite that!'

Once more, there is an element of truth in the story. At the end of the 1915/16 season Celtic – and other clubs – faced a congestion of fixtures so that the campaign could be concluded by 30 April, the traditional end of the season.[2] Celtic were due to face Raith Rovers at Parkhead on 15 April, and also agreed to play Motherwell at Fir Park in the evening; they defeated Raith Rovers by 6–0, travelled through to Motherwell and won there by 3–1, and Celtic did win the league very comfortably.

However, Celtic were not alone in playing two matches on that same day as Motherwell, for example, also completed a fixture at home in the afternoon, losing 3–0 to Ayr United. Celtic's manager Willie Maley was so insistent on playing both matches that he actually contributed £10 to the gate for the Motherwell–Ayr United fixture so that those clubs would not lose money. Because Motherwell had offered them only the bare guarantee from a league fixture, apparently, the Ayrshire side were reluctant to sanction the evening match.

And yet one Celtic supporter complains to this day about those two fixtures, no doubt seeing it as an attempt by the authorities to make life more difficult for his team.

---

[1] Mr. McCluskey also felt aggrieved at the newspaper's coverage of the incident and, encouraged by legal advice that he had a strong case, seriously considered suing the tabloid but decided against it reluctantly.

[2] The country was fighting in the First World War at this time, and midweek football had been ruled out as the result of an agreement with the War Office on the grounds that it might interfere with overtime at factories engaged in essential war work.

This book is a more honest attempt to examine the causes of this so-called paranoia in an objective manner, to see if there is any justification for the Celtic fans' persistent feeling that they, their team, and their club have been ill-treated down the years by the football establishment.

In discussing the controversial incidents covered in this book I would suggest that one issue be considered in each and every case.

Was the treatment accorded to Celtic similar to that received by all other clubs in Scotland?

Let me explain the methodology used in researching this work. It was important to be consistent in the approach used throughout and, accordingly, I determined to rely principally on four newspapers. This, I felt, would provide a reasonably diversified account of the events, and I should stress that this decision was made prior to starting the book. The newspapers chosen were the *Glasgow Herald* (renamed *The Herald* in 1992), *The Scotsman*, the *Scottish Daily Express*, and the *Daily Record*.

I felt it necessary to quote from these newspapers in order to give the flavour of the times and to be accurate. Sometimes, it was preferable to change the order of sentences in an extended quotation but I was most careful not to distort the sense of the reporting. The quotations remain true to the spirit in which the match reports and other accounts were written.

It was essential to quote extensively in order to provide 'evidence' of the point under discussion, but I was aware that citing four newspapers on the same issue would lead to a certain amount of repetition. Because part of the overall thesis of the book is the role played by the media in depicting Celtic Football Club, this overkill appears inevitable. Sometimes, excerpts from other newspapers – most notably the *Glasgow Observer*, the *Evening Times* (Glasgow) and the *Sunday Mail* – were used to illustrate particular points.

I interviewed directors, managers, players, journalists, referees and officials in the writing of this book but, because of the sensitivity of some of the issues raised, I decided not to include their names in a list of acknowledgements as is customary. Their contribution to the authenticity of this book is invaluable and much appreciated by the author. When I have used direct quotations from persons connected with football, those statements were already in the public domain and a matter of record. In writing previous books, I had also had contact with many other football men, and I referred to my notes to verify my personal recollections.

CHAPTER ONE

Days of Infamy

Within a period of ten years – between September 1941 and January 1952 – Celtic Football Club was forced to endure the following indignities: the closure of their ground for a month with the subsequent loss of revenue; several instructions to post notices warning supporters of their conduct; warnings about possible future closing of Celtic Park; harsh suspensions and censuring of prominent players; and, ultimately, a serious threat to the very existence of the club through expulsion by the ruling body in Scottish football.

No other club in Scottish football has been so consistently badly treated over such an extended period of time.

It has become a journalistic cliché to label the Parkhead club's frequent distrust and suspicions about the motives of the authorities as paranoia. Given the accumulation of injustices suffered by Celtic throughout this relatively short period of time, it is not surprising that directors and most managers, players and supporters should feel aggrieved. One former director smiled when I told him about the subject of this book and made the jocular comment: 'Just because you're paranoid, doesn't mean that they're not out to get you.'

Celtic have always been identified as a 'community club', representing the hopes and aspirations of a community, described generally – if somewhat mistakenly – as an Irish-Catholic enclave in Scotland. More than most followers of football, their supporters have been passionately involved in Celtic Football Club, rejoicing in its triumphs and despairing in its setbacks but never indifferent to its fate. Celtic supporters have long memories and, in many traditional Celtic families, this folk-memory is passed down from generation to generation. Thus, any insult, injury, or hint of injustice is remembered, often to an unhealthy extent.

My own daughter, on a visit from Canada and attending her first-ever football match in 1998, was astounded to hear the other four Celtic supporters at the table reel off without any hesitation or prompting the names of the side that won the Empire Exhibition Trophy in 1938 – a mere sixty years after the event. Other clubs may have their passionate followers also, but the sense of tradition among Celtic men is almost palpable; it is perhaps significant that one of the lines in the official Celtic Song should read as follows: 'And, if you know their history.'

Where does one start?

My original intention was to begin almost immediately after World War

II and to proceed chronologically from there. The reasoning was simple: most serious historians of the game agree that, if Celtic do have a case to make about ill-treatment, that period would provide the best source of evidence for a series of 'injustices' both on and off the field. The sense of grievance that habitually distorts the reasoning of present-day Celtic followers stems from that period, consciously or not.[3]

However, a Rangers vs. Celtic league match, played at Ibrox Park on 6 September 1941 and won 3–0 by the home side, might be considered the real starting-point of much of Celtic's subsequent *angst*. The controversy included all the basic ingredients for Celtic's so-called paranoia: poor refereeing, injured Celtic players, trouble on the terracing, a typically heavy-handed reaction from the SFA, and a sense of helpless outrage from Celtic sympathisers.

Let us try to look at this game from a more objective perspective.

It was a wartime game, played under the auspices of the Scottish Southern League and, therefore, 'an unofficial match'. In the early stages of the war, because of the valid fear of German air raids on Britain, attendances at football matches were restricted drastically but this measure was gradually being relaxed. In fact, a relatively large crowd of some 50,000 attended this particular fixture.

An hour or so before the kick-off Celtic were informed by the Scottish League secretary, Willie McAndrew, that a problem existed about the eligibility of Willie Fagan. The inside forward, a pre-war Celt, was registered with Liverpool but had turned up in Glasgow unexpectedly and was available to play for Celtic. Mr. McAndrew indicated, however, that if he were fielded in the Old Firm match he might not be eligible to turn out for Liverpool during the remainder of the season. The Celtic directors were perturbed about this opinion and the lateness of it, but they decided that Fagan should not be risked under the circumstances.

In fairness to the League authorities, the organisation of wartime football was still chaotic and the question of eligibility had not yet been fully addressed. The only newspaper to suggest anything sinister in this development was the Catholic weekly, the *Glasgow Observer*: 'First sensation at Ibrox was the news that Willie Fagan, old Celtic favourite now with Liverpool, would not appear in the forward line. Seems that the ordinary wartime regulations regarding players from English clubs do not apply when said player wishes to play for Celtic! Some enlightenment is required here!' (12 September 1941).

The fixed odds betting reflected the reality of wartime football: Rangers were favourites at 4–6 on, in contrast to the odds of 3–1 against Celtic. It was

---

[3] I am very much aware that many 'Celtic-minded people' consider that the club has been victimised since its inception in 1887.

no surprise as Rangers were by far the dominant side in Scottish football during the war; Celtic virtually operated as a part-time outfit, much to the chagrin of their supporters. The first-half play in this particular match suggested that the bookmakers had calculated things exactly right: Rangers led by 2–0 through goals by Beattie and Gillick, although Celtic were playing with some spirit and threatening frequently.

The *Glasgow Observer*, that most partisan of newspapers in a football sense, stated that Celtic had been badly treated in that first half and blamed it on questionable decisions by the referee (W. Webb, Glasgow). The newspaper complained that Rangers' opening goal by Beattie from a through pass by Adam Little in fourteen minutes was scored from an offside position, as both the scorer and Jimmy Smith looked suspiciously in the clear but no flag was raised. Shortly afterwards, Dawson, Rangers' goalkeeper, appeared to carry the ball over the line in attempting to deal with a fierce shot from Crum, an incident which happened at the Celtic end of the ground and which infuriated the nearest spectators.

The match finally erupted with a goalmouth incident at the Celtic end of the ground only three minutes before the interval: Jimmy Delaney, a constant threat to the Ibrox defence with his pace and opportunism, was fouled in the penalty area and injured. The referee immediately awarded a penalty kick, and it seemed the only decision possible but he was immediately surrounded by Rangers players protesting against the award and at times the official was jostled by the players. All the while Delaney was being treated by the trainer, and eventually removed from the pitch to behind the goal; the Celtic fans were in a fury.

Jimmy Delaney, Celtic idol of the 1940s. His injury during an Old Firm match in 1941 sparked a riot.

It would be impossible to assess the worth of Jimmy Delaney to Celtic throughout those difficult seasons, as he was a genuinely inspirational figure – a never-say-die performer and a player of both skill and courage. Delaney was a talisman, but his career had already been put into serious jeopardy for more than two years because of a broken arm. The sight of Delaney being borne from the pitch was a cause for anxiety and anger for the thousands behind the goal, as was the spectacle of the referee being badgered and man-handled by the Rangers players.

Delaney's previous injury had occurred in a home fixture against Arbroath in April 1939, when both major bones in his left arm were badly broken. The surgeon at the Victoria Infirmary, a Mr. Beattie, felt initially that the best course would be to amputate the arm but was persuaded to attempt an operation only because Delaney was an athlete. Delaney's recuperation period was long and agonising and, in fact, he had returned to the Celtic line-up to a rapturous welcome on 2 August 1941, only a month before the match at Ibrox Park.

When the penalty kick was eventually taken, it was not too surprising that Murphy's shot was saved by Dawson, the Rangers keeper who had been very much involved in the incident with Delaney.

The tensions erupted into rage at that moment; a sizeable contingent of Celtic supporters disrupted the match by throwing 'beer bottles, milk bottles and other missiles in the direction of the pitch' although there was little chance of the players being struck or injured because the Ibrox Stadium of 1941 was a vastly different ground from the present-day one. There was only one massive stand, which seated about 10,500 people, and so the remaining 40,000 at the match that day stood on the terracing or in the enclosures. Round the pitch was a full-scale running track, used at athletic events such as the annual Rangers Sports, while between the track and the goal lay a crescent-shaped piece of ground, some twenty-five yards wide at its centre.

Thus, there was little possibility of any missile hurled from the terracing ever reaching the playing field and injuring players or officials. Any victims of the bottle throwing would be fellow-supporters at the front of the terracing. The outbreak, while serious, was a symbol of frustration rather than malice.

The *Evening Times* in its match-day report described it thus: 'A shower of bottles descended on the track, and fights broke out ... the empty bottles fell on the track and on the turf behind Rangers' goal. Fights broke out on the ter-racing and, when the police concentrated on the spot, they were met by a shower of bottles. Several men were led away by the police only after batons had been used and a soldier was removed on a stretcher.'

However, it was a tense minute or two before contingents of the Glasgow police were able to restore some semblance of order to the terracing. The atmosphere remained volatile throughout the interval, and a police officer who had ventured among the visiting support, apparently to ask for the removal of a flag or banner, had his helmet knocked off before 'the crowd scattered in all directions' (*Evening Times*, 6 September 1941). At one stage in the disturbances a squad of mounted police appeared at the exit ramp between the main stand and the Celtic end of the ground, ready to be called into action.

Although no further outbreaks of violence took place on the terracing during the second half, the controversy was far from over. Celtic resumed the attack and pressed Rangers into defence: 'Divers headed into goal following a corner by Murphy. Delaney rushed to connect and Dawson dived at his feet. This time Delaney was carried off on a stretcher, but still no penalty' (*Glasgow Observer*, 12 September 1941).

The Celtic fans were incensed at the treatment meted out to their idol. The nearest modern-day comparison in public adulation would be to Henrik Larsson. Consider this hypothetical scenario in which Larsson returns to first-team duty at Celtic Park after recovering from his leg-break, and imagine the feelings roused if he were to be fouled repeatedly in an Old Firm match, and finally badly enough to be removed from the pitch for prolonged treatment.

By then the tensions on the terracing had transferred to the playing surface: 'When the rioting on the terracing stopped, some of the players began to introduce something of a similar nature on the field and the second half was completely spoiled by indulgence in shady stuff. For twelve minutes Celtic were without Delaney and Crum who were both carried off on stretchers to shrieks of delight from the hooligan element on the East terracing' (*Daily Record*, 8 September 1941).

Again the *Glasgow Observer* was more specific: 'Crum went to centre (to replace Delaney) to be badly fouled by Woodburn and he too was carried off on a stretcher. Woodburn was not even booked' (12 September 1941).

The reporter for the *Glasgow Observer* expressed disgust at the proceedings:

> To tell the truth I stopped taking notes after ten minutes of the second half had been played, I was so nauseated at witnessing the most disgusting scenes it has ever been my misfortune to witness on a football field. Remember the principle of cause-and-effect? I hold no briefs for hooliganism ... but Delaney did finish up behind the goalpost injured, a fact which should, in my opinion, have weighed much more heavily in the decision of the responsible official. So many fouls were committed against Delaney in the opening minutes that one could be pardoned for thinking that Jimmy had been labelled 'Dangerous – must be stopped at all costs!' (12 September 1941)

Fortunately, Delaney managed to resume after twelve minutes' absence although limping noticeably and, in fact, was able to recover enough to turn out for Celtic the following Saturday; Crum, on the other hand, was forced to miss several subsequent matches through 'bruising to the kidney area'.

The newspapers immediately dubbed the match as 'a bottle party' and Sir Patrick Dollan, Glasgow's Lord Provost, raised the possibility that 'Old Firm matches could well be prohibited until the end of the War. The Chief Constable has such power and, if he cares to exercise such power, he will have the support of all citizens.'

A report on the trouble at the match was given to Tom Johnston, the Secretary of State for Scotland, who was expected to consult Mr. Herbert Morrison, the Minister of Home Security. However, the key man was the Chief Constable of Glasgow, the martinet-like figure of Percy Sillitoe, whose recommendations were most likely to be followed, given that he had the support of the Regional Commissioner for Scotland, Lord Rosebery. Sillitoe, of course, had gained his reputation as the man who had done much to eliminate Glasgow's infamous image as portrayed in the sensationalist and sordid novel, *No Mean City*. In the 1930s he had threatened to end Old Firm matches unless behaviour improved drastically, and he was viewed as an authoritarian figure who might well impose draconian measures in the cause of public order.

The *Daily Record* led the way in calling for the SFA to act: 'And what of the ruling body of Scottish football? Will the SFA lie back in undignified silence or will they step in and take action? Surely they will not have it said, as has been said in the past, "If it had been wee clubs, there would be a lot of aftermath but it's Rangers and Celtic and so nothing will be done?" Grounds have been closed for a lot less than happened at Ibrox' (8 September 1941).

The newspaper indicated some of the possible outcomes and cited the Glasgow Police (Further Powers) Act, Section 9 which read as follows: 'The Magistrates Committee may from time to time make bye-laws and regulations for the safety and comfort of the public for maintaining order in theatres or other places of entertainment, and they may provide the bye-laws for the suppression of disorderly conduct.'

For football matches to be held and admission charged for entry a licence was required, which was granted on an annual basis. If the police authorities withheld the licence to a club for any reason, home fixtures could not be fulfilled, and the club would effectively be suspended. This was a serious matter as any club so punished would lose the revenues necessary to continue, and the league programme so affected would be thrown into disarray.

Another alternative would have been for the authorities – either civic or football – to order reductions in crowd size, as had already occurred in the early days of the war, or to make football fixtures all-ticket events. Had these latter measures been implemented as a universal policy, all the clubs in Scotland would have suffered as a consequence of the happenings at the Old Firm match at Ibrox.

Scottish football waited anxiously for the outcome.

If a ground were to be closed as a punishment, which one should it be? The current practice seemed to suggest that the home club was responsible for the conduct and behaviour of all spectators on its ground and, of course, was responsible for hiring sufficient policemen and ambulance men to deal with any situation. In most cases, this was a reasonable provision but Old Firm fixtures for decades were the only occasions on which a self-imposed segregation was undertaken by the spectators; thus, it was easier to identify the culprit following.

Undeniably, some Celtic supporters had misbehaved badly, but the trouble had occurred on Rangers' ground. Could the police effectively close down Celtic Park for events which happened at Ibrox? I put the question to a legal friend who volunteered this answer after some thought: 'Yes, probably – especially as it was in a war-time emergency situation, but it would have been unwise. I'll give you an analogy. Suppose a busload of people from Glasgow attend a pantomime in Edinburgh, and create a disturbance. Would the Glasgow police then be reasonable in closing down the theatres in Glasgow as a punishment?'

It would be relevant to cite the wording of the SFA Article of Association dealing with such a case: 'Each club in membership shall be responsible for the conduct of its spectators on any ground, and misbehaviour by spectators during or at close of matches shall render a member [club] liable to fine, or closure of ground, or suspension, or all of those penalties.'

The administrators were going to have to make a Solomon-like decision, and the pressure was on the football authorities to come up with an acceptable solution.

On 12 September the SFA War Emergency Committee met to discuss the matter, and announced its findings:

1. Celtic Park was to be closed for one month, until 17 October 1941, and Celtic were not allowed to play on opponents' grounds in Glasgow during that time;
2. warning bills, advising spectators of the effects of future misconduct, were to be posted at Celtic Park on or after 17 October;
3. the committee noted and deplored an increasing prevalence of dissent, and felt it was too much in evidence on the part of Rangers players. Accordingly, an instruction was to be issued to all clubs about dissent, referees were advised to take prompt action, and any referee not complying was to be removed from the list;
4. the Chief Constable of Glasgow was to be assisted in any action that he might choose to take in dealing with hooliganism;
5. the Magistrates were to be encouraged to impose harsher court penalties on those found guilty of hooliganism;
6. Celtic deserved some sympathy in having to deal with 'a section of supporters of an undesirable type'.

Colonel John Shaughnessy, a long-time Celtic director, commented on the committee's conclusions, especially on the closing of his club's ground: '... a very bad precedent because, up to the period of the throwing at the match, Celtic players did absolutely nothing to rile the crowd in any way. It is because of what the opposition did that we are hung up. That seems to be a very material factor. Nothing was done by our boys to give any excuse to the crowd to start bottle throwing.'

For the highly respected Celtic director to blame the rough tactics employed by Rangers and weak refereeing as the primary causes of the troubles may well have been accurate, but it is doubtful if those grounds were enough to excuse the outbreak of hooliganism and rioting perpetrated by Celtic fans, and Celtic could have expected punishment. Ironically, Celtic spokesmen had helped to frame the rule which held clubs responsible for the conduct of their supporters home or away. Tom White, Celtic's chairman, had presided over the Scottish League/SFA conference in 1922 set up to deal with concerns about the misconduct of spectators and Willie Maley, Celtic's manager, had been one of the Scottish League's delegates at the same conference.

This was not the first time Celtic Park had been closed by the football authorities: after a field invasion at Celtic Park in April 1920 had caused the abandonment of a league fixture against Dundee, the ground was ordered closed for a month as a punishment, and the result (1–1) allowed to stand as it did not affect any league positions.

However, several prominent public figures also came to Celtic's defence. Sir Patrick Dollan, Glasgow's outspoken Lord Provost, was also quoted in the *Glasgow Herald*, describing the verdict as:

> ... the most cock-eyed judgement I have ever read. I hope the government and the police who have the final say in this matter will correct a judgement which is more like Nazi philosophy than British fair play and see that both clubs are treated alike. Both clubs were responsible as, according to my information, most of the trouble was caused by players contravening the rules. The football authorities have always been lopsided in their judgements and I recommend the Scottish authorities to go to England and see how the Association and the League there manage football. Unless the Scottish authorities adopt a similar policy, and administer it without fear or favour, they will become the laughing-stock of the sporting world.

Astutely, as an elected politician, he added the following: 'My sympathies go out to Rangers and their followers. The Celtic have been made the martyrs. The sporting world may think that Rangers and their followers have been treated with favouritism but, knowing them, I believe this is the last thing they would wish' (18 September 1941).

Clearly, the Lord Provost – who might reasonably be assumed to have some awareness of local issues – was suggesting that there were factors present in the climate of the West of Scotland noticeably absent in England.

The *Glasgow Herald* devoted a rare editorial to commenting on the disgraceful scenes and their aftermath: 'The committee's decision may be thought of by some non-partisan lovers of the game to bear too heavily on one club, while the other suffers no penalty beyond its being named as numbering among its players some whose conduct was contrary to the best traditions of the game' (20 September 1941).

'Waverley' in the *Daily Record* also commented on the reputation for poor sportsmanship at Ibrox: '... the recommendation, especially where

Rangers players are concerned, that badgering of the referee is not to be tolerated. Many provincial clubs have been grumbling for long enough that whistlers generally are yes-men for the Light Blues. I have frequently wondered why referees stood as much questioning of decisions by Rangers players' (18 September 1941).

A week later, the same journalist – W.C. Gallagher, a highly respected and experienced commentator – would return to that theme, indicating disquiet within member clubs of the SFA: 'Clubs whose players are recognised as properly behaved strongly object to their players being classed with the Light Blues whose behaviour has brought an official rebuke.' He also had spoken recently to a referee who had had dealings with poorly disciplined players at Ibrox, and who was quoted as saying, 'On three occasions I have reported an internationalist for his behaviour. Nothing is done. What's the use of reporting them?' (26 September 1941).

The question of the partiality of referees towards Rangers – particularly during the wartime seasons – was frequently raised by the more responsible journalists. In the official history of the Scottish League, *The First 100 Years* (Glasgow, 1990), Bob Crampsey felt compelled to comment on the situation. He quotes another respected journalist, Sandy Adamson of the *Glasgow Evening News*: 'Then came one of those dreary penalty awards to Rangers, and the next thirty minutes were hard to endure.'

No doubt existed in the minds of most sports writers in Scotland; throughout the war years, referees were infamous for the favouritism extended to Rangers – although, given the make-up of the average side fielded by Rangers, this partiality was not really needed. The primary reason lay in the fact that wartime football was essentially a part-time business and the referees were recruited along the same amateurish lines. The standards had fallen at this time understandably, and the ranks of referees were swollen by less objective types simply unable to act in an unpartisan manner.

A letter printed in the *Sunday Mail* of 17 October 1943 makes this point exactly:

> Dear Rex,
> A lot is made of Rangers' popularity with Scottish referees, and I concede that quite a lot of it is true. But, as it is so very evident with most things nowadays, it's the 'utility' referees we are burdened with who cause most of the bother,
> 'Good Rangers Man'
> Cranston Street, Glasgow.

At the end of the day, what was accomplished in the wake of the incidents at Ibrox Stadium on 6 September 1941?

For undoubted misbehaviour at Ibrox Park by spectators claiming to be Celtic supporters, Celtic Park was closed for a month; for clearly reprehensible conduct on the pitch by Rangers players, a mild rebuke was issued to the

Ibrox club; for ineffective refereeing by the official, no comment was made nor action taken. Little may have been accomplished except for the fact that Celtic were left in no doubt that they could expect little mercy or justice from the SFA.

Therefore, it became imperative that Celtic maintain complete control over the behaviour and conduct of their players and spectators, as a repetition might lead to even harsher punishments. The club, of course, recognised its responsibility for the conduct of the players sent out on to the field, but they were placed in a hopeless quandary with regard to the spectators. Celtic could select their players and dispense with their services if the players' behaviour was unacceptable, but they could not choose their followers.

The solution, of course, was already in the hands of the civic authorities. If people acted badly at a football match and disturbed the peace, Celtic would have no objection at all if the police made arrests nor if the magistrates imposed harsh sentences in order to deter future misbehaviour. However, the club felt keenly that the spectators had not come to matches with the express intention to misbehave and riot. Their misbehaviour was almost always attributable to some happening on the field, not necessarily a bad result but most often a perceived injustice to the players on the pitch, and the conviction that those injustices were not always accidental.

Celtic were to renew their demands for stronger and fairer referees, but for some time were doomed to disappointment. In fact, things were to get worse, not better.

***

Five years later a more disturbing series of incidents took place, when Celtic faced Rangers in 1946 on neutral ground in the Victory Cup. This tournament was set up in haste to celebrate the end of World War II, and served to take the place of the Scottish Cup which had been mothballed for the duration of the war. It was an early experiment in summer football and Celtic, in surprisingly sparkling form, advanced comfortably to the semi-final stage having disposed of St Johnstone, Queen of the South and Raith Rovers.

They faced Rangers at Hampden Park on 1 June 1946. The weather was excellent, and the crowd of 66,000, basking in the sunshine and in a cheerful mood, watched the vigorous and fairly contested match. Rangers dominated the proceedings, and Celtic owed a great deal to Willie Miller in goal for the 0–0 scoreline. The goalkeeper, doubtful prior to the match with a wrist injury, made several fine saves and outshone Rangers' Bobby Brown playing in one of his early games for the Ibrox club.

The replay took place in mid-week on a cool, blustery night and the match was fated to enter the Old Firm list of infamous encounters:

A scene remarkable in Scottish senior football occurred in the second half and completely spoiled what had previously been a hard and sporting game. About 20 minutes from the end Rangers were awarded a penalty kick when Thornton, their centre-forward, was tackled and fell. After a protest by the entire Celtic team the referee ordered off Paterson, the Celtic inside-left, who had been warned in the first half about appealing against a decision. Celtic continued to protest and, after the ball had been replaced for Young to take the spot-kick, Mallan kicked it away. The left back was immediately ordered off in turn. Then, when Young, the Rangers' centre-half, had converted the penalty, one of the 43,000 spectators broke on to the field. Play was stopped until he had been arrested by the police, who made three further arrests. (*Glasgow Herald*, 6 June 1946)

The Scotsman thought the field invasion worthy of inclusion in its news pages, rather than its sports section:

Immediately afterwards a man was seen running across the field towards the referee. He aimed a blow at the official with a bottle, but Mr. Dale ducked and avoided injury. By this time several other men had rushed on to the field, but were quickly stopped by the police. There seemed to be stone throwing behind the East goal and a number of officers went in among the crowd. The trouble speedily subsided after this, but not before many of the spectators had left the ground. (*The Scotsman*, 6 June 1946)

On the surface it would appear that Celtic players had lost their heads in the second half when the referee (M.C. Dale, Glasgow) awarded that penalty kick, but the trouble had started long before that.

Two Celtic forwards – Jimmy Sirrell and Jackie Gallacher – had been injured, and had taken up position on the extreme wings since the early minutes of the second half. The use of substitute players in competitive matches was not sanctioned in Scotland until 1966; unofficially, the authorities cited 'tradition', and the feeling that it could be considered 'character-building' for a side to continue the match short-handed. One of the injured players (Sirrell) had been hurt after a fierce tackle by Shaw, Rangers' left-back who was significantly nicknamed 'Tiger', but the referee had not taken any action against the defender; Gallacher had picked up two knocks in the match, but neither was attributable to rough play. However, Celtic were harbouring a sense of injustice at having to play with two 'passengers' in such an important contest. In fact, long before the end both players were forced to withdraw, leaving Celtic to complete the match with seven fit players.

The refereeing had been highly suspect from the opening whistle of the replay with several dubious decisions going Rangers' way in the first half. What had become quickly apparent to the players on the field was that the match official was not in the best of condition to referee any football match, let alone an Old Firm cup-tie. Not too surprisingly, Celtic – the victim of those decisions – had begun to question them heatedly.

George Paterson, Celtic's captain and normally the most unflappable of players, when being spoken to in the first half, was the first to recognise the specific nature of the referee's problems. Mr. Dale had awarded another free kick to Rangers a few yards outside Celtic's penalty area, and stooped to place

Bobby Hogg, Celtic captain in the mid-1940s, leads out his team at Dens Park followed by Miller and Mallan. The latter was given a lengthy, but unjustified, suspension by the SFA in the wake of the Victory Cup semi-final of 1946.

the ball for the kick – and momentarily lost his balance. Paterson, helping him to his feet, asked him pointedly if he was feeling all right, and the referee cautioned him for dissent. Paterson had realised that the referee had been drinking before the contest and, within a few minutes, other Celtic players were sharing their captain's suspicions, insisting later that they also could smell liquor on his breath.

At half time they voiced their misgivings to Celtic's manager who passed them on to his directors. One director, almost certainly Bob Kelly, approached the secretary of the SFA, George Graham, in the directors' lounge before play had resumed to voice his concerns, and he was reassured that 'it would be dealt with'.

It was an awkward situation for the directors and football officials: Celtic, having informed the authorities of the situation could only wait for some action. It is not known what action, if any, the secretary took, but Mr. Dale emerged for the second half still in nominal charge of the match. Later, the Celtic directors were adamant that he should have been withdrawn at the interval at least for medical reasons. Desmond White summed it up admirably on one occasion: 'If the man was not capable of driving a car, how could he referee a Celtic–Rangers match?'

The situation degenerated on the pitch: the wind made playing conditions difficult, and Celtic's injuries had distorted the contest although they were still making a fight of the match. The award of a penalty kick to Rangers in seventy minutes, when Thornton tumbled inside the area, was an extremely harsh one for such a simple tackle, and it marked the last straw for most Celtic players.

David Meiklejohn, a famous Rangers captain in the pre-war days but by then a journalist, wrote these words on the day following the replay, and they suggest that he too had his doubts about the validity of the award: 'Whether it was a penalty or not is beside the point. I know what it is like to be on the field when such a decision is given against you, and you disagree. It is a galling experience and you feel like throwing discretion to the wind, but that does not condone the attitude taken up by some Celtic players' (*Daily Record*, 6 June 1946).

On the field, acting as captain, George Paterson led the protest, refusing to hand over the ball until he had been heard by the referee at least and, for his pains, he was ordered off; Jimmy Mallan had stood on the penalty spot dragging his feet while the arguments were raging and, when the ball was eventually placed there, he kicked it away and he too was dismissed by the official, who had clearly lost complete control of the situation. In all, it had taken six minutes from the award of the penalty kick until it was taken.

The *Glasgow Observer* was the only paper to attribute words to the Celtic players, suggesting that Paterson had simply said, 'You should keep the ball; you deserve it.' Reports, published many years later, were to suggest more earthy language but Paterson, incidentally a non-Catholic, did have the reputation of being a most level-headed and calm personality, not a man known for intemperate speech and the ordering-off marked the only time in a lengthy career he had fallen foul of referees.

Mallan's case was slightly different, as he had spent some minutes over the penalty spot in disgust, apparently trying to obliterate it, and the *Observer* indicated that he had told the official, 'There's no penalty spot, ref.'

To their credit Rangers attempted to play out the last fifteen minutes, content with the two-goal lead that the penalty converted by George Young had provided, and the match finished quietly enough. All the players still on the pitch were anxious to conclude the tie without causing any more trouble on the terracing.

After the match, the referee had 'considerable difficulty in making out his report, and required physical assistance to do so, and eventually handed over his third attempt to the authorities for them to complete.' One has to assume that representatives of the SFA, alerted by Kelly's halftime complaint, were playing a helpful part in the completion of the report. I was assured of this in 1970 by Cyril Horne of the *Glasgow Herald*; Horne, a long-standing personal friend of Bob Kelly, presumably had been informed by the Celtic chairman of the backstage drama.

One bizarre footnote was added to the situation when the name of Celtic's Matt Lynch was now included in Mr. Dale's report to be disciplined. Lynch, redheaded and wholehearted, had not been involved in any incident during the match, nor on the way to the pavilion afterwards.

The sequel was disastrous for Celtic.

George Paterson and Jimmy Mallan were both suspended for three months from the start of the following season, extremely harsh sentences for ordering-off crimes which did not involve violent conduct. Mallan had been ordered off earlier in the 1945/46 season for striking a St Mirren player in a league match at Love Street, and this previous blot may have been a factor in his suspension. However, Paterson had always been considered the most gentlemanly of players and his sentence undoubtedly was excessive. In fact, George Paterson, a member of Celtic's 1938 Empire Exhibition side and capped for Scotland during the war, lapsed into a mild depression because of this suspension and was transferred to Brentford before its completion 'for his own peace of mind'.

Most astonishingly, Matt Lynch, who had not been ordered off nor spoken to by the referee, was also suspended for one month. Lynch, a fiery competitor but one who had resolutely kept out of this fracas, was so incensed at the injustice of it all that he contacted Jimmy Duncanson, his immediate opponent in the match, and asked him for help in an appeal against the sentence. Duncanson, a most sporting player and a prolific scorer against Celtic, was pleased to write a letter on his opponent's behalf, and Matt Lynch was so gratified by the gesture of the Rangers player that he retained the letter till his dying day, joking that 'it will help get me into Heaven'.

'Waverley' pointed out that the appeal subsequently lodged by Lynch – one of the few players in Scottish football who was a university graduate – was unprecedented: 'The SFA Council will for the first time in its history consider an appeal by a player against a decision of the Referee Committee. Previously an appeal was heard only by the committee who tried him – which invariably meant only one thing' (*Daily Record*, 3 July 1946).

Unfortunately, the Council dispensed the same form of summary justice as the committee:

> The Celt gave it as his word of honour that he had tried everything he could to restrain his more hot-headed colleagues, and denied strongly that he had invited his mates to leave the field of play. His efforts were devoted to trying to get them clear of the penalty box and to enable the game to continue. Mr. Robert Williamson, chairman of the Referee Committee which meted out the punishment, declared that the player had said nothing new and that the committee had made a most exhaustive inquiry. They were satisfied that they had come to the right decision on the evidence offered them. (*Daily Record*, 4 July 1946)

The fact that the Council's vote was unanimous is scarcely surprising; it suggests most clearly that the representatives in the SFA Council were prepared

55 Walter St.,
Glasgow. E.1
22/6/46.

Dear Matt,

In certain circles my writing to you would have the same effect as a bomb exploding, but I felt that, if we are to live up to the name of sport, then I must say something. I knew, like many others, that two Celtic players had to appear before the S.F.A. for being ordered off the field, but no one was more surprised than I when, on the morning after the S.F.A.

meeting, I read in the papers that you had been suspended for a month. As you may well know, I had been asked by dozens of persons for my impression of this "scene". Believe me Matt, not once in all my explanations to these people did I have to incriminate you as an instigator, with the result that when they asked me why you had been suspended I just had no answer for them. If my memory serves me right, and I am sure it does, when the referee gave his decision he was immediately surrounded

by Celtic players. It was then, and about this I am positive, you came walking over to me and said "I don't want to get mixed up in any trouble here, Jimmy, I have been in enough of that." It was then that I said to you to try and get the Celtic players who were still protesting to keep their heads cool. You then walked back to the penalty area and appeared to me to be doing just that. You can imagine my surprise then, Matt, when I read you had been suspended for a month. I thought perhaps you would

have appealed, but so far I have seen no word of it.

I remember someone discussing the game afterwards, asking me how the players of both teams were conducting themselves prior to the penalty incident, my reply was that I thought it was one of the best old time games for some time and that if I always got as clean a game as I get from Matt Lynch then it would be a pleasure to play every Saturday. In closing let me wish you every success in the new season.

Yours in sport,
Jimmy Duncanson.

The letter written by Jimmy Duncanson of Rangers on behalf of Matt Lynch of Celtic. Lynch's appeal to the SFA against his suspension was unsuccessful.

15

to rubber-stamp recommendations from the various committees without considering them too carefully.[4]

The original committee, in judging Lynch, of course, had heard evidence from the referee concerned or, in his absence, had managed to decipher his report and make their decisions on that basis. That committee's report included the following statement on Lynch's participation: 'The referee also noted that, following J. Mallan's dismissal, M. Lynch, Celtic FC, invited and incited the rest of Celtic FC to leave the field.'

Equally surprising was the comment on Bobby Hogg, the veteran full back and another player who, in the eyes of most observers, had appeared to be acting as peacemaker: 'The Committee also expressed their disapproval of the conduct of R. Hogg who, as captain of the Celtic team, had the responsibility of maintaining discipline amongst his players on the field and should have shown them a better example. This fact will be recorded with the referee's caution on the player's record card.'[5]

Remarkably, Celtic did not do very much to back their players in any further appeals against the harshness of the punishments, nor in their complaints against the referee. Why not?

The directors later felt the club, after rightly drawing to the attention of the appropriate officials the physical condition of the referee, had been finessed in this matter. Their actions had taken place at half time, and Celtic felt they had been assured by the Secretary of the SFA that the matter would be remedied. The bizarre events of the second half unfolded on the pitch in a quite predictable way, and the Celtic players *en masse* lost any remaining trust in the match official. The directors apparently decided that any accusations against the referee might bring the game into further disrepute, and perhaps they were encouraged to drop the matter with the vague promise of better treatment in future.

However, the treatment meted out to their players by the SFA was little short of scandalous, and was a foretaste of similar injustices. The invasion of the pitch by three or four misguided individuals had not helped Celtic's case in any way, the blame for the whole fiasco now turning to the connection between dissent by the players and hooliganism on the terracing.

And Celtic, after the closure of the ground in 1941 felt vulnerable, but aggrieved.

The club did comment acidly in the next annual *Celtic Football Guide*, in

---

[4] In 1948, for example, Willie Kelly of Morton received much the same treatment when he appealed aghast his *sine die suspension* levied in December 1946. His case was heard, considered, and dismissed within a thirty-second period.

[5] Most newspapers reported that George Paterson was Celtic's captain on this occasion, although Bobby Hogg had frequently acted as the side's captain. Possibly, Hogg had resumed the captaincy after Paterson's dismissal.

which the manager's report on the season included this sentence: 'History will surely record that indiscretions in refereeing and harshness of punishment have imposed an undeserved penalty on club and players alike.'

It is widely believed that the principal writer of the *Celtic Football Guide* (and the later match programmes) was, in fact, Cyril Horne freelancing from his post at the *Glasgow Herald*. The club was fined later by the SFA for those comments, and also ordered to post warning notices at Celtic Park for their supporters.

Unfortunately, the gesture on Celtic's part was merely preaching to the converted, and quite typical of the club's current supine posturing against officialdom. Of course, it guaranteed only that the club's followers would continue to feel persecuted – and helpless against the football authorities.

In fact, it was not until the publication of Sir Robert Kelly's autobiography that Celtic paid due attention to George Paterson's suspension:

> The most unfair punishment ever meted out by the Referee Committee of the Scottish Football Association, however, was to a Celtic player, George Paterson. The cruelty of Paterson's sentence was shattering to both player and club. What horrified all of us at Celtic Park was that Paterson, a man of most temperate language, had never in a career of eleven years been sent off or asked to appear before the Disciplinary Committee. We were forced to the conclusion that he was punished as he was for one of two reasons – (1) he was adjudged to have provoked the misconduct of some of the spectators; (2) he had annoyed someone or other by making allegations against the referee at half time. (Sir Robert Kelly, *Celtic*, Glasgow 1971)

Some newspapers of the time had started to advocate an obvious solution: 'Why not the one suggestion which would bear most fruit – have an English referee at Celtic–Rangers games? It was scarcely a revolutionary idea as, back in 1905 after Celtic and Rangers had finished the league schedule tied in points, an English official was appointed for the play-off match at Hampden Park on 8 May. Incidentally, Celtic won that game by 2–1 to start off their celebrated run of six championships in a row but the impetus for that referee's appointment had come after poor discipline on the field and crowd trouble had marred the proceedings in Rangers' 2–0 triumph at Celtic Park in the Scottish Cup on 24 March.

Referees do not live in a vacuum: they have full-time jobs outside football, live in neighbourhoods, lead a social life. They do not emerge as qualified referees in their early twenties without previously having had some interest in football, and no doubt at some stage in their development they actually supported a football team.

In Scotland, or more particularly in the West of Scotland, this club is more than likely to be one member of the Old Firm. At the end of the Second World War, Rangers had been the dominant club in Scotland for a number of years; both common sense and demography would suggest that most emerging referees had supported them as boys at one time or another. This is not to say that some of those referees were biased in their judgements, but, when a man is faced with a split-second decision to make – no matter how well-trained or schooled he is – sometimes instinct does take over.

Bob Kelly, in his years as a Celtic director and chairman, was surprisingly tolerant of the awkward position some referees found themselves in:

> We have to recognise that most Lanarkshire referees, at least 90% of them enter football, supporting or having supported one member of the Old Firm ... and there's no denying that. What happens to a referee in the split-second that a player goes down in the penalty area? If he is a Rangers' supporter – and the player is a Ranger – the referee, despite all the training in the world, still sees that incident as a supporter. If he were not on the pitch refereeing, then he would be out there on the terracing screaming for a penalty. It's human nature – and there's nothing you can do about that. Don't consider that the referee is cheating because, thinking like a supporter, he sees it instinctively as a supporter.

Kelly is not alone in this view; a prominent journalist has written of the same syndrome as:

> ... a fact of human nature. They maybe won't go out of their way to favour the team they support or supported, but they will naturally see things from their perspective. Therefore if Rangers are all over Stenny [Stenhousemuir] in the last five minutes, and tackles are flying and a Rangers player goes down in the box, they automatically assume the defender has made the desperate tackle of one who knows the game is up. They may also be swayed by 40,000 people shouting 'Penalty' at the same time. After all, which of us does not react with the mob in a mob situation? They may also have millions of pounds' worth of internationals turning to them at once screaming for the decision and be swayed by this pressure. (Bill Leckie: *Pavement and Penthouse*, Edinburgh, 1999)

There is a tacit assumption on the part of both commentators that the majority of Scottish referees will have been Rangers supporters at one time or another – an understanding which does reflect the demography of Scotland reasonably accurately.[6]

Mr. M.C. Dale was such a man. It was widely recognised in the 1940s that he was a supporter of Rangers and, after his retirement as a referee, it was reported that he frequently travelled to football matches on a Rangers supporters' bus. In fact, he had previously been involved in controversy over his handling of Rangers matches, most notably a match between the Ibrox club and St Mirren in 1940; surprisingly, St Mirren were making a strong challenge for the Scottish Southern League and went into the fixture only one point behind Rangers.

W.C. Gallagher was normally the most phlegmatic of sports writers but

---

[6] Jim Farrell, the former Celtic director, was approached by a young referee for his advice. The problem was that the young man had once been a keen Rangers supporter, and he was wondering if that would prove a handicap in his career. Farrell advised him that if he could referee matches without being influenced by that fact, then he should continue with his plans. He added jokingly (?): 'It shouldn't hold you back in refereeing – most of the others are too.' The would-be official took his advice, and became a Class 1 referee – and was never involved in any major controversy when handling either member of the Old Firm.

his column on the match was headlined: 'We Must Not Have Such Refereeing!' and his opening paragraph read as follows: 'In 20 years of sports reporting I've seen some bad decisions by referees. I've been at soccer grounds where the field has been invaded. I've been in boxing clubs where revolvers have been drawn. Honestly, I don't believe I have ever been eye-witness to such a glaringly bad verdict as I saw at Ibrox on Saturday' (*Daily Record*, 23 September 1940).

The decision that sparked the reaction by the veteran reporter was Mr. Dale's decision to turn down a penalty for St Mirren at a stage when Rangers were hanging on grimly to a one-goal lead: 'When Stead was being attended to, I wrote in my notebook, "St. Mirren awarded a penalty seventeen minutes after the interval." Then I looked up and I could hardly believe my eyes – Referee Dale was signalling for a free kick inches outside the eighteen-yard area. For a moment I thought either Dale or myself had gone crackers. It was so clear-cut, so obvious that, in my opinion, there is absolutely no excuse whatever for the referee.'

Later in the contest Rangers were awarded a penalty kick, apparently correctly, but the Paisley players, led by Craven, after Venters had converted it, protested immediately on the grounds that Gillick had been following up so closely into the area that the goalkeeper was not sure which Ranger was taking the kick:

> Two paramount errors in one game! Dale in the closing half-hour appeared to have lost control of the game and it was a good thing that St. Mirren players kept their heads. They almost lost them when Craven was ordered off ... nearly all his mates wanted to join him in the march to the pavilion. If officialdom fails to make an enquiry, officialdom is letting down football. According to some of the players, words were used on the field [by the referee] that are absolutely foreign to sport, and the allegations must be probed. Mr. William MacAndrew, the League secretary, and Mr. James Bowie, the president of the League, were at the match. I feel sure they will read with sympathy whatever complaint St. Mirren make. (*Daily Record*, 23 September 1940) [7]

'Waverley' was only one of several reporters who felt that Rangers were getting too many breaks from the officials and, in his report on the Glasgow Cup final between Celtic and Rangers the following week, he could not resist alluding to the general suspicion. The match was played at Ibrox, and Celtic won 1–0 through a goal scored early in the second half by Gillan from an offside position: 'I thought he was [offside] and, if I am correct, then the fates turned their backs on Rangers for once. After receiving so many questionable decisions in their favour, the Light Blues now know how chagrined Queen's Park, Falkirk, and St. Mirren and others must have been on highly important occasions' (*Daily Record*, 30 September 1940).

---

[7] Thus, it can be seen that two different sides [Celtic and St. Mirren] considered walking off the pitch in matches against Rangers in protest at Mr. Dale's handling of the games.

Earlier that season (1940/41) Mr. Dale had been in charge of a Celtic–Rangers fixture in the Western Division of the wartime Scottish League and had become almost inevitably embroiled in controversy.

The first incident had involved a clash between Malcolm MacDonald (Celtic) and Alec Venters (Rangers); according to the *Glasgow Observer* – admittedly not the most objective of newspapers – MacDonald was fouled 'in a way that should have meant retiral for Venters but instead Calum [MacDonald] was told off' (12 April 1940). The second controversy took place within a minute of the restart for the second half. Once more the *Glasgow Observer* was highly critical of the referee's decision: 'Venters did a swan-dive in the Celtic penalty area, and Dale gave a penalty from which the injured (?) Venters equalised.' The referee, in the eyes of the reporter, simply added insult to injury by denying Celtic's claims for similar awards: '... two glaring penalties were refused Celtic; Mr. Dale must have been blind when he did not see Woodburn [Rangers' centre half] throw his arms round Crum's neck to prevent him reaching the ball.'

However, the *Glasgow Observer* was not alone in its criticism: 'Jaymak' in the *Evening Times* match-day report described the penalty award 'which the Celtic players protested vigorously was rather harsh', and 'Rex' in the *Sunday Mail* a day later was even more emphatic in his condemnation: 'As an exposition of Venters' histrionic art, it was superb. As a punishment for the crime, it was a washout. The Ranger appeared to me to have started his dive before he was tackled' (7 April 1940).

Mr. Dale's 'refereeing' was, no doubt, the most blatant example of the favouring of Rangers in those days but Bob Kelly, of course, was less charitable to those in power in Scottish football: 'Referees react in a split-second; administrators don't have that excuse.'

However, any indirect complaints or comments by Celtic and other clubs were largely ignored by the SFA, and similarly any reporting or criticism of such irregularities published in the Scottish press were brushed aside as irrelevant. In matters pertaining to football the SFA was supreme, apparently oblivious to any criticism.

In the wider area of social justice the SFA also seemed oblivious to the fact that one of their member clubs was actively practising a policy of discrimination against Catholics by excluding them from employment. It would be difficult to find any evidence or indication of any member of the Council or secretariat expressing an opinion condemning this shameful practice.

In law, silence is often viewed as a form of consent or approval; one can reach only the same conclusion about the attitude of the football authorities in Scotland.

CHAPTER TWO

The Ghetto Mentality

Celtic and their followers have often been accused of suffering from a paranoia arising from a ghetto mentality.

This attitude might be summed up as the collective feeling that, apart from one's fellow nationalists or religionists, the world is a hostile place, that outsiders are not to be trusted too far, and that one should be prepared to endure unjust sufferings and punishments. The principal ghettos that spring to mind are the Jewish communities within the major European cities prior to and during World War II and into which the Jews were largely confined and limited. In Scotland poverty forced most of the Irish immigrants to crowd together in districts which, because of the overcrowding and unsanitary conditions, quickly degenerated into slums; in the late nineteenth century in Glasgow the Gorbals and the Calton, and the Cowgate in Edinburgh, would be prime examples of this phenomenon.

A ghetto can be a reassuring place psychologically. It is much easier to deal with life when surrounded by others in exactly the same boat and, if the outside is indeed hostile, it becomes almost imperative to share the beliefs, attitudes and customs of the fellow sufferers. Every immigrant community, no matter where, shares this collective experience, and the Irish who were forced to flock to Scotland (and England) in order to survive were no exception.

It was an unfriendly and critical environment, as indicated by the words of one Scottish professor berating the newcomers: 'They are responsible for most of the crime committed in Scotland, which otherwise would be the most law-abiding country in the world. Wheresoever knives and razors are used, wheresoever sneak thefts and mean pilfering are easy and safe, wheresoever dirty acts of sexual baseness are committed, there you will find the Irish in Scotland with all but a monopoly of the business' (A. D. Gibb, *Scotland in Eclipse*, 1930).

James MacMillan, the Scottish composer, who delivered an important address in Edinburgh on the eve of the 1999 International Festival pointed out a tendency towards revisionism:

> A foreign academic brought it to my attention that the *Collins Encyclopaedia of Scotland* has no entry for the Irish in Scotland or the Catholic Church. Foreign visitors to Edinburgh attended an exhibition a couple of years ago at the Scottish Records Office, recounting the history of immigration to Scotland. Large displays set out the history of the immigration of Flemish weavers, Jewish traders, Asian shopkeepers, Chinese restaurant owners, black bus-conductors, and rightly praised the contribution they had all made to Scottish society. The

massive Irish immigration in the 19th and early 20th century was dealt with in something like three sentences, as follows: 'In the mid-19th century an increasing number of seasonal Irish farm labourers who worked in the summers in lowland Scotland stayed over due to poor economic conditions in Ireland. Many of them became a burden on the local Parish Poor Laws.'

As Dr. MacMillan – and other historians – suggest, the Irish were viewed with suspicion by the native Scots, who resented the vast influx of largely unskilled labourers into Scotland in successive waves of immigration in the nineteenth and early twentieth centuries.

Because of that treatment it is scarcely surprising, therefore, that the Irish in Scotland would suffer from a persecution complex; perhaps the word 'complex' should be removed from the phrase because the persecution was real.

The treatment meted out to the newcomers was brutal and discriminatory but often the stories of injustices remain anecdotal and, because of their essential subjectivity, they cannot stand unverified as evidence – although the frequency and similarities in the stories do suggest their accuracy. There was widespread discrimination against both Irish immigrants and Catholics in the basic matter of employment. These two groups – although the words 'Irish' and 'Catholic' seemed almost interchangeable – were offered work only in unskilled categories and in the lowest-paying. This practice appeared calculated to maintain the *status quo* within Scotland. The anecdotal evidence – from which community values are often derived – may have been exaggerated at times, but it is virtually impossible to be objective when the viewpoint is from the bottom end of an impoverished society – and with no prospect of improvement.

Apologists for the resident Scots could claim also that the occasional letter or newspaper article written by a native, and excessively critical of the Irish, might be dismissed as one man's individual opinion, and not representative of the attitudes of the majority. Such revisionism is not uncommon among social historians or, at least, those with an agenda.

However, one particular document stands out, and remains as the best possible example to illustrate the thinking about the Irish at that time. The subject was simple, and fully justified consideration: 'the alarm and anxiety ... occasioned by the incursion into Scotland of a large Irish Roman Catholic population within recent years.'

It was a Report submitted by the Committee on Church and Nation, and received by the General Assembly – the annual meeting of the Church of Scotland held in Edinburgh – on 29 May 1923. The General Assembly received the Report, 'thanked the Committee for their diligence, discharged them [the Committee], and commended the Report to the earnest consideration of the ministers and members of the Church.'

The Assembly then went on to discuss it and, among other recommendations, called upon the Government to amend the Education (Scotland) Act of 1918 – which had largely relieved the financial burdens on Catholic schools – and recommended that the whole Report be considered by individuals and groups within the Church, and that a progress-report be presented at the next Assembly.

The Church of Scotland, the established church of the nation, fully endorsed the document, as witnessed by the principal recommendation: 'The General Assembly, impressed by the facts set forth in the Report, urge the Government to appoint a Commission to inquire into the whole situation, with a view to the preservation and protection of Scottish nationality and civilisation.'

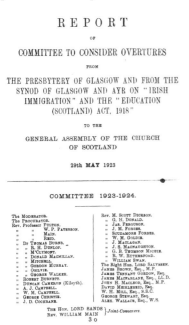

The report to the General Assembly of the Church of Scotland in 1923.

This was not a report submitted by an obscure committee, and slipped past an inattentive General Assembly late in a crowded schedule. The Report was discussed at length, and continued to be debated seriously at subsequent General Assemblies for more than a decade. The Committee on Church and Nation is probably the most important of the Church of Scotland's committees, and its members had worked hard throughout the previous year in preparing this document. Consider the composition of the committee: the Moderator, the Procurator, four Reverend Professors, eight Reverend Doctors, seventeen Reverends, two MPs, three lawyers (one LL.D, one Solicitor to the Supreme Court, and one Writer to the Signet), and two Lords.

As late as 1969 a similar 'Church and Nation Report' could say: 'The Church of Scotland itself can rightly claim to be the national Church and to have a unique right to speak with an independent voice on behalf of the nation and to be the nation.' Back in 1923 it represented an even more substantial cross-section of the Scottish Establishment.

It must be admitted at the outset that the Report is well written in clear prose, and admirably organised, but a detailed examination of the document's content might be more illuminating. I make no apology for quoting at length from this document as it represents the thinking of the Scottish people on this most difficult of topics.

First of all, the Committee narrowed the areas of concern by discounting 'the Scottish Roman Catholic population ... who have a right to call Scotland their country, in common with their fellow-countrymen of the Protestant Faith.' Significantly, the Committee was unconcerned about another incursion into the nation: 'Nor is there any complaint of the presence of an Orange population in Scotland. They are of the same race as ourselves and of the same Faith, and are readily assimilated to the Scottish population.'

Instead, the Report centred exclusively on 'the problem of the Irish Roman Catholic population in Scotland. They remain a people by themselves, segregated by reason of their race, their customs, their traditions, and, above all, by their loyalty to their Church, and gradually and inevitably dividing Scotland racially, socially, and ecclesiastically.'

It traced the history of Irish immigration and gives due credit to the Irish for their contribution to the development of the modern Scotland:

> ... a demand for cheap labour arose. Industrial firms and great contractors advertised for labour in the Irish Press, and crowds of Irishmen and their families emigrated to Scotland to engage in building railways, to work in coal mines, in the great shipyards on the Clyde, and in the jute mills of Dundee, and to labour in the construction of public works, such as the Loch Katrine water scheme. When they had settled down they invited relations and friends to come across to Scotland, promising to find work and a home for them. All were welcomed by the employers of labour. The Irishmen worked well, accepted almost any kind of habitation, and were content with small wages.

The Report bemoaned a parallel migration of Scots from their native land, and unjustifiably linked that with the incoming of the Irish:

> ... a great exodus of the Scottish race. They wished for better conditions of life, higher wages, and wider prospects. Compelled by the economic pressure of the Irish race, young Scottish men and women – the flower of the nation – left their native land, and sought to build up their fortunes in America and the Dominions. It was certainly to the advantage of the countries to which they went that the best of our Scottish people should have gone there, but it was a grievous loss to the land of their fathers.

After linking these two events – the increase in Irish and the decrease in Scots – the Report went on to spell out the dangers to Scotland, and did so through the use of statistics, mostly culled from the Report of the Registrar-General. Among the findings are the following: 'The Irish population has almost doubled in the last forty years' and, using the figures from 1881 to 1921, it points out that: 'In the twenty years, 1881 to 1901, the Irish population increased by 32.3 per cent, while the Scottish population for the same period increased by only 18.5 per cent. In the twenty years, 1901 to 1921, the Irish population increased by 39 per cent, while the Scottish population increased by only 6 per cent.' The committee members concluded from these statistics that: 'from 1881 to 1901 the increase of the Irish population was nearly twice as great as that of the Scottish population, and from 1901 to 1921 the increase of the Irish population was 6.5 times as great as that of the Scottish population.'

The Report also included the statistics from 1919 to 1921 provided by the Education Authorities of Glasgow, Lanark, Dumbarton and Renfrew, and these figures verified this demographic trend. The authors of the Report were quick to point out that the figures involving children on the school rolls were not related to family size:

> There is a widespread impression that the rapid increase of the Irish population relative to the Scottish increase is due to the alleged fact that the Irish family is, as a rule, larger than the Scottish family. This is not true. The fertility of the Scottish working-class family is just as great as that of the Irish working-class family. The tendency to restrict the size of the family does not – as yet, at any rate – affect the Scottish working-class any more deeply than it does the Irish working-class.

The Report indicated that, given the above 'fact', 'the increase in the Irish population and the relatively small increase in the Scottish population are due mainly to two causes – immigration of Irish into Scotland, and emigration of Scots from Scotland.'

Having established a case for its legitimate concern, the Committee members reached a sombre conclusion:

> The time is rapidly approaching when, through this racial imcompatability [sic], whole communities in parish, village, and town will be predominantly Irish. It is, in fact, a sober and restrained prophecy to say that through the operation of the various factors now at work – immigration of Irish and emigration of Scots, disinclination of Scots to work alongside and live among Irishmen, partiality of Irish foremen for employing Irishmen – the great plain of Scotland stretching from Glasgow in the west to Dundee and Edinburgh in the east will soon be dominated by the Irish race. If, therefore, the Scottish people wish to safeguard their heritage, they cannot afford to lose time in taking whatever steps may be necessary to secure this just and patriotic end.

Throughout the Report so far, the references to 'the Irish menace' had been racial or social in tone, but the emphasis now switched to the religious – and the Committee expressed concern about the Vatican's plans for the conversion of Scotland:

> If Scotland be won for the Roman Catholic Church, a mighty lever for the control of England – the greatest prize of all – will have been put in the hands of the Church. Already the Roman Communion is the largest in Glasgow, the second city of the Empire. This achievement could only have been regarded as the dream of a visionary fifty years ago. But when such dreams come true, who can say that dreams of yet vaster triumphs will never be realised?

The Committee reminded the General Assembly of the social changes effected in Scotland already, ones familiar to the representatives through their involvement in Scottish life at a local level:

> Even now the Irish population exercise a profound influence on the direction and development of our Scottish civilisation. Their gift of speech, their aptitude for public life, their restless ambition to rule, have given them a prominent place in political, county, municipal, and parochial elections. They [the Irish] have had an unfortunate influence in modifying the Scottish habit of thrift and independence. An Irishman never hesitates to seek relief from charity organisations and local authorities, and Scotsmen do not see why they should not

get help when Irishmen receive it. Generally speaking, they [the Irish] are poor through intemperance and improvidence, and they show little inclination to raise themselves in the social scale. The Scottish reverence for the Sabbath day is passing away. It may be that there is in the Scottish mind a tendency towards the secularisation of the Sabbath, but indubitably this tendency has been increased and stimulated by the influence of the Irish race.

The final target for the anger of the Report's authors was the Education (Scotland) Act of 1918. This historic legislation – significantly still a major debating point within Scotland – transferred the control of Catholic (and Episcopalian) schools to the local education authorities but those churches still retained important powers: the appointment of teachers, the assurance of religious education by qualified staff, and provision for religious observances throughout the school year.[8]

Consider the tone of the Report:

The Education Act of 1918 – passed through Parliament when Scotland was deeply and painfully preoccupied with the problem of the war – has proved an immense boon to the Roman Catholic Church. It has made her in proportion to her numbers the most richly-endowed Church in Scotland. Every year £283,023 are paid in salaries to the Roman Catholic teachers of Glasgow, and the expenditure per annum on rates and taxes, fuel, light and cleaning, books and stationery, and repairs reaches the enormous sum of £107,225. Meanwhile the Roman Catholic Church, loaded with wealth received from an overburdened nation, is using it for the purpose of securely establishing a Faith in their land that is distasteful to the Scottish race, or of supplanting the people who supplied these riches by a race that is alien in sympathy and in religion.

The Report concluded on an emphatic note:

Fusion of the Scottish and the Irish races in Scotland – just as it was in Ireland – will remain an impossibility. The Irish are the most obedient children of the Church of Rome; the Scots stubbornly adhere to the principles of the Reformed Faith. Already there is bitter feeling among the Scottish working-classes against the Irish intruders. As the latter increases, and the Scottish people realise the seriousness of the menace to their racial supremacy in their native land, this bitterness will develop into a race antagonism, which will have disastrous consequences for Scotland. The loss of the Scottish race to civilisation would be immeasurable. In science, theoretical and applied, in art, poetry and prose, in government and industry, in philosophy and theology, their contributions to the advancement of knowledge and civilisation have been remarkable.

Appropriately, for a Report commissioned by a Church, it ended with a Biblical flourish, albeit an Old Testament one:

God placed the people of this world in families, and history, which is the narrative of His providence, tells us that when kingdoms are divided against themselves they cannot stand. The nations that are homogeneous in Faith and ideals, that have maintained unity of race, have been ever the most prosperous, and to them the Almighty has committed the highest tasks, and has granted the largest measure of success in achieving them. It is incumbent on

---

[8] In order to compensate for school time lost to 'Holy Days' the Catholic schools in Glasgow traditionally started two weeks earlier than their secular counterparts. Both the Catholic and Episcopalian Churches, who had benefited through the Act, felt that the 'public system' was Presbyterian in philosophy and practice – and in effect already a denominational educational institution.

the Scottish people to consider, before it is too late, the grave situation in their native land, and to devise means which, while they do no injustice to the Irish people whom they allowed to come into their country, shall preserve Scotland for the Scottish race, and secure to future generations the traditions, ideals, and Faith of a great people, unspoiled and inviolate.

Scotland in the 1920s was in a poor way economically and every responsible institution in the country had reason to be concerned. The Church of Scotland, as the established church had a perfect right – if not responsibility – to comment publicly on these concerns.

World War I with its devastation and carnage had been a turning point in public consciousness: thousands of young men had marched off for a patriotic adventure, and returned – if at all – shell-shocked both physically and emotionally. Hundreds of thousands of young men lay dead and buried on European soil, a mute testimony to the ineptitude of the Generals, and the failure of politicians. The survivors of that lost youthful generation returned in a short-lived atmosphere of triumph only to be disillusioned at home.

The sacrifices seemed to have been in vain: thousands affected by mustard gas in the trenches lived out their remaining years in poverty and despair, social reforms hinted at and promised during the conflict were postponed, apparently indefinitely. Worst of all, the country was entering a most predictable economic slump and those heavy industries, revived and geared up for a war economy with a working-class labour force, had few plans to deal with the situation in peacetime. The economic decline was a particularly severe one in Scotland, with its accompanying side effects of massive unemployment and emigration on a large scale:

The low morale of Scottish public opinion ... was due to a variety of factors coinciding: the disproportionately high casualty rate of the Scots in the First World War who had flocked to the colours in greater numbers than people anywhere else in the United Kingdom; the crisis of Scottish heavy industry upon which rested the local economy, that was triggered off by the post-war fall in demand for ships, engineering products and coal, but was made worse in Scotland by the failure of conservatively-minded industrialists to diversify into other areas; and the conversion of much of the working-class to parliamentary and even extra-parliamentary forms of socialism which, in their different ways, were seen to pose a threat to the security and cohesion of Scottish and British society. (Tom Gallagher, *Glasgow: the Uneasy Peace*, Manchester, 1987)

Any nation in a situation like that is quick to seek out scapegoats, fairly or unfairly, and in Scottish society the designated victims were inevitably the Irish, set apart from the native Scots initially by nationality and accent but more permanently by religion and low social status.

On its very first page the Report had accused the Irish of 'gradually and inevitably dividing Scotland racially, socially, and ecclesiastically.' Unfortunately, the Report itself – and by extension its authors – is overtly racist, elitist and sectarian. I am aware that it might be unfair for us to judge and criticise the statements and actions of more than seventy years ago by the more enlightened standards of 2001. But, considering the qualifications and lineage of the members of that committee, the Church of Scotland could – and should – have done a lot better.

I am not alone in condemning the Report.

T.M. Devine in his *The Scottish Nation* considers it 'notorious' and refers to it as *The Menace of the Irish Race to Our Scottish Nationality*, the title given when it was later published as a pamphlet – a clear indication that the contents had met with widespread public approval.

James E. Handley, perhaps better known as Brother Clare, wrote two important books on the subject: *The Irish in Scotland (1798-1845)* and *The Irish in Modern Scotland* which covered the period from 1845 until 1938. In the chapter entitled 'The Scoto-Irish' Handley demolishes the arguments put forth in the Report.

Similarly, Tom Gallagher in his *Glasgow: the Uneasy Peace* is critical of the Report's tone and noted the importance of the timing of the document composed by:

> ... a small but growing number of ministers whose church was not as confident of its identity and was thus an accurate barometer of Scottish opinion. Now that most of Ireland had withdrawn from the United Kingdom, a good few Kirk ministers felt that any restraint about mentioning an alien presence in their midst could be lifted. It is no coincidence that *The Menace of the Irish Race...* report emerged when the new Irish Free State had still to reach its first birthday.[9]

All the historians cited above criticise the statistical evidence produced by the Report, and consider it seriously flawed. Handley is particularly effective in pointing out the invariable linking of the two words 'Irish' and 'Catholic' in the Report and other publications of a similar frame of mind. As he shows, a large percentage of those designated as Irish had been born in Scotland, and their families had lived in Scotland for some generations. As subjects who had lived and worked in Scotland, and who had fought and died under the Union Jack, they had fully earned the right to be designated as Scottish. He also indicated that a number of Catholic children considered to be Irish were of Italian, Polish, or Ukrainian descent.

The Report had chosen to assume that everybody who arrived in Scotland from Ireland was Catholic, despite the preponderance of recent arrivals from Ulster. The statistics used by the authors of the Report regarding immigration from Ireland were equally suspect. Every reliable barometer indicated that the peak period of Irish immigration had passed; for example, the total number

---

[9] The texts cited are as follows: *The Scottish Nation, 1700 – 2000* by T.M. Devine, (London 1999); *The Irish in Modern Scotland* by James E. Handley, (Cork 1947); *Glasgow: The Uneasy Peace* by Tom Gallagher (Manchester 1987)

who moved from Ireland to Scotland between 1911 and 1920 was 4,423 and of those no fewer than 2,964 came from Ulster.

The *Glasgow Herald*, rightly considered the most influential newspaper in the West of Scotland as the one read by the members of the business community, decided to investigate the facts about the Irish immigration into Scotland. Despite the newspaper's impeccable Protestant credentials, its researchers reached different conclusions from those of the Church of Scotland – which had continued its campaign at subsequent General Assemblies.

The five articles, lengthy and comprehensive, appeared in the newspaper in March, 1929.

The first examined the historical background logically and dispassionately and dismissed out-of-hand the fears expressed by the Church of Scotland and others that immigration had continued unabated: 'After an extensive, painstaking, and impartial examination of such evidence I am satisfied that the current Irish immigration is not large, that compared with the stream of the past it is the veriest trickle, and that it is practically negligible in bearing upon the development of the Irish community in Scotland. That development proceeds almost entirely from the multiplication of the Scoto-Irish – natives of this country, but of Irish extraction' (*Glasgow Herald*, 20 March 1929).

The second article, which appeared in the newspaper the following day, examined the oft-repeated claim that the Irish were flocking to Scotland in order to benefit materially through poor-relief and unemployment insurance benefits, small as they were. The investigator(s) reminded the readers that the newcomers could not be considered eligible for unemployment insurance benefits until certain conditions of employment and time had been met – and that the attraction of such rewards was minimal. The findings for the Glasgow poor-relief were revealing: at the present time (March 1929) there was not one single native of Ireland on the roll as a recipient of outdoor relief; and, out of a total of some 58,000 receiving relief from the city, only ninety were natives of Ireland who had been less than six months in Glasgow.

On 22 March the newspaper considered the Church of Scotland's stated views on the changes in the country's population: the Church was on record as believing that the unfavourable statistics were due solely to the continued 'stream of immigration', while the Irish community's representatives felt that the disparity was primarily due to a higher birth-rate among the Scoto-Irish. The newspaper's investigator(s) were inclined to accept the views of the Irish Catholic community as being more credible; using the official statistics, it was pointed out that there were 144,145 births recorded to the Catholic population of Scotland – estimated at 650,000 – between 1921 and 1927, while there were 760,346 births to the Protestant population of 4,250,000. The logical conclusion reached was that the birth-rate within the labouring-classes,

Scottish and Irish, Protestant and Catholic, was virtually identical, while the birth-rate among the more affluent – and in Scotland that meant the native population – had declined. The newspaper also revealed that the Catholic birth-rate had actually started to fall: between 1901 and 1905, 99,946 births had been recorded but, in a similar five-year period between 1923 and 1927, the number had slipped down to 98,659 and these figures were more significant when one realises that the total Catholic population in 1901 was 431,900 and in 1927 was 650,000.

Clearly, the conclusion reached by *The Menace of the Irish Race to Our Scottish Nationality* had been unduly alarmist in terms of population changes, and the statistics had been doctored consciously to heighten the fears of the Scots.

The investigators pointed out another serious flaw in the Church of Scotland's methodology: the notorious 1923 Report – and further publications – failed to consider the possibility that any of the Irish immigrants might move on to other destinations such as America and the Dominions. Not too surprisingly, in view of the nature of their welcome in Scotland, many of the newcomers were quick to consider this country as a mere stepping-stone to other lands. In essence, the 1923 Report stated that all immigrants from Ireland, North or South, had to be Catholic, and that all emigrants from Scotland had to be Scottish. And it assumed as fact that all people of Irish extraction, including those descendants whose families had lived in Scotland continuously since 1845, remained Irish rather than Scottish.

It is tempting to recall Disraeli's famous remark about such reasoning: 'There are three kinds of lies: lies, damned lies, and statistics.'

The next article (published on 23 March) considered the consequences of the current trends. The conclusion of the newspaper's researchers was that the Catholic community within Scotland amounted to some 650,000, equivalent to 13.26% of the whole population. That was not to be considered alarming in itself, but the comparative birth rates did suggest a present and future bias slightly in favour of the Catholics. The journalists did express legitimate social concern about the numbers of Catholics (and Irish) within the West of Scotland, indicating that 450,000 lived in the archdiocese of Glasgow, which extended into Lanarkshire, Ayrshire, Renfrewshire and Dunbartonshire. This concentration of a poor, working class, Irish and Catholic community within such an area was bound to cause problems culturally and socially.

The last article appeared on 25 March and dealt with the issue of 'the Scottish nationality'. The writer unashamedly stated the Church's guiding premise and it was a valid one from the perspective of the majority inside Scotland. The appeals for action to curb immigration had been inspired by worthy Scottish traits: the continuation of intellectual freedom; the moral and democratic values provided by a Presbyterian nation; the preservation of a national identity and religion, both of which were worthy of preserving.

The newspaper considered, however, that any Scottish demand to curb Irish immigration would be ironic, and make the Scots a laughing-stock: '... in inviting those Irishmen, appealing to them by glowing advertisements in the Irish press to come over to build your railways, make your roads, work your coalmines, help in your Clyde shipyards and your Dundee jute mills, lead Glasgow's water supply from Loch Katrine, and then, after they have performed with acknowledged efficiency innumerable and invaluable services, tell them you have no further use for them?'

The writer agreed in part with the Church of Scotland's position that 'Scotland is being gradually divided into two great racial camps, different in ideals, with different traditions, and with widely diverging characteristics. The two races do not fuse to any appreciable extent. The tendency is the very reverse. The Irish race in Scotland keep largely by themselves, and their habits are such that our Scottish people do not readily mingle with them.'

The 'fault' lay in the Catholic Church's refusal to recognise 'mixed marriages' unless certain conditions regarding the upbringing of children were met, and in the segregation accomplished by the 1918 Education (Scotland) Act. It was to be hoped, the newspaper continued, that a national and uniform system of education could be worked out in the near future with the co-operation of all concerned.

Considering the nature of the *Glasgow Herald* and the bulk of its readership, the tone of the articles was surprisingly tolerant. The statistics cited by the Church of Scotland were to be regarded as highly suspect and to be dismissed, but a threat did exist to the nature of Scottish society and to the unquestioned ascendancy of the Protestant religion. However, the prospect of Scotland being overrun by the descendants of the Irish Catholic immigrants was so remote that any present-day speculation was merely academic.

The furore over Irish immigration was scaremongering of a high order. The only conclusion to be drawn from the publication of the Report and its general acceptance is that it represented the views of the majority of Scots living in the Central Belt, and nothing can hide the fact that it was a racist and sectarian document masquerading as legitimate concern. More refreshingly, the series of articles in the *Glasgow Herald* – perhaps astonishing in view of the newspaper's traditional stance – represented a softening of that visceral prejudice. However, the advantages to be derived from a multi-cultural, multi-ethnic Scotland were simply beyond the imagination of the commentators of 1923.

The real problems for Scotland in the period between the World Wars were massive unemployment and sub-standard housing. When ordinary people were struggling just to survive, differences such as race and religion were exaggerated to an unhealthy degree.

In Europe, difficult economic times helped to foster the rise of fascism with leaders like Hitler, Mussolini, and Franco; Scotland produced a minor league version with the emergence of the Scottish Protestant League (in Glasgow) and Protestant Action (in Edinburgh). These extreme right-wing groups fielded candidates for municipal elections, and during the 1930s managed to get substantial representation on the councils of both Glasgow and Edinburgh.

Their leaders, while capable of mustering local support, were not impressive. John Cormack of Protestant Action would serve as an illustration. He had served in the British Army in Ireland during the War of Independence – a term of duty which confirmed his anti-Catholic feelings – but he left the forces in 1922. For a time he worked in the Post Office in Edinburgh – where he was suspected of tampering with the Archbishop of Edinburgh's mail. He was accused of stealing postal orders and letters, but never formally charged, and eventually he was dismissed from his employment.

Despite his chequered past, he was able to influence crowds with his oratory and physical presence, a combination which pandered to the feelings of the mob at public meetings. In 1933 he formed the Protestant Action Society, being elected for North Leith in the municipal elections the following year.

His platform was based on a vehement anti-Catholicism. He advocated the expulsion of Catholics from Scotland in particular, and their electoral disenfranchisement throughout Britain. He proposed that Catholics be removed from all public employment, and the restrictions on their public processions be enforced. In 1935 he and his followers interfered violently in a civic reception accorded to the Catholic Young Men's Society; astonishingly, his followers numbered more than ten thousand and a detachment of Gordon Highlanders from Edinburgh Castle had to be placed on full readiness in order to safeguard the guests who included the Archbishop of Edinburgh.

Clearly, he and his party had tapped into a vein of anti-Catholic or Irish feeling in Scotland. Later in the same year, his party interrupted and marred the ceremony in which the Australian Prime Minister – a Catholic named Joseph Lyons – was being given the freedom of Edinburgh.

Throughout that same summer, Catholics had to stand on vigil outside their chapels to guard against vandalism and damage from Protestant extremists in the wake of the Eucharistic Congress held in Edinburgh in June. This particular celebration – exclusively Catholic – infuriated Cormack and Protestant Action. He organised a demonstration on 24 June near the Waverley Market, where Catholic women were holding a service, and four priests were attacked. The height of the disorder came on the 25th with the climax of the Congress at an open-air procession of the Blessed Sacrament in Canaan Lane in Morningside. The decision had been made to hold this service in Morningside, one of the most respectable and genteel of Edinburgh's districts, in order to avoid any disruption within the Old Town. However, the

scenes of disorder, orchestrated by Protestant Action, were alarming; according to *The Scotsman*, 'an estimated mob of 10,000 had gathered around
Morningside Road ... special coaches containing women and young people
were stoned ... fighting broke out in the crowds, the police were attacked, and
baton charges were made in retaliation' (26 June 1935).

These events, it should be noted, took place in Edinburgh – and not in the
more volatile West of Scotland. Protestant Action at the height of its influence
gained almost twenty-five per cent of votes polled in Edinburgh local elections and attained a membership of 8,000 in that city.

However, the views and actions of Cormack and his party were not taken
up by the mainstream of Scottish society. The Church of Scotland did not lend
its support, tacit or otherwise, to Protestant Action; nor did the Orange Order,
a more middle-of-the-road Protestant organisation. Even more significantly,
the popular press did not approve of its extreme views and inherent violence.
In fact, Cormack's decline as a political force was traced to the actions, at the
height of the disturbances in Edinburgh, of a Glasgow newspaper (*The
Glasgow Weekly Herald*) which published a letter from him exactly as
received, filled with basic errors in spelling, grammar and punctuation. The
ignorance of the man was revealed, and any widespread public approval of his
aims and methods was gradually withdrawn by the populace.

Because nothing permanent ever came of these two extreme right-wing
parties, it is too easy to downplay their importance in the life of the Catholic
and Irish communities in Scotland. They represented a real threat to the well
being of a sizeable percentage of the population, and hinted at an iceberg of
prejudice that still existed.

The question of possible repatriation of the Irish was an intriguing one and
another precedent was recalled: an Anglo-Russian convention between the
British government and the Kerensky regime in Russia in 1917 allowed for the
forcible repatriation of male Lithuanians who had emigrated to Scotland to
work in the Lanarkshire coalmines back to serve in the Russian army; few, if
any, of those conscripts were ever able to rejoin their families in Scotland.

Tensions still existed between de Valera's government in the Free State
and its Westminster counterparts and, if that situation had escalated into a
near-war scenario, it is very likely that Irish-born immigrants to Scotland
might have been deported, or placed in some form of custody. It should be
recalled that, during the Second World War, after Italy under Mussolini's leadership had joined Nazi Germany in 1940, many male Italians of adult age,
although they had lived in the United Kingdom for decades, were placed in
internment camps for the duration of the hostilities.[10]

---

[10] I do not know how much significance to attach to the fact that all of these 'communities' [the Irish,
Lithuanian, and Italian] were predominantly Catholic.

Distrust of the Irish was rife in Scotland in the inter-war period and it was by no means confined to the lower end of the socio-economic scale. Consider the words of Andrew Dewar Gibb, Regius Professor of Scots Law at Glasgow University, writing in 1930:

> In the heart of a dwindling though virile and intelligent race there is growing up another people, immeasurably inferior in every way, but cohesive and solid, refusing obstinately, at the behest of obscurantist magic-men, to mingle with the people whose land they are usurping; unaware of, or if aware, disloyal to all the finest ideals and ambitions of the Scottish race: distinguished by a veritable will to squalour [sic] which is mainly responsible for Scottish slumdom; squatting and breeding in such numbers as to threaten in another hundred years to gain actual predominance in the country. (*Scotland in Eclipse*, 1930)

Another prominent Scot, George Malcolm Thomson, a journalist, wrote of his visceral reaction: 'The sight of three Irish Catholic priests walking in Princes Street came upon me with the shock of a portent. I waited for some demonstration of wrath from heaven. I looked around appealing to some solid outward symbol of Knox's presence in his own land to fall down and crush the papistical intruders.'

Today, in the second year of the new Millennium, public attitudes have changed considerably. For one thing, such blatant and widespread employment practices that existed for the first fifty years of the twentieth century have been declared illegal, and a general feeling that such discrimination is indeed shameful has grown within Scotland. Similarly, racial taunts or abuse is against the law and frowned upon – with the possible exception of football grounds where it still appears to be a part of that particular folk-culture, and generally ignored by the authorities.[11]

Apart from a few pockets – where it is difficult to prove actual prejudice – the situation has improved for all minority groups and, of course, for the Irish. Following the Wildcat Theatre production of *The Celtic Story* the following comments were recounted by a successful Glasgow professional man: 'Do you know what this story is about? It's about us. My grandfather came from Kildare, and worked for the railways, and yours came from Donegal and was a labourer. Now, two generations later, I'm a psychiatrist and you're in insurance.'

There was a justifiable pride in that statement, and perhaps a slight sense of wonder.

In fact, it seems almost ludicrous today to label the descendants of those

---

[11] On 27 October 2000, Pope John Paul II condemned violence and racism at football matches, stating that enthusiasm for one team should not descend to insults for the other. Of course, John Paul II was a keen footballer in his youth, and has apparently retained an interest in the sport. In the audience for the Pope's homily were several players from Lazio, including their Yugoslav defender Mihajlovic who had recently felt obliged to make a public apology for his taunting of an Arsenal opponent in a Champions' League match.

people who flocked to Scotland in search of better prospects 'Irish'. After several generations they are largely indistinguishable from the native population in almost every way and any latent prejudice against 'the Scoto-Irish' – in Handley's phrase – may now be cultural and social rather than racial or sectarian. It might be time to throw this nomenclature into the dustbin of history.

The one exception to the validity of this statement may be the West of Scotland in which sectarian differences still appear to be 'celebrated' openly, although in a more muted form. The situation might have improved, but the frequent outbreaks of hostility are a national disgrace and very often football seems to be an excuse, if not a focus, for those disorders.

No doubt exists that the 'Irish' have become more integrated into the fabric of Scottish society, but the memory of the treatment accorded their ancestors is still a factor in the consciousness of the present-day descendants. Given the evidence of the attitude already shown in this chapter, and the virulence with which it was held, it would be truly astonishing if the 'Irish' were not distrustful.

For many of those people this sense of persecution seems to persist, and in some perverse way almost be accepted, in their collective attitude towards football. For some, the different treatment accorded Rangers and Celtic by the media, the performance of the officials in charge of matches, and of the legislators of the SFA itself, represents the vestigial traces of a discrimination which was once much more widespread.

One Celtic supporter, apparently with a knowledge of medicine, explained it to me: 'It might seem daft to remember all the previous injustices, and make the same complaints year after year ... but it's like a human being having an appendix. It's there, and it serves no useful function, and should be ignored ... but in isolated cases it can suddenly flare up without any warning. Bigotry is like that; often when you think it's all in the past, it erupts again – just like an appendix.'

In 1999 the Scottish composer James MacMillan caused widespread controversy with his speech delivered in Edinburgh when he chose the occasion to deliver a sombre 'state-of-the-union' message. Although a modern and intellectual composer, MacMillan is a keen follower of football and a passionate Celtic supporter, admitting that his work *The Berserking* was prompted by suffering through an epic match between Celtic and Partizan Belgrade in European competition. Celtic won that match by 5–4 but were eliminated on the away-goals rule, victims of a last-minute counter; MacMillan comments wryly that this work is imbued with 'the motif of squandered energy'. He is also on record as having said: 'The sound of 50,000 committed, partisan people is incredibly exciting, a sort of exhilarating cacophony; I love to hear the rise and fall of the fans' chants, and I'm continually thinking about it as an inspiration for new music.'

The amount of publicity generated by the speech, and the astonishing number of responses in articles, columns, and letters to the newspapers, seem to indicate that in some way MacMillan's words had touched a raw nerve in the Scottish psyche. The interest aroused suggests all too clearly that the composer's words contained more than a kernel of truth. If, as was claimed by his critics, the speech represented nothing more than the mistaken or deluded thoughts of one individual, why such a furore? For some weeks it seemed as if every academic in the country was anxious to disassociate himself from MacMillan's comments, without having read the complete text of the speech.[12] In fact, one such person volunteered and submitted a rebuttal to the newspapers even before the composer had delivered his speech in Edinburgh.

However, in the year following the speech, the composer has been gratified and encouraged by noting a gradual change in his critics' thinking, characterised by a more thoughtful attitude to the problems raised.

After starting off by commenting on the sense of optimism apparent in Scotland with hopes for the success of the new Scottish Parliament and a renewal of aspirations at the Millennium, MacMillan lamented the fact that the Scottish artistic tradition was enervated by one of the defining moments in Scottish history: the Reformation.

According to him, speaking as a musician, only 'remnants' and 'fragments from a broken past' remain. He condemns this 'religiously-inspired conscious destruction and abandonment of our musical heritage' and puts the blame on the restricting effects of the Reformation on Scottish life. However, he does acknowledge that: '... the world of the Arts is the one arena where I have never encountered anything approximating to the visceral anti-Catholicism which so disfigures many other walks of life in our society.'

He warned against complacency in the modern age by reminding his listeners that: 'In many walks of life – in the workplace, in the professions, in academia, in politics and in sport – anti-Catholicism, even when it is not particularly malign, is as endemic as it is second nature. ... Many of us are either happy to live with, or to deny completely, the existence or the importance of, an anti-Catholicism which is still a significant element of Scottish culture.'

He made several references in his address to football: 'On my trips abroad or to England, I am often asked curious, probing questions about my country, and specifically about the extreme nature of our anti-Catholic past and rumours of a still-prevalent sour anti-Catholicism. This is mainly sparked by the activities of our referees and our sporting bodies.'

Rather courageously, MacMillan raised the question of the present-day

---

[12] Defenders of James MacMillan point out accurately enough that most critics of the address were credited in the media with the authority their academic positions warranted, while Dr. MacMillan was depicted often in a rather patronising way as 'the modern composer' and his credentials as an academic and professor were ignored.

attitude towards Catholics in Scottish sport – a somewhat ambivalent one in view of the continental signings by Rangers in recent years:

> My interest in football tends to lead to easy, animated and good-humoured discussion any-where I go in the world but, because I am Scottish, the gentle ridicule and barely repressed sniggers I generally encounter is not just due to the decreasing quality of our national game. Scotland, after all, is known as the only country in the footballing world where a player can be given the referee's red card for making the sign of the cross. I've just come back from Australia where the only piece of Scottish news in three weeks to make it into TV, radio and newspaper coverage was the national team manager frantically defending himself against the charge of singing anti-Catholic songs. In the light of the precedent set by Donald Findlay none of the Australians I spoke to about it seemed the slightest bit surprised. In what other country do retired referees boast of having done their best to help one team against another? And in what other country is there a special kind of rage in the press reserved for those who cry foul in these matters?

In Scotland far too much importance is given to a part of life which is meant to be a recreation or a hobby. But nobody can deny that football does indeed play an inappropriately significant part, and that is unfortunate. However, it may not be an exaggeration to claim that sometimes this passion can act as a metaphor for Scottish life itself – at least in the broad issue of sectarianism. In a society acknowledged as both anti-Catholic and anti-Irish, it would have been surprising if referees and other football officials had somehow managed to avoid the malaise.

The Very Reverend Dr. Andrew McLellan, a Moderator of the General Assembly, recently stated (8 July 2001) that: 'People of my background think that the effect of anti-Catholicism is less serious than it is said to be, that people like us would never encourage divisions in society, and that sectarianism is limited to a tiny element of society in certain well-defined geographical areas. Now is the time for my community to recognise that all of these are illusions.'

On the same day Ian Bell, writing in the *Sunday Herald*, claimed:

> Many will allege ... that the mutual loathing you can still see, hear and feel at an Old Firm game is a relic of the past, fading fast. Anyone who raises the issue, as James MacMillan did not so long ago, is sent off with a flea in his ear ... It is called being in denial. The observable fact may be that the sort of loathing which scars football in Glasgow is merely the echo of a wider and deeper division in Scottish society. It penetrates the professional classes as surely as it penetrates the housing schemes.

Some Celtic followers still believe that events in football, on or off the pitch, represent the lingering traces of a bitter anti-Catholic and Irish feeling; a cancer of the mind, or heart, which is notoriously difficult to keep in remission. Jack Ramsay, the Grand Secretary of the Orange Order in Scotland, was quoted in July 2001 as feeling that the Orange Order might become some form of paramilitary organisation in the event of Scotland gaining complete independence. He also claimed that comments by James MacMillan and Frank Roy, a Lanarkshire Member of Parliament, were: 'unadulterated nonsense. They are describing some Scotland that used to exist in the 1950s.'[13]

In a modern society which has outlawed discrimination, football may be one of the areas in which such anti-social tendencies may be safely expressed openly in the stands, or administratively in a subliminal manner, without fear of retribution.[14]

---

[13] The MP raised a considerable furore in early 2001 when he suggested that the proposed visit of the Irish Prime Minister, Bertie Ahern, to Carfin in Lanarkshire in order to dedicate a memorial to the victims of the Irish Famine could spark public disorder because of the close proximity of a Rangers–Celtic match. Significantly, the dedication was postponed and took place uneventfully several months later.

When I showed Ramsay's words to a devout Catholic, he commented bleakly: 'When I was growing up in the 1950s I was told that discrimination against Catholics in Scotland was something that existed in the 1920s – and that I should not be paranoid.'

[14] Celtic were not the only Scottish club to suffer outrageous treatment because of their background. Hibernian have more legitimate claims than the Glasgow club to be considered *the* Catholic and Irish club in Scotland and their early years comprise a catalogue of injustices and insults, well documented and indisputable. The club was founded by Father Edward Hannan, an Edinburgh priest, and membership was restricted to members of St Patrick's Catholic Young Men's Society. St. Patrick's was the Roman Catholic church in the Cowgate, the overcrowded slum in Edinburgh's Old Town popularly called 'Little Ireland'.

Before they could play any competitive matches, Hibernian had to become members of both the SFA and the Edinburgh FA; neither association was willing to welcome the newcomers. Apparently, the SFA's initial response to the new club was insultingly abrupt: 'We are catering for Scotsmen, not Irishmen,' and the Edinburgh Association dutifully endorsed this response, going so far as to instruct other clubs within their jurisdiction not to play the newcomers. It took a year of hard lobbying before the Edinburgh F.A. were to approve Hibernian's application for membership; the SFA also followed suit but so grudgingly that they barred the new club from that season's Scottish Cup competition.

Similarly, Dundee Hibernian were to encounter the same hostility, to such an extent that they eventually changed their name to Dundee United in 1923 to become more acceptable. It is encouraging to note that the club's change-strip for 2000/2001 reverts to their original colour of green to honour their founders.

CHAPTER THREE

The Cox-Tully Affair

Every Old Firm match is played out in a tense atmosphere, either on the terracing or on the pitch, and the Glasgow Police are usually highly relieved
when the weekend of a Rangers–Celtic clash is over. Several historians have
attempted to describe the atmosphere at an Old Firm confrontation:

> No one watching a Rangers–Celtic game today could come away from it under the illusion
> that all he had been to was a football match. On the one side of the ground is a sea of green
> and white, sprinkled with the tricolour of the Irish Republic; on the other, a mass of red,
> white and blue scarves set against a vigorous waving of Union Jacks; from one end come
> rebel songs in praise of the Republic backed up by chants denouncing the UDA; from the
> other come songs in praise of being up to one's knees in Fenian blood, recalling the glories
> of the Sash and the victory at the Boyne, and backed up by chants of an uncomplimentary
> nature about the Pope and the IRA. The hatred that fills the air at these games is almost
> physical in its impact, as Glasgow plays out in bloodless microcosm the tragedy being
> enacted in Ulster. (Bill Murray, *The Old Firm*, Edinburgh, 1984)

Despite this awareness, at the start of the 1949/50 season, Celtic were due to
face Rangers four times between 13 August and 24 September: twice in
League Cup sectional play, once in the Glasgow Cup, and once in the League.

This was surely a recipe for disaster.

Interest was even higher than usual in 1949 because Celtic, after their
scandalously part-time approach to football during World War II, and a skir-
mish with relegation in 1947/48, were at last making a serious effort to
improve.

In July 1948 they had appointed a coach in the person of the venerable
Jimmy Hogan, almost sixty-five years of age but a man respected throughout
Europe for his knowledge of the game. So highly regarded was he that he
attended the famous 6–3 rout of England at Wembley by Hungary in 1953 as
a guest of the Hungarian FA. And Celtic had finally started to buy quality
players at considerable expense: Lesley Johnston, formerly of Clyde and
Hibernian, and Charlie Tully from Belfast Celtic for some £8,000. In addition,
a couple of promising newcomers had arrived from the junior ranks in time
for the 1949/50 season: Mike Haughney from Newtongrange Star, and the
tiny Bobby Collins from Pollok. The teenage Collins, an outstanding
prospect, had been the subject of an acrimonious dispute between Celtic and
Everton, but the Parkhead club managed to secure his services eventually.

It was felt throughout Scotland that Celtic were now in a much better
position to mount a challenge to Rangers, apparently the perennial champions,

and to Hibernian, the emerging force in Scottish football. The crowds had flocked back to Scottish football after the war, and in particular to Celtic Park after the arrival of Charlie Tully in 1948.

With the renewed enthusiasm came higher expectations, and the possibility of disappointment.

The first Old Firm match, in the League Cup, took place at Celtic Park on 13 August 1949 before a crowd of 71,000 and was a typically hard-fought encounter. The match was played at a torrid pace despite the heat and brilliant sunshine; both sides were awarded a penalty kick, converted by Waddell of Rangers and McPhail of Celtic. Celtic scraped through by 3–2, the winning goal scored by Haughney, making his debut for Celtic as was Collins on the right wing; and the match was handled impeccably by J.A. Mowat (Rutherglen).

An all-ticket crowd of 95,000 filled Ibrox Park for the return fixture on 27 August, and the match turned out to be a highly controversial affair. Celtic took the initiative from the start, and Haughney broke through to strike the crossbar in twenty minutes but, shortly afterwards, came the incident that rocked Scottish football. Sammy Cox was allowing the ball to go through to his goalkeeper, and Charlie Tully was a few yards behind, following up; the referee, Mr. A.B. Gebbie (Hamilton) was some thirty yards behind the players, a reasonable distance in the context. As the ball was being cleared by Brown, the Rangers goalkeeper, Cox turned and kicked Tully, who immediately went down in agony. The referee saw Tully fall to the ground, but waved play on. The Celtic trainer, Alec Dowdells, raced round the track to treat his player who had rolled behind the goal, and attended to him for some minutes while play continued.

The incident had happened at the Celtic end of the ground in full view of the massed Celtic support, initially angered by the assault on their star player and now inflamed by the fact that it had gone unpunished by the referee. The situation turned uglier by the second: the howls of outrage from the Celtic supporters were followed by prolonged booing, an outbreak of fighting on the terracing, and the throwing of bottles and other missiles in the general direction of the pitch. Police reinforcements rushed to the scene behind the goal to deal with the situation as did ambulance men to cope with injured spectators struck by the missiles. Hundreds of spectators left their places near the foot of the west terracing to seek the safety of the track and the area behind the goal.

It was a horrible scene, and a highly dangerous one – a minute or so that could easily have developed into a full-scale riot. The author was at the match as a fourteen-year-old and had a perfect view of the crucial incident:

I was at the Celtic end of Ibrox, about ten rows from the front, and level with the edge of the six-yard box. It was always going to be Rangers' ball, and Cox was steering it back to his goalkeeper with Tully behind him. Cox turned and kicked Tully as Brown collected the ball. It was so blatant that it was almost unbelievable, in the way that traffic accidents can be. You can see it happening, but your mind refuses to believe what you are seeing. In defence of the referee, I think he was in a direct line with the players and he could not see the actual kick because Tully himself was obstructing his view.

The charismatic Charlie Tully, who signed for Celtic in 1948.

Tully was a victim of his own talent to a certain extent. The charismatic Irishman had been a breath of fresh air to the staid Scottish game since his arrival a year earlier and the newspapers were full of his antics and his legendary cheek. Like his Ranger counterpart in this incident, Tully could stand as a symbol of his club at this time: he was a superstar, newsworthy all the time, a centre of attention, no matter how well or badly he was playing. But he was inconsistent, an artiste rather than a worker, fragile rather than durable.

In his most famous game to date, against Rangers at Celtic Park on 25 September 1948, Tully played magnificently and ran Rangers' famous 'Iron Curtain' defence ragged. Celtic won by 3–1, and Rangers immediately dropped Ian McColl, Tully's marker and a future Scottish internationalist, for several weeks as a punishment. Celtic supporters immediately hailed Tully as the new Moses who would lead the team into the Promised Land and restore the club to its pre-war glories.

However, throughout his longish career with Celtic, Charlie Tully never had the reputation of trying to get other players into trouble by feigning injury. He could be a master of other forms of gamesmanship: irritating, contrary and irksome, distracting opponents with his line of patter; but it would be difficult to recall too many instances in which he dived or feigned an injury in order to get an opponent into trouble with the referee. In fact, this type of behaviour was generally foreign to players of that era.

The newspaper coverage of the events at Ibrox was varied.

The Scotsman reflected its pretensions to be a quality newspaper with an emphasis on cricket, golf, and racing. The sport was found on the second back page, which it shared with farm news including livestock prices and lamb sales,[15] and the following extract constitutes the *entire* match report: 'In a game watched by an all-ticket crowd of 95,000 Rangers reversed their earlier defeat by Celtic. The latter, with much more of the play, just could not finish off some very pretty football. Rangers were more direct, and got the goals. It was a pity the game was marred by those terracing troubles which seem to happen so frequently at the "Old Firm" meetings' (29 August 1949).

Cyril Horne, a writer more noted for an antipathy towards Rangers than a preference for Celtic, was already anticipating in the *Glasgow Herald* that the authorities might take action against Celtic for the misbehaviour of their supporters at Ibrox, and referred to previous sanctions:

> On 17 September 1941, the SFA announced that the Celtic ground would be closed for one month and during that period they would not be allowed to play on opponents' grounds in Glasgow. The Parkhead officials were also ordered to post bills to intimate to their supporters on their reopening that it had been closed by order of the Association because of 'the serious misbehaviour at Ibrox Stadium on 6 September' and to warn supporters that more serious punishment would befall Celtic if there was a recurrence of such behaviour on any ground.

> The SFA decision was not at all acceptable to many people besides Celtic, who officially stated at the time that none of their players had given the crowd any reason for creating trouble before the disturbance on the terracing started. Will Celtic again be held responsible for the actions of a small section of alleged supporters of the club whom neither they nor anyone else wants in football? How indeed can this unruly element be kept out of the various grounds? No solution so far has been found. But if clubs ensure that their players do not, by their actions on the field, encourage hooliganism, there will not be so much of it.

> So far as Saturday is concerned neutral members among Scottish Football legislators should have no trouble apportioning the responsibility for the trouble. (29 August 1949)

What had enraged the Celtic following was the realisation or the feeling that, acting in cold blood, Cox had chosen a moment when he might escape punishment for his action. Some felt that he had calculated the odds to perfection, banking on the fact that a referee might be reluctant to order off a Rangers player at Ibrox in an Old Firm match. It was recalled that the fierce-tackling Cox, normally a left-half, had been switched to right-half for this match specifically to mark Tully – as had also happened the previous season in the wake of another Celtic victory in the same competition.

Cox, a two-footed player, was a most versatile performer. Regularly fielded at left-half, he could be switched to right-half and, according to Rangers' needs, he was frequently fielded in either of the full-back positions and on occasion even played at inside left.

The Saturday mayhem at Ibrox Stadium provided a busy Monday at the courts in Glasgow. Bailie Joseph McKell of Govan Police Court sentenced Henry Finn (22) to twenty days' imprisonment, commenting as he did so:

---

[15] It is possible that a post-war shortage of paper was a contributory factor in the cramped pages of the newspaper at this time. Besides, as an Edinburgh-based newspaper, it concentrated that day on the Hibs–Hearts clash rather than on the Old Firm.

'Football supporters are the most unsportsmanlike people I know; they go only to see one team win. Every club has supporters of this kind whom they could do very well without.' The magistrate had heard evidence from the Fiscal, John Boss: 'A disturbance took place on the west terracing and a fight broke out among spectators. Police worked their way towards Finn and apprehended him. This was the signal for a number of bottles and other missiles to be thrown, and a number of people were injured.'

Cornelius Cassidy (18) was arrested at Bridgeton Cross where a large crowd had assembled an hour after the match at Ibrox. He was seen taking a bottle from his pocket and throwing it at a supporters' bus, smashing a window. He was charged by the police on duty at this traditional flashpoint, and given a thirty days' term on the Monday.

Immediately after the match the Celtic directors had asked the SFA to conduct an Inquiry into the events at Ibrox. They were afraid that the club would be held solely to blame for the mayhem, and were anxious about the consequences for Celtic, given recent decisions by the SFA against the club, and the threat made by the SFA after the previous trouble at Ibrox in 1941.

They also felt most strongly that their player had been brutally treated and that the referee had erred grievously. With the score 0–0 and Celtic on top, they should have been awarded a penalty kick, and Cox should have been ordered off. Their view was shared by every newspaper report in the country, although it was recognised that nothing could – or perhaps should – change the result of a football match influenced by a genuine mistake on the part of a referee.

Nevertheless, such public disorder was rightly a matter for the authorities, and the Glasgow Magistrates requested a meeting with representatives of the SFA. The magistrates indicated pointedly that the SFA had considerable powers and listed them for the benefit of the public: the Association had complete control over players and could impose disciplinary measures upon them; it had the authority to close football grounds as a punishment; and it had the authority to appoint referees.

Clearly, the city magistrates were suggesting that the football authorities clamp down severely on all forms of misbehaviour: by clubs, players and officials. Spectators, it seemed, were not the only ones on trial in this case.

The *Glasgow Herald* still hoped that football could handle its own affairs adequately:

There have been few cases of serious disturbances at football matches that were not caused by incidents that took place on the playing pitch. Clubs and their players must be given a final warning that they will suffer severe punishment if the blame for trouble on the terracing can be laid at their door. If, on the other hand, a trouble-provoking incident is not immediately dealt with by the referee, either because he has not seen it or through incompetence on his part, football club officials should prove their honesty of purpose by themselves punishing the perpetrator or perpetrators. (3 September 1949)

Cyril Horne, a well-informed journalist, must have realised that Rangers would be most reluctant to punish their player for his part in the incident. He knew also that Celtic had dropped their full-back McGuire for the Ibrox clash because of doubts about his temperament, and Bob Kelly would not hesitate to act against other Celtic players who had misbehaved. At that time Horne was virtually a lone voice in criticising the Ibrox club; indeed, his editor on one later occasion had to hire bodyguards to protect him following death threats received at the newspaper in the wake of his reporting a Rangers European match.

Horne continued to pursue the matter of refereeing standards most diligently. In one column, printed on 17 September, he made several suggestions for improvement. Too often, he argued, referees had been appointed because of their knowledge of the rules, based on written or oral tests, and not because of any aptitude for the job, while too many linesmen were content to be only linesmen and did not aspire to become referees. He felt that a greater degree of professionalism could be attained by paying the match officials the same amount as the players instead of the current £4. 4. 0, and that the payments should be made through the SFA or the Scottish League. He also pointed that the antiquated system whereby the referee was paid directly by the home club's manager (or even the gate-checker) was open to abuse in several ways.

A few days later the chairman of Elgin City, J.R. Hamilton, entered the discussion with a letter to the editor of the *Glasgow Herald*:

> Referees have a difficult task. They may have the most proficient knowledge of the rules of the game and orally and in writing solve many problems. The construing of those rules on the field of play involves an instantaneous decision. Who is ever infallible? Certainly not referees whose slightest slip is immediately greeted with disapproval. This is where the player can play his part. His acceptance of a decision against him, even if he knows his action is blameless, will react on the onlookers and mollify their wrath. Indeed, his sporting action will help him to gain in stature in the eyes of the spectators.

Understandably, Mr. Hamilton was taking the establishment point of view – that referees were men of integrity, honest enough to make decisions as they saw them. Given the nature of the Rangers–Celtic divide in the West of Scotland, this may well have been an idealistic perspective.

Cyril Horne, for one, had not been overly impressed by the impartiality of officials; on 17 September he ended his column: ' ... and, in the not too distant future, (the SFA) should consider whether any club or clubs have in the past decade or so received much more than their fair share of the breaks of football.' Clearly, he was suggesting that the preferential treatment accorded Rangers by referees during the war was being continued.

The activity in the newspapers had been stirred by the fact that the Referee Committee had released its report on 7 September, in advance of submitting it to the full SFA Council on 28 September. The preamble stated that the committee had conducted 'an exhaustive inquiry and felt duty-bound to take a serious view of the matter.' The committee was 'satisfied that the rowdyism on the terracing was incited by the actions of the two players, S. Cox and C. Tully, and also in some measure by an error of judgement on the part of the referee.' The committee put forward six minutes to be approved by the SFA Council:

1. Notices shall be posted at every entrance to the grounds advising that admission will be refused to anybody carrying flags, bottles and any other possible missile; that anybody inside the ground in possession of any of the above shall be removed, and may be prosecuted; and that the police and the magistrates have been informed of the steps taken;
2. Any refreshment kiosk inside the grounds that sells bottled refreshment shall be closed on the occasion of Rangers-Celtic matches;
3. Both clubs are requested to place notices inside the dressing-rooms reminding the players of their responsibilities and of the SFA's determination to deal very severely with any player found guilty in these matches of any misconduct on the field which incurs disciplinary action by the referee;
4. S. Cox and C. Tully should be severely reprimanded, and that these reprimands shall count in any future disciplinary actions;
5. The referee should be informed that his failure to take appropriate action in the incident in which S. Cox and C. Tully were involved might have precipitated a more serious situation but, in view of his previous good record, no further action should be taken against him;
6. It was proposed that the Scottish League Management Committee be asked to consider whether, owing to the frequency with which Scottish referees come into contact with the players in their various matches, it would not be advisable in matches such as those between these two clubs where tension is likely to be great, to appoint a referee from another British association or, if such a suggestion does not find favour, they should discontinue the practice of balloting the referee for these matches and appoint the referee by other means.

The report ended with appreciation for the prompt and effective action taken by the police, and an acceptance of the Glasgow Magistrates' invitation to meet on Tuesday 13 September. This was, ironically, the date for the next Celtic–Rangers match at Celtic Park.

Celtic had been claiming for some time that the refereeing in Old Firm matches had often been most unsatisfactory, and the Referee Committee's sixth recommendation proved the point exactly.

It is astonishing to note that, apparently, the choice of referee for even an important fixture was still a matter of luck as the official was appointed by a ballot. However, this could not have been enforced too strictly as Peter Craigmyle (Aberdeen) was not assigned any match involving his home-town team for many seasons, and Willie Webb (Glasgow) had not refereed a Rangers–Celtic match for eight years, a tacit recognition of the fact that Webb lived above Jimmy Smith, Rangers' centre forward, in Mosspark.[16]

The chief writer for the *Daily Express* at that time was Tommy Muirhead, and he also wrote of the difficulties encountered by referees: 'To say that a meeting between Celtic and Rangers should be just another game and that any

---

[16] I can vouch for this personally. During the Christmas holidays in 1955 I worked for the Post Office and found that Smith and Webb were indeed neighbours. Webb, of course, refereed the infamous match at Ibrox which led directly to the closing of Celtic Park for a month in 1941.

referee should be able to take charge is bunkum ... the greatest and most tense club game in the world is more difficult to control than any international, and just any referee is not good enough for an international' (19 September 1949). As a journalist, Muirhead had the added advantage of having represented Scotland eight times, and had participated in Old Firm clashes as a Rangers player during the 1920s and 30s.

The training, promotion and selection of referees was still haphazard as this list of officials for a typical Saturday in August 1949 might suggest: H.P. Anderson (Edinburgh), J. Anderson (Edinburgh), W. Bowman (Motherwell), J.S. Cox (Rutherglen), C.E. Faultless (Glasgow), P. Fitzpatrick (Glasgow), A.B. Gebbie (Hamilton), D. Gerrard (Aberdeen), W.G. Livingstone (Glasgow), R.M. Main (Glasgow), G. Mitchell (Falkirk), J.A. Mowat (Rutherglen), F. Scott (Paisley), and W. Webb (Glasgow). Some of these officials were, or went on to become, outstanding referees but this was largely through their own talents and efforts to improve rather than through any system established by the SFA.

Revealingly, and to Celtic's delight, the sixth minute cited above indicated clearly that part of the problem lay with the calibre of officiating, or perhaps with the unfairness of asking Scottish officials to handle such a fixture given the unnatural level of hostility normally aroused by it. Unfortunately, nothing was to come of this proposal then – and nothing has ever come of it when it has been resurrected usually in the wake of subsequent Old Firm 'shame-games'.

At first sight it appeared as if the SFA were prepared to act. The directives seemed resolute: clubs had been reprimanded, players censured, referees reproved, and spectators warned – but Celtic were far from happy.

Their directors met soon afterwards to discuss the report, and deemed it 'unacceptable to Celtic'. Their primary objection lay in the preamble and in the fourth minute of the report. Rightly, Celtic could not accept as fact that their player had contributed to the rowdyism in any way, other than being the victim of an unprovoked assault. They announced their intention to renew their request to the Executive Council of the SFA for an independent inquiry, and stated that they would be giving their approval of Tully's intention to appeal against his reprimand.

The club received some backing, and from one unexpected source. The Scottish Players' Union had been founded only a year or so previously and that organisation contacted Celtic (and the media) volunteering to help with any appeal lodged by Tully. Several members of the Players' Union had attended the match as spectators and were willing to act as witnesses. In 1949 there was no opportunity of a 'trial by television'. If the SFA had wanted to pursue the matter further, the testimony of such qualified witnesses would have been invaluable. As the biggest and richest clubs in Scotland, Rangers and Celtic, however, were suspicious of union activity and, not too surprisingly, Celtic informed the Players' Union that the club would be dealing with the matter alone.

On 9 September Alec Millar, the president of the fledgling association, had commented on the weak refereeing prevalent in the game and had been quoted in the *Glasgow Herald*:

> Things are different nowadays. I could mention one referee, Mr. Martin of Ladybank. When he was in charge of a match, I have heard players in the dressing room advise one another not to take liberties. Mr. Martin was recognised by every player in the game as a just and strong official, one who would stand no nonsense. Looking at referees today, it seems to me that advisory notices are more required in the Referee's Room than warning ones in the players' pavilion.

Cyril Horne also branded the recommendations as 'unsatisfactory', and wrote: 'It is no exaggeration to say that even Rangers followers were convinced, if at the same time astonished, that their player by his foul on his opponent was primarily responsible ... their [the Referee Committee] finding implies that both players were equally to blame; that, so far as those who saw the incident can reason, was not the case' (*Glasgow Herald*, 8 September 1949).

In fact, virtually without exception, the Scottish press deplored the findings, as indicated by this excerpt from the *Glasgow Observer*: 'That the committee had made an obvious miscarriage of justice was shown by the immediate reaction of indignation among neutral sportswriters and football followers who lost no time in taking up the cudgels on Tully's behalf' (9 September 1949).

Meanwhile, Celtic had been drawn against Rangers in the semi-final of the Glasgow Cup, and the match was played at Celtic Park on 13 September. Both teams, conscious of the need to be on their best behaviour, seemed intent on concentrating on football, and the large crowd enjoyed the proceedings. John McPhail put Celtic in front from the penalty spot in the first half, and Billy Williamson headed the equaliser a few minutes after the interval.

The trouble started with only a few minutes left. The referee (W. Davidson, Glasgow) decided that Roy Milne, Celtic's left back, had handled the ball some thirty-five yards out. The defender started to protest strongly that he had chested it down. Several other Celtic players in the vicinity agreed with him, and surrounded the referee while registering the protest. Most reporters later felt that the referee's decision had been wrong and, given the fact that the players had been clearly instructed to accept the official's decisions without question and had done so until the eight-seventh minute, Celtic's appeals against that decision would seem to have had some added justification.

Worse was to follow because, while the referee was being confronted by the protesting Celtic players, a Rangers forward slipped the ball forward to Findlay inside the penalty area and that well-known 'poacher' netted the ball, and awaited developments. The referee wheeled around in time to see only the finish of the move, but he awarded a goal. He had not signalled for the free kick to be taken, had not seen from where it had been taken, and could not have been aware that the ball was in motion when the kick was taken. Some newspapers suggested that Findlay was also in an offside position but, as the linesman was in a perfect position and had not raised his flag, this should not have been another issue.

Celtic players were incandescent with fury; Rangers were almost embarrassed, and few of them had bothered to congratulate Findlay. The Rangers end of the ground cheered momentarily and lapsed into silence, intrigued by the events on the pitch, while the Celtic followers regained their voices after some seconds of sheer disbelief at the referee's decisions. Police reinforcements quickly appeared on the track to quell any possible invasion but they were not needed. The events had been almost too farcical to provoke the extra ingredient of violence.

The game was delayed while Celtic players continued to argue with the referee, and among themselves. There was not the slightest doubt that several members of the team were actively considering leaving the pitch in a form of protest against a rapid-fire sequence of outrageous happenings so late in the match. The Celtic fans were in a strange sort of mood, almost light-headed, with many encouraging the players to leave the field but most still shaking their heads in total disbelief, feeling that once more a referee's decision had adversely affected Celtic in the course of an Old Firm match.

Eventually, after a delay of several minutes, during which the Rangers players remained lined up in their half of the field and the referee stood defiantly in the centre circle, the game was resumed. A clearance from a Rangers defender went down the right wing in the direction of Waddell, and Boden, Celtic's centre half, raced across to deal with the situation; his tackle for the 50-50 ball was waist-high and the Rangers winger escaped injury only by jumping several feet in the air. Seconds later, the referee ended the game, wisely, in view of the mood of the aggrieved players.

Cyril Horne pointed out the wrongness of Mr. Davidson's decisions at the free kick, but he also stated quite categorically that Tully should have been sent off for attempting to persuade and lead his colleagues off the pitch, and for delaying the game, and that Boden also should have been ordered off also for his attempt to dismember Waddell. Ironically, the match had been played in a most sportsmanlike manner by both sides up to the last three minutes.

The other quality newspaper – from its Edinburgh viewpoint – was more detached in its reporting: '... the match was carried through in an orderly manner. There was a tense moment in the last two minutes, however, when Rangers scored a disputed winning goal to give them victory by two goals to one. For a few seconds it looked as if there might be trouble on the terracings and on the field but the tension quickly blew over and the game was resumed'

(*The Scotsman*, 14 September 1949).

After these tumultuous events, the last thing Scottish football needed was more of the same. Yet another Rangers–Celtic fixture was looming: the Scottish League match at Ibrox on 24 September.

Celtic were in a quandary: their supporters had misbehaved badly at Ibrox on their last visit, and some of their players had done so at Celtic Park in the Glasgow Cup-tie. Accordingly, the directors sent a letter to the Scottish League almost immediately after the Glasgow Cup-tie asking that their forth-coming league game with Rangers be postponed or, if the committee thought fit, cancelled altogether. In case anybody considered that this was an attempt to deprive Rangers of gate-money, Celtic also suggested that they would agree to the cancellation of the return league game at Celtic Park on 2 January 1950.

The National Secretary of the Celtic Supporters' Association, H. McGrechan, announced that the association was totally behind any action that the club was contemplating to resolve the situation. He added that the mem-bers of the Supporters' Association, which numbered some 12,000, might stage an effective protest by boycotting the fixture if it were still scheduled.

The football authorities, most particularly the Scottish League, were placed in an embarrassing situation, and attempted to get Celtic to change their minds. On 17 September the matter was given a prominent place on the front pages: 'Efforts will be made today to get Celtic Football Club directors to withdraw that letter to the SFA suggesting that matches with Rangers next Saturday and on New Year's Day be postponed or cancelled' (*Daily Express*, 17 September 1949).

Despite the concerted efforts being made to persuade Celtic to withdraw their proposal, the club was determined to see this matter through against the opposition of the sport's authorities. The *Daily Record's* principal reporter, W.C. Gallagher was, as always, frank about the issues: 'While the consensus is that the committee should turn down the request for postponement, there is considerable sympathy for Celtic and there are clubmen to say that, in taking up the cudgels, the Parkhead club are fighting for clubs other than them-selves. It appears certain that one good thing will emerge from the business – that the refereeing problem will be firmly tackled. And high time too' (19 September 1949).

The League Management Committee was forced eventually to consider Celtic's letter, and decided that the fixture should go ahead as arranged, and that Mr. M.A. Mann (Perth) would be the referee. Later in the same day, four members of the League Management Committee – Bob Kelly (Celtic), W.C. Johnston (Queen of the South), H.M. Dickson (Queen's Park), and W.B. Palmer (Falkirk) – went as a delegation to a conference with the SFA in order to discuss the question of refereeing in general. However, no statement was issued as a consequence.

Understandably, Rangers were reluctant to take part in any public debate over the issues and their chairman, John Wilson, answered a question posed by a *Daily Express* journalist on 19 September: 'Rangers have no grumbles about anything.'

'Waverley', who had reported on football for more than thirty years, had summed up Celtic's position frankly a week earlier: 'In the two most recent of this season's three games with Rangers, Celtic emphatically believe that they did not get justice from the referee. My opinion is that they were victims of weak refereeing. However, Celtic down the years have never believed that they were the sufferers of the controlling official's weakness as much as his prejudice. Indeed, there are responsible people connected with the club who go so far as to employ the word 'persecution' (*Daily Record*, 12 September 1949).

There was no way that the authorities could agree with Celtic's request without acknowledging there was indeed something rotten within Scottish football. Thus, the Scottish League dismissed Celtic's plea, and the fixture went ahead at Ibrox before a crowd estimated at 64,000. This marked a decrease of 31,000 on the previous Old Firm match at the same stadium on 27 August. Clearly, the boycott, called by the Supporters' Association and backed by Celtic, had worked.

Predictably, the match itself was an anti-climax, Rangers running out easy winners by 4–0 as Celtic, playing to their chairman's strict instructions, avoided any excessively physical challenges. The referee had no trouble at all in controlling players 'who would have paid homage to a schoolma'am refereeing a girls' hockey match'. At the conclusion, 'the handshaking was so general as almost to be suspect. Rangers' victory could not have been more complete, but it was as hollow in the circumstances as it was decisive' (*Glasgow Herald*: 26 September 1949).

The one exception to Celtic's pacifism was the right-back Jimmy McGuire who gave away a late penalty for a crude challenge, cheered lustily by those Celtic fans still in the ground, on Rangers' left back, 'Tiger' Shaw who was by then playing on the wing because of a shoulder injury. In the first match of the season at Celtic Park on 13 August, McGuire had conceded another penalty against Rangers by downing Findlay in the area. At Ibrox, Bob Kelly was so incensed at the player's continuing lack of control that he ordered the manager to drop McGuire, and the player made only one more appearance for Celtic that season before being released on a free transfer.

Celtic had also decided to withdraw Charlie Tully from the line-up, although they claimed that he was suffering from a leg-strain, and he was also to miss the following week's match against Raith Rovers at Celtic Park. Tully did not attend the match at Ibrox even as a spectator and, surprisingly for a player requiring treatment for an injury, was allowed to return to Belfast for a week's break. Most people assumed that Tully had been given a club suspension for his role in the closing minutes of the Glasgow Cup-tie and, if so, it was another indication that Celtic were enforcing disciplinary actions against their own players without prompting from the authorities. It would have been perfectly in character for Celtic's chairman, Bob Kelly, to have enforced these measures.

The controversial report from the Referee Committee on the Cox–Tully affair was considered by the SFA Council on 28 September, and presented by its chairman, Mr. Angus Forbes (Inverness). In his address Forbes reiterated his claim that the Inquiry had been exhaustive, and had heard seven witnesses, including the referee and his linesmen. He came to the defence of Mr. Gebbie, claiming: 'The referee had not had a clear uninterrupted view of the incident, but he had, indeed, erred in not asking his linesmen for their opinion.'

He then inflamed Celtic's feelings by his remarks about Tully's involvement: 'Tully simulated any slight injury he might have received, and his actions might have been as blameworthy as an admitted indiscretion by Cox.' He added that Tully had later on been cautioned but that the player had denied this when giving his evidence.

Subsequently, Tully was to appeal against the SFA censure on the grounds that he had not been cautioned during the match. His case, surprising as it sounds, did have some merit and it would be supported by the club. In 1949 it was difficult to ascertain if a player had been officially cautioned. Referees did not brandish yellow cards and usually spoke to the player, or sometimes made a point of writing the offender's name in his book. Of course, after the match, referees were not allowed to discuss incidents with reporters or others. The *Glasgow Observer* of 2 September 1949 described the incident as follows: 'He [the referee] appeared to caution Tully and take Cox's name although Tully seemed the instigator in this instance. This action by the referee seemed an acknowledgement on his part that he had erred earlier by not reprimanding the Rangers' halfback.'

Bob Kelly, representing Celtic but also the President of the Scottish League and a Vice President of the SFA, was unhappy at the growing acquiescence of the Council and pointed out a major discrepancy in the referee's statement. At the Inquiry, according to Mr. Forbes, he had claimed not to have seen the incident clearly, yet 'A high League official, not connected with any of the clubs, questioned the referee at half time during the match and was told by the referee that he did not think that the infringement committed by Cox was deliberate and that, therefore, he had ignored it.'

Had the referee seen the incident, or had he not? An advocate acting for Celtic's defence in open court would have leaped upon this discrepancy, and Kelly wanted to have it cleared up immediately.

Other representatives started to seek further clarifications: R.A. Dustan (Welfare) asked if a verbatim copy of the evidence heard at the Committee meeting was in existence but George Graham, the secretary of the SFA, had to admit again there was none available. [17] Mr. T. Paterson (Amateur) asked about the terms of the Inquiry and whether it was about one game in particular or football in general. Graham responded by stating that the Inquiry had been held as a consequence of a letter to the SFA from the Glasgow Magistrates and the Chief Constable.

Celtic also had requested a Special Inquiry immediately after the match, but was told at this meeting of the SFA Council that such a request was 'out of order'. Bob Kelly then asked Mr. John Lamb (Arbroath), the chairman, about what steps a club could take in order to have a matter such as this investigated, adding that he had searched the rule-book for guidance but could find none that justified turning down such a request. However, the chairman of the SFA was unable to provide any further enlightenment, nor could the secretariat offer any guidance.

Graham, in his capacity as secretary of the SFA, was asked to read out the correspondence dealing with Celtic's request for a further hearing and he read four letters to the Council: from Celtic asking for a Special Inquiry; from the SFA asking Celtic to state the specific grounds and detailed reasons for such an Inquiry; from Celtic saying that the reasons could be found in the Press, and from those SFA members who were at the match; and from Charlie Tully appealing against his severe reprimand, citing support from his club in the appeal. The sequence of letters suggests an increasing chilliness between Celtic and the secretariat.

Mr. Forbes (Inverness) appeared anxious to lay the matter to rest, and criticised other members of the Council who had involved themselves in the discussion: 'I am going to be blunt. If Celtic have a grievance or a grouse, let them come forward and say it instead of leaving it to other people.' At this point an irate Bob Kelly wanted to say something in reply and rose to speak, but was ruled out of order, and a vote was called for.

Accordingly, Kelly moved that the minute concerning the responsibility of the players should not be accepted; pointing out that he had no objection to the other five minutes. His motion was seconded by W. Waters (St Mirren), another club which had suffered several contentious decisions in fixtures against Rangers, who added pointedly: 'Refereeing is steadily becoming worse.'

Throughout the whole affair, Celtic were supported and encouraged by

---

[17] In the *Daily Express* (9 September 1949) Alec Millar, president of the SPFA, was quoted as saying: 'It was wrong to put the major portion of blame on the players. It was the failure of the referee to take appropriate action that was the main cause of the trouble. Players will always be guilty of indiscretions on the field of play but these won't cause terracing rowdyism such as we saw at Ibrox if the referee takes appropriate action.'

other Scottish League clubs, most notably St. Mirren, Partick Thistle (Tom Reid) and Clyde (Willie Dunn). Significantly, these were West of Scotland clubs, who felt in particular that in fixtures against Rangers they had been short-changed.

However, the Council voted on the motions, and approved the minutes of the Referee Committee by twenty-five votes to five. Charlie Tully duly received his severe reprimand.

It was scarcely surprising that the Council should have approved these minutes. Normal practice would suggest that recommendations from important committees to the full Council were passed almost automatically and it would be fair to say that most members of the SFA Council were not exactly household names, nor were the clubs or the organisations they represented in the foreground of Scottish football.

In 1949 there was no public television in Scotland, and therefore the members of the SFA, unless they had attended the match, had to accept only the evidence presented to them. They would not have been bombarded with reruns of the incident, showing in detail exactly what had happened. In fact, Cox's assault on Tully was so unprovoked, and so astonishingly unexpected, that none of the massed photographers a few yards behind the goal managed to capture it on camera. The legislators had to rely almost exclusively on the referee's report, and their perspective would have been influenced by newspaper accounts or photographs of the hooliganism which erupted *after* the incident.

Those elected, or appointed, to administer the national sport in Scotland were quite prepared to accept the perks of office: deference, expense-accounts, tickets, and the occasional foreign trip. But they seemed reluctant to accept any responsibility in important decisions. It was much easier to receive the 'guidance' and 'direction' of the SFA's secretariat in dealing with such matters. The *status quo* – the labyrinthine procedures of the SFA, the committee system established by its bureaucrats – had a seductive appeal for such men, albeit with some notable exceptions.

The Celtic programme for 1 October 1949 included this excerpt in its editorial:

> The last Rangers programme contained remarks about the present tension and offered the advice to forget the controversy and the events which caused it. Twice in recent years we have done that but this time we do not feel disposed to do so because we consider that better and stronger handling of all games by the men in charge is of the utmost importance to the game. If teams can take the field confident that the officials in charge are strict and fearless, it will allow them to concentrate on playing and enjoying the game to the best of their ability and thus provide the public with first-class entertainment.

But there may have been another, altogether less obvious factor at work. It certainly might not be too far-fetched to suggest that, not for the first time, recent events in Northern Ireland had influenced the situation in Scotland.[18]

The football rivalry between Belfast Celtic and Linfield matched that waged in Glasgow between Celtic and Rangers. There were other similarities: Belfast Celtic represented, in general terms and not exclusively, the Catholic community, and Linfield the Protestant; the two teams wore the same strips as the Old Firm in Glasgow; fixtures between the pair had often degenerated into violence on the field, and hooliganism off it. Similarly, Belfast Celtic, although a symbol for the Catholics in Northern Ireland, did not practise a restrictive signing policy; Linfield, on the other hand, were exclusively Protestant.

Like their Glasgow counterparts, Belfast Celtic suffered from inexplicable decisions on the field of play and found themselves frequently the victims of administrative injustice off it. Latterly, because of the tensions aroused, referees from the mainland had to be imported to handle these explosive matches; Jack Mowat (Rutherglen) earned a well-deserved reputation for his firm and fair handling of this fixture.

Although representative of the minority in Northern Ireland, Belfast Celtic were a much more successful side than Linfield, and this fact apparently rankled with their opponents' supporters. After one derby match against Linfield on 27 December 1948, during which two players were ordered off and a mob invaded the pitch at the end, Celtic players were attacked and one – Jimmy Jones, ironically a Protestant – was badly injured.

As a direct consequence Belfast Celtic simply decided to withdraw from football at the end of the season, and to disband altogether. It is difficult not to conclude that the bitter sectarianism in Northern Ireland had claimed another victim; but football in the province was the real loser. Genuine interest in the sport gradually declined until it had reached its present unhealthy and apathetic state, and the loss of Belfast Celtic was a major factor in that decline. During the turmoil near the end of the Glasgow Cup tie at Celtic Park on 13 September, according to Jack Harkness of the *Sunday Post*: 'People turned towards the directors' box and pleaded with club officials to "do a Belfast Celtic".'

A trip to North America had already been arranged for Belfast Celtic, and this now turned out to be a farewell tour, a highly emotional affair for the club and its large expatriate support in the United States. The Scottish international side was also touring at much the same time and the American organisers were anxious to arrange a match between them. The match was played on 29

---

[18] In 1922 a riot broke out at Cappielow during a Morton–Celtic fixture on the last day of the season. Many observers felt that the tense situation in the newly formed Irish Free State had contributed to the outbreaks of violence in the Greenock–Port Glasgow area. And, of course, the infamous Church of Scotland report of 1923 was published within a year of Eire's founding. The *leitmotif* of 'the Irish problem' affecting matters in Scotland became more and more obvious to me as work progressed on this book.

May in New York before a crowd of 15,000, and the Scots, playing in their first match of the tour, were shocked by the Irish club side – and their enthusiastic support.

It erupted into a fiercely-contested clash and tempers frequently were near breaking-point: Waddell (Rangers) and O'Flannigan, the Belfast Celtic inside-left, came to blows early in the second half but were merely spoken to by the referee; Evans (Celtic), after being tripped in the penalty area by Ahearne, chased his opponent for forty yards in a vain attempt to exact retribution, but at the end Scotland were defeated by 2–0 to the great delight of the majority of the Americans in the crowd, the large Irish community in New York turning out in number to support 'their team'.

The report in the *Glasgow Herald*, filed by a special correspondent, described it as 'the football surprise of the century'. The Scottish tour had got off to a disastrous start, and the officials of the SFA were mortified, nobody more so than the secretary, George Graham.

A month or so after the return to Scotland, he spoke to the Rotary Club of Glasgow on 6 September 1949 about 'The American Tour' and mentioned this fixture in particular.[19] The SFA secretary was still embarrassed by that result, and he informed his douce audience that the game was 'played much against the inclination of the touring party' and that it turned out to be 'no exhibition match'. The Scotland side, he claimed, 'tried to display as much of the art and craft of football as they could, while their opponents were determined to win, and win they did'.

Clearly, there was a lingering animosity towards the Irish club among the embarrassed SFA officials, and this hostility may well have been later redirected at Belfast Celtic's Glasgow cousins.

***

One unexpected consequence of the Cox–Tully affair was that an issue normally considered beyond the pale was raised in the media. And, of all places, on the BBC. On 24 September 1949, on the Home Service, the well-known broadcaster John McAdam announced, presumably to a bemused radio audience, that 'a few moronic fanatics have persisted in attaching Catholic and Protestant labels to Celtic and Rangers, and it is no good telling them that all along Rangers have signed Catholic boys when they wanted them for football – and it's been the same with Celtic.'

At last somebody, albeit mistakenly, had raised the issue in public of dis-

---

[19] The tour, despite that shock defeat by Belfast Celtic, was a success at least socially. After all the travelling expenses for the players and a large number of officials had been deducted, it was announced that the profit on the trip amounted to a mere £20.

criminatory practices by the two Glasgow football rivals. Celtic had little to be ashamed of in this regard; although founded as 'a Catholic/Irish club', a strictly Catholic policy had very quickly been abandoned and many of the club's most famous and popular players had been non-Catholic.[20] Rangers, on the other hand, did have something to hide, although it was an open secret in the West of Scotland.

It may have been general knowledge throughout football circles, but the matter was never raised within the media. At that time, the BBC's football coverage was under the control of Peter Thomson, memorably described by Jock Stein as 'Blue Peter' and that department, while employing several competent and outstanding commentators, did not employ Catholics no matter how well qualified.

Similarly, some newspapers practised the same type of discrimination – even up to relatively recent times, as James MacMillan recounted in his speech in Edinburgh in 1999:

> 'When I was appointed editor of the *Glasgow Herald* in 1981', he [Arnold Kemp] writes, 'the then managing director of the publishing company came to me in great embarrassment. A board member, evidently confused by the fact that I was a Hibs' supporter, had insisted on knowing whether I was a Catholic. When I answered in the negative, a cloud lifted from his brow. Some days later, I was visited by a rather sinister member of the personnel department, who wished to assure himself that I would observe the company's traditional recruiting policies. This meant that applicants' letters would be placed in three piles – "probables", "possibles", and "those you won't want to see". This last was a euphemism for those whose name or educational history betrayed their religious affiliation.'

The newspapers in the late 1940s, tabloid and broadsheet alike, simply continued to ignore the fact that the country's most successful club was practising a policy of discrimination against members of one religious faith. And, of course, anybody who referred to this discrimination in conversation, especially if he complained about it, was considered 'a trouble-maker'. If such 'paranoid' thinkers were so correct about the existence of the longest-running scandal in Scottish football, one is forced to wonder how many of their other beliefs were justified.

When the media, decades later, were forced to face up to the issue openly, no attempt was ever made to apologise for their singular lack of courage throughout the previous seventy-odd years.

---

[20] Much of Celtic's early history is to be gleaned from Willie Maley's *The Story of the Celtic* (Glasgow, 1939). Maley, the long-time Celtic secretary/manager, also contributed several short histories of the club to different newspapers over the years. In one of them, printed in the *Daily Express* of 3 March 1931 he specifically referred to Celtic as 'this great Glasgow-Irish club'. Somewhat ironically, Maley appears to have been a royalist, despite his Irish birth and parentage. He was very proud of having been introduced to Princess May of Teck (later Queen Mary) prior to the international against England in which he played. Also, when proprietor of The Bank Restaurant in Glasgow's Queen Street, his business card featured a photograph of him being introduced to King George VI during a wartime (1940) visit by the monarch to Glasgow.

At the time the only newspaper to pick up on the BBC broadcast was the *Glasgow Observer* on 7 October, 1949 with an article headed, 'Did Catholics Play for Rangers?'. The sports writer also had the gumption to contact Rangers: 'I checked up at Ibrox Park where I was informed that, to the best of their knowledge, no Catholics had ever played for Rangers.'

The following week produced a letter to the *Observer* from Pat Lafferty, a Catholic from Rutherglen, who pointed out: 'Rangers competed for the English Cup in the 1880s. I was one of the team.' Others contributed letters to the newspaper, and within a week or so a list could be compiled of the number of Catholics who had been signed or who had played for the Ibrox club.

It proved a pathetically small list, numbering only twelve or thirteen and should have been a shocking indictment of Rangers' discrimination, but the mainstream Scottish press appeared unwilling (or afraid) to pursue the matter, and many Celtic supporters continued to feel themselves considered as 'second-class citizens', still unwanted and unaccepted because of their religion.

What else did the Cox–Tully incident show about Scottish football?

For one thing it revealed clearly and without doubt that Scottish refereeing was still in a mess; even the Referee Committee of the SFA had tacitly admitted as much in their minutes and recommendations. Many club officials were concerned about it, and the newspapers were frequently critical about the inconsistency of referees, and their personal lack of professionalism and fitness.

With regard to the most potentially explosive fixture in the football calendar, Malcolm McCulloch, Chief Constable of Glasgow, had already suggested a simple solution: 'Some of the trouble in the past has been caused by the impression that the referee was biased one way or the other. I did suggest to the football authorities that it would be well worthwhile trying out a referee from over the border.' However, a statement issued following the meeting between the Referee Committee (SFA) and the League Management Committee (Scottish League) was predictably bland and evasive: 'We discussed several points affecting referees with a view to solving minor problems.'

The SFA, responsible for the recruitment, training and certification of referees, was most reluctant to accept any of the criticism. In fact, George Graham, the SFA Secretary since 1928, was the most vulnerable in this regard as he was the person who had initiated and 'improved' the training scheme. Previously, he had been quoted as being confident about success: 'In two more years or so the refereeing in Scotland will be as near perfect as we can hope to achieve' (*Daily Record*, 20 August 1947).

In September 1949 he was notably quiet in the debate about refereeing standards and performance, although he went on record as saying, in an incredible defence of the SFA's beleaguered officials, 'Rangers and Celtic are just another two teams to us. If a referee is on the First League List, he should be able to tackle any game.'

It showed also that the SFA were content to lay the blame for some 'incidents' equally on both members of the Old Firm rather than having the moral courage to judge each particular event strictly on its merits. In this way a facade of impartiality could be preserved.

For other 'incidents' Celtic were punished alone. It is difficult to find any instance of the SFA deciding to punish only Rangers for their part in Old Firm mayhem although Rangers supporters may have been the only ones at fault.

Consider the case of the League Cup final played at Hampden Park on 23 October 1965, when Celtic beat Rangers by 2–1 after a hard-fought battle before a crowd of 107,000. After being presented with the trophy the Celtic players went down to the pitch with it and had attempted a semi-lap of honour by making towards their celebrating supporters still massed in one end of the ground. The sight was just too much for some hundreds of Rangers supporters, mainly youths who streamed over the retaining wall and raced towards the jubilant Celtic players. No doubt they intended to wreak physical harm upon the players and some Celtic players had to take evasive action while others prepared to defend themselves and each other. The police quickly put a stop to the situation but, throughout this unsavoury business, at a time when their heroes were in danger of being attacked, the Celtic support, without exception, remained in their places on the Hampden terracings.

The reaction in the media was remarkably muted: some newspapers felt that the towsiness of the cup final had been a contributory factor – five players had been booked, and Celtic had been awarded two penalty kicks! Others suggested that the Celtic players had been provocative in showing the trophy to their followers. This latter argument does not stand up under the weight of evidence: on two other occasions when the Old Firm had met in cup finals and the matches had been held up in order to deal with a field invasion or with major disturbances behind the goal, Rangers supporters had been at fault – and no lap of honour had been involved. The only common factor in the equation was the fact that Celtic had won those games convincingly: by 7–1 in 1957 and by 4–0 in 1969.

No member of the press rushed to advocate that Ibrox Park should be closed down as a punishment, although it was obvious that only Rangers supporters had been involved in the disgraceful and dangerous scenes; few recommended massive fines for Rangers in view of their fans' behaviour. Celtic supporters with memories thought back at that time to the Old Firm matches in 1941, 1946 and 1949 when such measures were proposed in the wake of behaviour perhaps less dangerous to others.

The 'punishment' inflicted this time was that on similar occasions in the future no laps of honour would be permitted. Celtic supporters in a triumphalist tone suggested that this punitive measure involved Celtic much more than Rangers in the years following 1965.

In 1949, however, there was no possibility of those capable of adopting such an ostrich-like stance ever discussing the underlying causes or roots of the sectarian cancer within Scottish football. And the silence in the Press was deafening on this particular issue, despite the opportunity afforded by the *Glasgow Observer* to raise the matter of Rangers' discriminatory employment practices.

The Cox–Tully affair also demonstrated that Celtic, thanks to the valid perception that they were an organisation in decline, no longer had sufficient clout at administrative levels to effect changes or, indeed, to get justice for themselves. The football authorities, noting the lack of success achieved by Celtic and drawing the conclusion that the Parkhead club was incapable of emerging from its long-time mediocrity, were not going to risk anything by being fair. In boxing terms Celtic did not 'punch their weight', and they were not going to get too much support from officialdom until they did so.

Celtic's greatest fear was that the SFA would use the events at Ibrox Park to close down Celtic Park and disadvantage the club in its programme of fixtures. It was a legitimate fear, given the background of some SFA office bearers. The directors also recalled that a similar punishment had been doled out on more than one occasion in the past.

The side effect was that Celtic remained reluctant to pursue issues to a definite conclusion and seemed content enough to claim the safety of the moral high-ground, and confine their criticism to gnomic statements to the converted in the annual *Celtic Football Guide*. They could draw some comfort from the awareness that most newspaper coverage was sympathetic, but the part-time legislators and the full-time secretariat at Carlton Place seemed impervious to outside criticism.

Finally, it suggested clearly that a bias against Celtic existed among the senior and influential members of the SFA bureaucracy, a prejudice inherited from the club's traditional association with Ireland, and perhaps also Catholicism. Institutionalised racism is scarcely a new concept within Scotland, and the SFA, under the pervasive influence of George Graham, was a most conservative and clannish organisation.

MEDIA COVERAGE

Rangers vs. Celtic
League Cup: 27 August 1949

... but for the prompt action of the police, a riot would have taken place at the west end of the ground. There is no doubt what caused the trouble – the foul committed by Cox, Rangers' right half-back on Tully, Celtic's inside left, after only 30 minutes of play, and the astonishing attitude of the referee in ignoring the offence and actually waving play on. The referee did appear to take the names of both players some minutes later when they were involved in an incident which, compared to the first, was trivial but, as he took no action when Cox committed the original offence, it is obvious that he cannot report that the original occurrence caused the scenes on the terracing. (*Glasgow Herald,* 29 August 1949)

The whole unsavoury business of police ducking bottles and quelling fights on the terracings while ambulancemen were bandaging heads and carrying away casualties could, I think, have been avoided if referee Gebbie had got hold of the Cox–Tully incident. It is possible he did not see what had happened – another player could have obstructed his vision – but, when he saw Tully writhing on the ground, he should have stopped play and made a point of finding out what had occurred. (*Daily Express,* 29 August 1949)

They [the SFA] will no doubt receive a report from the referee. That report must be probed in emphatic manner as an earnest that the Committee's repeated declarations about keeping the game clean are no mere pious, meaningless phrases. After twenty minutes' play ... the ninety-odd thousand spectators were thoroughly enjoying the game and I had visions of a repeat of the hard, clean and wholesome contest between the teams a fortnight ago.

Then, a yard or so from the Rangers by-line on the stand-side of the Govan end, where the Celtic supporters were massed, Cox and Tully engaged for possession. Next, a terrific howl of anger from the terracing as Cox went off with the ball and Tully writhed in pain on the ground, the victim of a foul. To everyone's astonishment, the whistler, A.B. Gebbie (Hamilton) signalled play to go on. Celtic's trainer Alec Dowdells rushed on to the field to tend the Irishman with the stadium in an uproar. The very least the referee could have done was to award a free kick against Cox. That, to a certain extent, might have appeased the hotheads but Mr. Gebbie's failure to carry out his obvious duty further incensed the crowd. (*Daily Record*, 29 August 1949)

Celtic vs. Rangers
Glasgow Cup: 13 September 1949

Celtic's chagrin knew no bounds then, and to the horror of those who have the interests of the game at heart, Tully was quite clearly seen to be urging his team-mates to leave the field. Almost reluctantly, several of them took the wiser council of others and the game was restarted ... the track around the field seemed to contain all Glasgow's policemen now and there had been more than a liberal sprinkling there and within the terracing all through. (*Glasgow Herald*, 14 September 1949)

After watching the last five minutes at Parkhead last night I unhesitatingly state that no further matches between the clubs should be allowed this season. With this view the Celtic officials are in agreement – if, as they say, referees who can completely control play and players are not available to handle such games. I can say now that Celtic, immediately after the Ibrox game of unhappy memory, seriously considered scratching from the competition (Glasgow Cup) since only a fortnight would elapse between the Ibrox match and the clubs' next encounter. (*Glasgow Herald*, 14 September 1949)

CHAPTER FOUR

The Eire Flag Flutter

In 1952 a decision made by the Council of the SFA, and defied by Celtic Football Club, threatened to put the famous Glasgow club out of existence.

An extravagant claim? Yes, but the climate of mutual hostility was so intense that such a possibility was mooted and considered before cooler heads prevailed. Those cool heads were motivated in different ways: those who could see the folly of the SFA persisting in an untenable legal position; those who felt that Celtic were being treated unduly harshly; and those who realised belatedly that Celtic would not back down from a principled stand, and that Scottish football would be infinitely poorer for their absence.

The final vote at the meeting of the SFA Council which saved Celtic was passed by sixteen votes to fifteen!

The whole affair began as a consequence of repeated crowd-trouble at Celtic Park, a matter which rightly concerned the SFA.

The first instance was alleged to have occurred on 3 November 1951 during and after a league match against Third Lanark at Celtic Park, an unsatisfactory 2–2 draw. Tully was involved in an incident with George Aitken, Third Lanark's rugged left-half and was ordered off immediately and correctly by the referee, G. Mitchell (Falkirk).[21] At the end of the match, the officials met with a stormy reception as they left the pitch; one of the linesmen complained later in the privacy of the dressing room about 'an assault by spitting' and this fact was duly recorded in the referee's report.

Conscious of the controversy during the match and the mood of the crowd following Tully's dismissal, a sergeant, supervised by the Assistant Chief Constable of Glasgow, had gathered six other officers near the tunnel. The referee and his linesmen were the last to leave the pitch and they were escorted the nineteen feet across the track and into the tunnel by the police. After learning of the linesman's complaint, Bob Kelly, a part-time JP, had taken the precaution of interviewing the police and was able to produce statements from the officers that they were prepared to swear in court under oath that they had not detected any spitting, and that they had not received any complaint from the linesman at the time nor at any time afterwards.

[21] Tully's subsequent suspension was of one month's duration at a time when the normal period for a first offence was two weeks. Clearly, the blots on his record from the previous incident with Cox had counted heavily against him.

62

Despite this evidence, however, the SFA instructed the club to post bills at the stadium until the end of the season warning spectators about their conduct. Kelly had absolutely no sympathy for Tully's lapse in discipline, although he was dismayed at the excessive length of suspension when the player was banned for a month instead of the customary two weeks. But he did object to the accusations of misbehaviour on the part of the spectators gathered in the enclosure in front of the stand, because he had been a witness to the whole affair.

He had every confidence in his club's being exonerated in full but he was astonished when the SFA Council on 12 December refused to consider his evidence, and dismissed it with the chairman's words: 'We have the linesman's word about what happened, and that is enough.' Kelly was further enraged when the SFA chairman, Mr. Robbie (Aberdeen), added gratuitously: 'Celtic will have to warn spectators that a repetition of such conduct may lead to serious action being taken against the club including possible closure of the ground.'

On 1 January 1952 Celtic faced Rangers in the traditional Ne'erday clash and violent scenes erupted among Celtic supporters midway through the second half. It had been a thoroughly miserable affair: the first snow storm of the winter had started about two hours before the kick-off, and the rain, sleet and snow, after threatening the cancellation of the fixture, discouraged many from attending. The crowd was estimated at 42,000 although it had been an all-ticket game.

Rangers played remarkably well considering the conditions, and the fact that 'Tiger' Shaw was stretchered off after sixty minutes, the victim of a clash with Tully. At that stage the score was 2–1 for Rangers, but the shorthanded Ibrox men scored two more for a very convincing 4–1 victory.

That was too much for some Celtic supporters to bear, and disturbances broke out in the covered enclosure and in the Celtic end of the ground but the police quickly restored a semblance of order. Several spectators were arrested for various 'breaches of the peace' including fighting and bottle-throwing: a Henry Donnachy (24) and John McGeachie (40) were jailed for twenty days when they appeared at Glasgow Eastern Police Court on the Monday and Patrick Mackin (35) and David Scullion (37) were fined £5, as an alternative to sixty days' imprisonment. At Glasgow Southern Police Court, Michael Duffin, who admitted three previous convictions, was given thirty days for throwing a bottle at a Rangers supporters' bus after the match.

The Glasgow Magistrates assembled on 8 January 1952 for one of their regular meetings and the scenes at Celtic Park and environs was on the agenda. The magistrates heard a report from the Chief Constable, and received a deputation from the National Association of Celtic Supporters' Clubs who represented 9,000 members and 120 clubs. Patrick Mooney, the General Secretary, deplored the various incidents and expressed his organisation's willingness to help the magistrates in every possible way. However, Bailie Dr. Gladys Dewar, the Senior Magistrate, was in a sombre mood, commenting menacingly: 'If the football authorities do not act, then the Magistrates will.'

On 16 January the magistrates supplied a list of four recommendations, which the SFA and the Scottish League were invited to consider:

1. that Rangers and Celtic should not be scheduled to play each other on New Year's Day again, as passions were likely to be inflamed by drink and more bottles carried than on any other day;
2. that, when these clubs meet, admission should be by ticket only and the attendance limited to a number consistent with public safety, the number to be decided by the Chief Constable;
3. that Celtic Football Club should be asked to construct numbered passage-ways at each end of Celtic Park in the interests of public safety;
4. that the two clubs should avoid displaying flags or emblems which might incite hostile feelings among the spectators.

The views of the magistrates certainly deserved to be considered seriously.

At that time Glasgow was infamous for drunken excesses at the New Year period and to stage such a volatile football match at that time has always appeared to many to be a deliberate and masochistic act of folly. Thousands of spectators turned up for these fixtures nursing a hangover from the previous night, and were prepared to continue the 'celebrations' with their football pals. And, it should be remembered that, in 1952, fans were still allowed to carry bottles of alcohol into the ground for refreshment. It was a situation virtually guaranteed to cause trouble, and deserved to be corrected.

In 1952 all-ticket games were not always the best answer because there was no effective way of screening the applicants. The tickets were on sale at the football grounds, and at selected outlets within the city. All sales were on a cash basis and there was no way of checking on the character of the spectators or even which team they supported. Limiting the number of spectators seemed an acceptable idea but the record attendances at Ibrox and Celtic Park are 118,000 and 83,500 respectively; the crowd at Celtic Park on 1 January, 1952 was a mere 42,000. The fact is that the vast majority of spectators at Old Firm matches do behave reasonably well, and the trouble is usually caused by a much smaller hooligan element among both sets of supporters and often is provoked by some incident on the field of play. Until recent times, there has been no effective way of ensuring that tickets for important fixtures do not fall into the hands of people likely to lose control of themselves.

The third proposal that Celtic construct passageways was a highly practical one, of great assistance to the police in controlling crowds and to ambulance men trying to render first aid to spectators injured or ill. It was a matter that Celtic should have dealt with already but, to their credit, the club acted on this proposal during the next close season. Ironically, only three were ever completed, and all were at the Rangers end of the ground, normally the more sparsely inhabited of the two terracings.

The fourth proposal was a coded reference to the sectarian issue but it seemed to be a measure aimed at Celtic exclusively.

The flag of the Irish Republic had flown at Celtic Park above the famous covered enclosure for many years without causing too much comment or interest. However, one representative of the SFA had raised the matter in September 1934, prior to an international match between Scotland and Ireland being played at Celtic Park. He claimed that the flag could be considered offensive to the visiting Northern Ireland side and hinted strongly that Celtic should remove it for the occasion at least. This official, almost certainly George Graham, six years into his job at the SFA, seemed to be the only person who had noticed the flag since it first appeared at the ground in 1921 when Eire took its place among the nations of the world.

At this point it might be worthwhile to trace the history of that particular flag. Celtic, recognising the ancestry of the majority of their supporters and in memory of the club's founders, had originally flown the flag of the once-united Ireland, a golden harp on a green background.

In 1921 Celtic substituted for it the tricolour of the recently formed Irish Free State, a gift from that country's government. This flag was placed on the pole at the Celtic end of the 'Jungle' and flew there until 1951, by which time it was badly in need of repair. Celtic's manager Jimmy McGrory was unable to find a flag maker in Glasgow or in Scotland to provide the club with a replacement. Remembering the club's successful tours of Eire and meeting with Eamon de Valera, the manager wrote to him outlining his predicament. Within a week the Premier of the Irish Republic had responded and sent a new tricolour to Celtic Park with his best wishes.

As every Celtic chairman has felt compelled to emphasise since the controversy erupted, the Union Jack has also flown at Celtic Park and from the highest point of the ground.

Celtic were incensed at the proposed ban on such a symbol of the club's origins and traditions, and prepared to fight to oppose it. Since the Second World War, Celtic had played the role of 'victim' but this time they were prepared to fight to the end. Inside the world of Scottish football they made their views known privately and at meetings, and an impasse was reached at the committee stage. Several meetings of various important committees were held without any resolution of the matter: on 28 January the Management Committee of the Scottish League discussed the matter and it was announced that 'talks would continue'. The Referee Committee met on 11 February for a one-hour meeting but no statement was issued.

The Magistrates of the City of Glasgow were becoming impatient, feeling that the matter of their recommendations was not being given due attention.

By that time, the SFA had written back about only one matter (crowd control) pointing out that all-ticket matches for the Old Firm was the practice, and that the clubs accepted the advice of the Chief Constable regarding the size of crowd. Later, the Management Committee of the Scottish League had discussed the matter of re-scheduling the traditional New Year fixture but 'were reluctant to interfere with a fixture of such long standing', yet another indication of the reluctance of Scottish football's legislators to change.

However, on 13 February 1952, the Referee Committee of the SFA met and considered the matter further. At the end of their deliberations a fateful decision was taken: Celtic were ordered to take down the Eire flag. As the Committee minute recorded: 'The Celtic club are instructed to refrain from displaying on their ground on match days any flag or emblem which has no association with this country or the game.' Ominously, the decision was unanimous.

On 16 February Celtic played Stirling Albion at Parkhead and *The Scotsman* commented about the issue that was beginning to develop into a crisis:

> Incidentally, the flag of Eire was still flying from the mast of the west side of the covered enclosure on Saturday. It was this emblem that the Referee Committee of the SFA asked should be removed when they inquired into the scenes at the New Year's Day game against Rangers. The flying of the flag was not an act of defiance by the Celtic management. They hold that the order will not be effective until the minute of the committee is finally ratified by the Council of the SFA. (18 February 1952)

Celtic had been bemused – and worried – about the effect of the magistrates' recommendations upon the football authorities. As a responsible club, they had no difficulty in accepting most of the recommendations but they had anticipated – and they were perfectly right – that some members of the SFA might concentrate an attack on the flying of the Eire flag.[22] Accordingly, they had immediately sought legal advice on the matter and were reassured by counsel's opinion that they had an excellent case for flying and continuing to fly the flag of a friendly nation, and one which honoured the origin of most of the club's original founders.

Things were different in the early 1950s. For one thing there was no great proliferation of scarves and banners and even the more rabid of the supporters did not dress in his team's colours. At Celtic Park the prevailing hue was the green of scarves, ties, pullovers and so on. Banners appeared only on special occasions: for example, the first time that I recall Eire flags or banners appearing on the terracing after World War II was at the 1951 Scottish Cup final between Celtic and Motherwell. On that occasion four or five flags were waved from the traditionally Celtic King's Park end of the ground, but more

---

[22] This suspicion might well have been construed as evidence of the club's paranoia but, in view of the situation that developed, the caution was entirely justified.

significantly the playing of the National Anthem was disturbed by shouts and catcalls from a number of Celtic followers on the terracing. However, compared to the sustained booing of the same anthem at the recent European Nations Cup play-off between Scotland and England, that disruption in 1951 was in a minor key.

Until the time of the next plenary meeting, some frantic lobbying was being done: a faction within the SFA, orchestrated by the secretary, George Graham, and led nominally by Harry Swan (Hibernian), the Acting President, was intent on forcing Celtic's capitulation, while Celtic were looking around for bad-weather friends to support them. It was going to be a showdown with implications for the future of the sport in Scotland.

On 25 February the full Council of the SFA met to receive the minutes of the Referee Committee and to discuss the issue. In addition to the instruction on removing the Eire flag, the minutes indicated that, according to the Rules of the SFA, responsibility for the conduct of spectators lay with the club, and that responsibility would not be waived by the club's employing a sufficient number of policemen.

And in the 1950s clubs did not employ stewards in any great number, as the vast majority of spectators stood on the terracings and were free to move from spot to spot on those terracings.[23] No football ground was equipped with police surveillance cameras, and Celtic were genuinely puzzled about how to comply with the magistrates' recommendations and the committee's minutes.

For example, the SFA indicated that the police could not take action until trouble had actually erupted but what could Celtic do in that case? Celtic were ordered to warn their supporters that any further transgressions could endanger the continuance of scheduled games at Celtic Park. This was the ultimate sanction available to the SFA and had been invoked against Celtic on several occasions in the past as a result of hooliganism by some of their supporters.

The club was then asked to refrain from displaying in the ground any flag or emblem that had no association with the sport or the country. Both Rangers and Celtic were ordered to take all possible steps to prevent the flaunting of provocative flags or emblems by spectators and to discourage by all means in their power any display of sectarian sentiments which, the Council members felt, were the cause of the problem.

Mr. J. Robbie (Aberdeen) was one of the leading opponents of the flying of the Eire flag at the Council meeting, but insisted that hooliganism was the real issue for him, pointing out that Celtic fans had been in trouble at Cappielow, Broomfield, Palmerston Park and Cathkin, as well as on two occasions at

---

[23] It was my habit to enter Celtic Park at the traditional Rangers End and, if Celtic were shooting into the Celtic End for the second half, I would spend the interval burrowing my way through the Jungle in the company of several hundred like-minded supporters.

Celtic Park that season. Bob Kelly was highly suspicious about the fact that the SFA chairman appeared extraordinarily well briefed on this matter and sensed that this issue was going to be the major one in his tenure as Celtic's spokesman. Mr. Robbie's logic – that the Eire flag at Celtic Park must come down to discourage acts of hooliganism on other grounds across Scotland – defeated many minds, including Bob Kelly's.

With withering sarcasm Celtic's chairman dismantled the argument: it was true that Celtic supporters had misbehaved, and that Celtic flew that flag at home games but, for more than thirty years, that flag had been flown there, and nobody – till now – had blamed it for any trouble. It was surely evident that the flag could not have annoyed Celtic supporters and, therefore, any trouble provoked by the flag must have been instigated by non-Celtic supporters, but manifestly that had not been the case. So, what had the flying of a flag to do with causing trouble among Celtic supporters?

Kelly had been advised that his best legal argument would be through the citing of Article of Association 114 which read: 'Each club in membership shall be responsible for the conduct of its spectators on any ground and misbehaviour by spectators during or at close of matches shall render a member [club] liable to fine, or closure of ground, or suspension, or all of those penalties.'

Celtic's case was based on the grounds that, although the club conceded the fact that the SFA did have the right to impose these sanctions on individual clubs, the SFA did not have any authority to go beyond the rules and establish new punishments. In other words, the SFA could go as far as to suspend a member club for the misconduct of its followers legally, but not for the flying of the flag of a friendly country.[24]

The meeting was heated at times, and prolonged, and discussion of the issue completely overshadowed the draw for the fourth round of the Scottish Cup, which was also on the agenda. Bob Kelly moved for the rejection of that part of the minutes which involved the banning of the Eire flag, and his motion was seconded by John Wilson, the chairman of Rangers. This should not be considered surprising as Rangers were aware that a Scottish League without Celtic was scarcely worth winning, and also because the Ibrox club did not want its own background in sectarianism to be examined.

Kelly, not always the best of speakers, gave a magnificent and impassioned defence of his club's traditions, and stressed that Celtic were a non-sectarian club. When the time came for the vote, both Kelly and Wilson were

---

[24] It would appear that anti-Irish sentiment was a strong undercurrent in this affair. One Celtic director informed me (accurately) that, when Scotland played a friendly international against Germany at Ibrox Park in 1936, the Swastika was flown from the flagpole without too much comment. However, when Rangers played opponents from the League of Ireland in European competition in 1968/69 the tricolour was conspicuous by its absence.

asked to withdraw from the chamber while the issue was decided. In their absence the recommendations of the Referee Committee were then upheld by the substantial majority of twenty-six votes to seven.

The mood after the taking of the vote appeared to be one of relief; many of those who had opposed the Parkhead club being quick to express sympathy. Some of those had been manipulated by the secretariat into voting against Celtic's position on the grounds that no club, no matter how large, could defy the democratic power of the SFA; others genuinely saw the banning of the flag as an appropriate punishment for unacceptable behaviour on the part of some Celtic followers.

At that time few members of the SFA Council realised that Celtic were indeed prepared to continue the fight: 'The matter is, of course, far from finished. Celtic took expert legal advice before they opposed the flag part of the decision, and I understand from club officials that their immediate reaction to the position is that they will ask the same legal advisers what their attitude should be now' (*Glasgow Herald*, 27 February 1952).

The Eire flag continued to be flown at Celtic Park in its customary place above the Jungle as the directors awaited further legal opinions. Not too surprisingly, the advice indicated that the SFA had no authority to enforce such an order and that Celtic should not fear the consequences of flying a symbol of its origins.

At the next council meeting (on 10 March) the battle-lines were drawn up quickly: Harry Swan (Hibernian), perhaps over-confident after the size of the previous majority, moved that Celtic be given a mere three days to comply with the order or be suspended from membership in the SFA.[25] Again the discussion was heated but Bob Kelly was remarkably calm, pointing out: 'In all the history of Scottish football suspension has only been ordered when a rule has been broken, and nobody in this chamber has proved to me that Celtic have broken any rule.'

The longer the meeting went on, the stronger Celtic's position became as the Council members began to consider the question again. What rule had Celtic broken? The ramifications of their actions became clearer: if Celtic continued to defy the SFA and were suspended, the rest of the league programme would necessarily have to be curtailed; adjustments would have to be made to the results of those games already completed by Celtic; and, most

---

[25] When Hibernian won the Second Division title in 1893/94, the Scottish League curtly informed them that they would not be providing a championship flag, as was the custom. The 'problem' lay in Hibernian's Catholic and Irish leanings, and the choice of flag: '... green with a yellow harp and no crown, with the inscription Hibernian Football Club *Erin Go Bragh*.' However, the decision was eventually reversed and the flag was presented and unfurled on 18 August 1894. What may have been worse was the fact that, although Hibernian had won the division, it was Clyde who were promoted upon a vote by the First Division members.

importantly, any club still due to face Celtic would now lose out on the assurance of a large gate.

In fact, Bob Kelly, a man known for a keen interest in horse-racing, had calculated the odds to perfection this time. He knew that he had the support of most clubs within the Scottish League and he used the often uneasy relationship between the SFA and the League to devastating effect. The Scottish League was still seething over the fact that it had been largely ignored as an organisation throughout the affair and its representatives – and, in particular, Rangers – were generally backing Celtic.

The other organisations, apart from the Scottish League, represented at the SFA were more difficult to convince, as they found it awkward to detach themselves from the influence of the long-time secretary.

In the end, the most telling factor was Bob Kelly himself. Not always the most talented public speaker, he surpassed himself. Utterly fearless and truly formidable, he had a cause to believe in, and a corner to fight; he had the boost of expert legal advice, and he had the air of a man capable of carrying out his promises – or threats.

A club – a founder-member of the Scottish League, and one with a glorious history – apparently determined to go out of existence as a matter of principle at least deserved to be listened to with great respect. And, at the back of most minds in the council chamber, was the financial clout wielded by Celtic's support both home and away.[26]

Ironically, those members of the SFA Council impressed by his confidence, and latterly by his argument, could scarcely have guessed that Celtic's chairman earlier had had to resist the arguments of other Celtic directors and shareholders in favour of pulling the flag down as a gesture of appeasement.

During the debate Harry Swan (Hibernian) was actually forced to admit as a result of a direct question by Wilson (Rangers) that George Graham had been approached by the Scottish League for a meeting to discuss all the aspects of the affair and that he (Graham) had turned down the suggestion. The visibly embarrassed Mr. Swan also had to admit that Graham had initially denied the approach at the previous Council meeting, thus 'inadvertently' misleading the Council.

Finally, a face-saving compromise emerged; an amendment was proposed that the grace period be extended till the season finished at the end of April and, at that point, if Celtic had not pulled down the flag, the club and its directors would be suspended. The members realised, of course, that 30 April

---

[26] In 1952 all gates were shared more or less equally between the two competing clubs. Thus, East Fife, for example, that season would have split gates of 15,000 at Methil on 15 December and 30,000 at Celtic Park on 22 March. At both fixtures Celtic's support would have constituted the majority of spectators.

marked the official end of the season and had been informed privately by Celtic that the Eire flag would not be flown during the close season. Thus, the SFA could argue, rather unconvincingly, that Celtic had complied with the order imposed upon them. The vote was taken and the amendment was carried by the narrowest of margins, sixteen votes to fifteen.

A disaster had been averted but only barely; the disaster, of course, would have affected the whole of Scottish football and not just Celtic, and the cynical observers could point out that the switch in voting was not out of principle but occasioned by the fear of losing money.

Of course, Celtic resumed the flying of the Eire flag at the start of the next season, and continued to fly the controversial emblem. At the same time, however, the club persevered with its criticism of supporters who flaunted such symbols, claiming that flag-waving in this vein was not a respectful reminder of tradition. This subtle distinction eluded many commentators in the media. Jock Stein helped to defuse the issue when he suggested, and his directors agreed, that the flags of a varied selection of the countries with whom Celtic had links should be flown on the flagpoles of the renovated 'Jungle'.

George Graham may have had his own reasons for dismissing the proposal of a meeting between the SFA and the Scottish League, but he had also sanctioned a meeting of the Referee Committee to discuss the matter. Perhaps he had already sensed that the tide had started to turn against him because, significantly, he had failed to inform Bob Kelly, the chairman of that particular committee, that a meeting would be held, although it was among the secretary's responsibilities to inform all committee members of the times and places of scheduled meetings. Kelly was tipped off by another member of the committee, and entered the room amid a shocked silence and assumed his customary place as chairman. His remarks were brief: 'I, as chairman of this committee, was not consulted about this meeting even though I may have had the most important information to give to the members of this committee about the subject to be discussed.' After that pointed rebuke to the secretary, he withdrew from the room, leaving the members in some disarray to discuss matters on an informal basis.

At the decisive Council meeting itself Bob Kelly must have been boosted by the realisation that the secretary had called in sick on the morning, another inkling that Celtic's stand was eventually going to prevail. The secretary's surprising 'illness' made him unable to attend the plenary session of the Council, and the *Glasgow Herald* pointed out that 'it was the first [meeting] he had missed in many years'.

On 7 April the Council met once more in an attempt to resolve the situation in an acceptable manner, and the members agreed unanimously that the threatened suspension be inoperative, pending a conference likely to be held in the near future between the SFA and the Scottish League.

Celtic – and Kelly – had won; Graham – and his cohorts – had lost. Within the members of the SFA a sea change had taken place and it was recognised tacitly that Celtic's principled and impassioned stand had won the day.

The whole shameful episode marked a considerable personal defeat for George Graham and many observers have traced the subsequent waning of his influence at Carlton Place to that public loss of face. Bob Kelly emerged from the saga with his reputation at its highest, accorded new respect within the SFA and at Celtic Park.

It marked also a significant setback for those within the SFA who had tried to use circumstances to punish Celtic. In fact, some zealous Celtic historians believe that this concentrated effort to attack Celtic was a last serious attempt to inflict harm on a club and institution which had done a great deal for Scottish football on and off the field. If those forces had succeeded, Celtic would have suffered grievously either by being forced in a humiliating capitulation to pull down the symbol of their origins and tradition, or by being forced out of Scottish football.

Whatever the outcome intended – and humiliation was the more likely – the motivation behind it lay in bigotry.

CHAPTER FIVE

Jousting Knights

The feud between Celtic's chairman and the secretary of the SFA had developed into open warfare with the protracted conflict over the flying of the Eire flag at Celtic Park. For some years Celtic had had ample reason to suspect the motives of George Graham, but by now the club was convinced that an undeclared state of war existed.

In a study of sectarianism in sport and society in Scotland, the author stated: 'Whether they liked it or not, Rangers and Celtic were still tied to their history and their society, and it was as respective spokesmen for influential sections of that society that Robert Kelly refused to take down the Eire flag and George Graham, secretary of the SFA ... seemed bent on forcing a humiliating capitulation' (Bill Murray, *The Old Firm*, op cit).

It is time to look more closely at the two combatants in this long-running vendetta.

Bob Kelly's Celtic roots went back a long way: his father, James Kelly, had captained the very first Celtic side assembled in 1888, and went on to become a fixture at Celtic Park, serving as a committee man and as chairman of the club from 1909 until 1914 and later as a director.

The younger Kelly was himself appointed a director of the club in 1932 upon the death of his father, and acted in that capacity until 1947, at which point he succeeded Tom White as chairman. The other members of the Board were Colonel John Shaughnessy, a Glasgow lawyer and a director at Celtic Park since 1911, and Desmond White, an accountant who had acted as Celtic's secretary since 1940 and who had become a director upon the death of his own father, Tom White, in 1947. Apparently, the younger White's first task as a director was to choose the new chairman by casting the deciding vote in favour of Bob Kelly.

It was not the best of times to become Celtic's chairman, as the club was toiling on and off the field. During the Second World War, with football on an unofficial status, Celtic had not made any great efforts to field a competitive team: several players left the club and went elsewhere, including Johnny Crum and John Divers of the famous Empire Exhibition side in 1938 who moved to Greenock Morton. A new manager, Jimmy McStay, had been appointed to replace the almost legendary Willie Maley but it quickly became clear that the newcomer had little authority within Celtic Park and few resources.

Other clubs fielded guest-players such as Stanley Matthews (Stoke City) and Tommy Lawton (Everton) who turned out for Morton, Frank Swift (Manchester City) who represented Hamilton Academical, and Torry Gillick and Jimmy Caskie (both of Everton) who played for Rangers. Matt Busby, stationed in Scotland, offered his services to Celtic but was ignored and went to Hibernian instead. No doubt, these players were offered some financial incentives to turn out for their new clubs and those costs would have been negligible although illegal. But Celtic had chosen not to adopt that route to success, and paid a terrible price during the war and for too many seasons afterwards.

With the death of an elderly and ailing chairman in 1947 and the appointment of a younger, more energetic leader in the person of Bob Kelly, now aged forty-five, it was hoped that Celtic's fortunes would change for the better. However, it soon proved difficult to turn things around, especially on the field and with a relatively inexperienced manager in Jimmy McGrory, a man with the reputation of being 'too nice to be a real manager'. Colonel Shaughnessy, a director for thirty-six years – and perhaps hurt at being rebuffed as chairman – was too old to be of real assistance to Kelly. On the other hand, Desmond White was still inexperienced in his role as director, although he had acted as the club's secretary and accountant for a number of years. Thus, Bob Kelly had heavy responsibilities to bear at Celtic Park.

The problems associated with running a successful football club were exacerbated by a management structure with a profound imbalance: the manager was weak, and the chairman was strong. Increasingly, Jimmy McGrory became 'an errand boy for the Board' while Bob Kelly took on more and more of the football responsibilities. Frankly, the arrangement did not work as Celtic continued to slump into mediocrity or worse; in fact, it required a nail-biting 3–2 victory at Dens Park in April 1948 in their last league fixture to ensure that Celtic were not threatened by relegation.

The interference by the chairman in the day-to-day running of the football operations continued for some years, and many Celtic supporters openly blamed Bob Kelly for the lack of success. Inconsistency on the field, despite a squad that contained some outstanding players, produced frustration for the supporters and was a major factor in the occasional outbreaks of hooliganism that dogged Celtic for some years immediately after the Second World War. And this deserved reputation for rowdiness did not help Celtic when dealing with the SFA.

Despite his travails at Celtic Park, Kelly was recognised as a leader within Scottish football as he had a coherent view of the problems besetting the sport and his opinions were forthright; his participation was largely welcomed within the Scottish League, where he was seen as being sympathetic to the plight of the smaller clubs. In short, he was 'a football man'.

His difficulties at Celtic Park were compounded by the unhelpful attitude of the SFA, or more specifically the secretariat under the rule of George Graham. It is hard, even for the blandest commentators on Scottish football, to escape the conclusion that the SFA waged 'an anti-Celtic campaign' for at least the decade comprising the wartime years and the immediate post-war period.

In fact, some have stated quite categorically in private that 'George Graham was openly anti-Celtic', a representative of the type of middle-class Scot who retains an aversion to things Catholic and/or Irish. This type, fortunately, is on the decrease but much of Celtic's present distrust of the SFA stems from the period of Graham's leadership.

During that time, George Graham was the organisation's secretary and most prominent figure, running the SFA at times as if it were a personal fiefdom. He took full advantage of a bureaucratic system which he had largely created and understood perfectly. Too frequently throughout its history the SFA chairmen have been mediocrities who had risen to the post through prominence in their own clubs or organisations, followed by years of dutiful attendance at SFA committee meetings; and the avoidance of controversy.[27] These men enjoyed the status but were terrified of making mistakes in public; more and more they relied on the expertise of the secretary, who had been in the office since 1928 and was understandably an acknowledged master of the rule-book.

It is not too well known that Graham's appointment to the post of secretary owed much to Celtic supporting his candidacy. Even more astonishingly in view of his later attitude towards Celtic, Graham was invited – or, in the manner perfected by SFA officials, wangled an invitation – to travel with Celtic on their European tour of 1922. Celtic's chairman Tom White, and the secretary-manager Willie Maley, had recognised George Graham's undoubted talents in administration, saw him as rising through the ranks at Carlton Place and were able to co-operate with him peacefully enough throughout the 1930s. It has been suggested that a little of Graham's open aversion to Celtic came after Willie Maley's abrupt and callous dismissal in 1940.

Whatever the reason, with the outbreak of World War II in 1939, Graham's attitude towards Celtic appeared to harden, and it is probable that the neutral line adopted by the Irish Free State during that global conflict contributed towards the secretary's increasingly hostile stance.

Lord Acton, the celebrated historian, commented: 'Power tends to corrupt, and absolute power tends to corrupt absolutely.' This appears to have been the case with George Graham who used his mastery of the procedures of the SFA to build up a personal base of power that became virtually unassailable. The

---

[27]   Mr. Charles Dempsey (New Zealand), who abstained in the voting for the venue of the 2006 World Cup, might be considered as representative of the type.

secretary, a permanent fixture at Carlton Place and later Park Gardens, had built-in advantages over the more transient representatives of Scottish football. Naturally, any newcomer to the committees of the SFA would welcome the advice and assistance offered so freely; of course, the secretary for a long time actually appointed the chairmen of these various committees – and these were positions eagerly sought after.

It was clear that Graham was in a position to influence matters at the SFA; it was scarcely surprising that a man of Graham's ambition and talents should wish to do so. Desmond White, another Celtic chairman, wrote in the foreword to an official history of the club, published in 1978: 'Progressively, over the years, he controlled to a greater and greater extent the committees of the Association by the power of his own personality, by freemasonry, and by tickets.' This was an astonishingly candid assessment of the former SFA secretary by the chairman of one of the country's most important clubs, and it bears examining in detail.

First of all, George Graham was not one to conceal his association with freemasonry, as his entry in the *Who's Who* of 1956 suggests:

> **Graham, Sir George (Goldie),** Kt., *cr.* 1952; O.B.E. 1947; D.L.; J.P.; Secretary of The Scottish Football Association since 1928; Director (Scottish Board) Legal and General Assurance Society; *b.* 10 Feb 1892; s. of William John Graham, Contractor, Glasgow; *m.* Mary Frances Watson, Glasgow; two *s. Educ.*: Allan Glen's School, Glasgow. Past Grand Master, Grand Lodge of Scotland; Chairman Sports and Games Committee of Scotland. J.P. 1940, D.L. 1955, Glasgow. O.St.J. 1951. *Address*: (business) 48 Carlton Place, Glasgow, G.5. *T.*: Glasgow South 2718/9; Glendoune, Milngavie, Dunbartonshire. *T.*: Milngavie 1324.

For the purpose of comparison only, Bob Kelly's later inclusion, in 1970, is reproduced here:

> **Kelly, Sir Robert (McErlean):** Kt 1969, J.P. Chairman Celtic FC Co. Ltd. since 1947 (Director, 1932); *b* 17 Oct 1902; *s* of James Kelly, J.P. *m* 1933, Marie Josephine Reilly; no *c*. Educ: St. Aloysius Coll. Glasgow; St. Joseph's Coll. Dumfries. President: Scottish Football League for six years; Scottish Football Assoc. for four years (Vice-Pres. for four years).
>
> *Recreations*: reading, gardening. *Address*: Marisdale, East Kilbride Road, Burnside, Rutherglen, Scotland. *T*: 041-6344078.

It should be noted that those who agree to have their names appear in this publication actually write and submit their own biographical material.

Membership in the Masonic Order is often an advantage in business and commerce, and was not to be hidden under a bushel. In fact, it is recalled in Glasgow that a large, ornately framed photograph of Sir George Graham in his Masonic regalia was given place of honour in the window display of a branch of the Provincial Building Society with which he had a connection.

All appointments to the SFA and promotions within came under the aegis of the secretary; it would again be astonishing if those appointments and promotions did not reflect the personality, preferences and prejudices of the secretary. James Farrell, a long-time Celtic director and a member of several SFA committees, told me an amusing story about one meeting. As the participants drifted in, one representative was relaying a particularly surprising piece of gossip to the growing incredulity of his listeners. Somebody dismissed it abruptly, but the narrator persisted in his account: 'I assure you it's true. Really true; I heard it at the Lodge.' A sudden silence greeted this comment, an embarrassed silence, until the speaker (a representative of Juvenile football) realised that not everybody present was a 'member'. He offered his apologies quite sincerely to the Celtic representative: 'I'm sorry, Mr. Farrell, I didn't realise you were sitting there.'

During the writing of this book and the period devoted to research I interviewed several people prominent in Scottish football either as administrators, referees, managers, players or commentators. I asked those who knew George Graham, or who were familiar with him through his work at the SFA, about their views on the long-time secretary. The one word which kept recurring in the interviews was 'bigot', and this was from people with no connection to or apparent sympathies with Celtic.

Bob Kelly, Celtic chairman, receives the Charity Cup in 1950 in Glasgow City Chambers. George Graham, SFA secretary, is standing alongside him (to Kelly's left).

Neither man – Graham nor Kelly – was ashamed of his origins and, in fact, proclaimed them. Graham openly acknowledged his Masonic affiliations and Kelly, in a more private manner, named his house 'Marisdale'. His nephew (Kevin, himself a later Celtic chairman) suggested that it was either named after Brother Walfrid, a member of the Catholic religious order, or his old school St Joseph's College, Dumfries, which was run by the Marists.

It was scarcely surprising that they should clash on a number of issues.

As President of the Scottish League, traditionally at loggerheads with the SFA over the running of football in this country, Kelly continued to have run-ins with Graham from 1949 to 1955. Everybody within Celtic Park was convinced rightly that Graham and his sizeable clique within the SFA were determined to harm Celtic; Desmond White, when I asked him some years ago about George Graham's attitude towards Celtic, replied: 'He'll be roasting in Hell for what he tried to do to our club.' The furore over Celtic's continued flying of the Eire flag at their ground in direct confrontation with the SFA's ruling did not ease the personal animosity between the two men.

Kelly, however, ably represented all the clubs within the league framework impartially, and was noted for a sympathy and understanding of the needs of the smaller clubs and this genuine feeling for Scottish football had gained him respect and a certain amount of wary affection from the league clubs. His strength and integrity as the League President was largely instrumental in the organisation's wresting a greater degree of autonomy from the SFA, much to his own personal satisfaction and to the chagrin of George Graham.

The conflict escalated when Bob Kelly was elected as the president of the SFA and found himself in a position where he could observe the workings of the bureaucracy at first hand on a daily basis.

Cyril Horne, a confidant of Bob Kelly and helper with his autobiography, told me that a public scandal had been narrowly averted some years previously.

It had been the task of George Graham to organise all the various activities of an international match: tickets, programmes, selection of teams, training facilities, crowd-control, hospitality for the visitors and, of course, the distribution of the gate-receipts for a crowd of 134,000 at Hampden Park. The members of the SFA were content to leave all these time-consuming arrangements in the capable hands of the SFA Secretary.

According to Cyril Horne, Bob Kelly started to realise that the lucrative market in the sale of programmes had somehow eluded the SFA and had been appropriated by the secretary as a private concern. Graham had been in the habit of arranging for the programmes to be printed, and distributed on the day of the match; he had paid for them personally and, of course, had pocketed the profits, with the SFA apparently unaware of the 'moonlighting'. Horne was told that Kelly, after verifying the details of the practice, confronted Graham face-to-face over this issue. After the confrontation the practice was halted forthwith.

The distribution of tickets for important matches was always another contentious issue. Graham's position within the SFA bureaucracy guaranteed him considerable power and licence, and the opportunity for abuse of privilege. Like other influential men in football he could re-route tickets to friends – personal and business – and, in turn, be granted favours in the future. Take a simple example: the owner of a garage is given – or pays for – tickets for an attractive fixture. Naturally, he is grateful for the courtesy extended him and at some time might reciprocate that favour by giving preferential treatment to the donor: chairman, director, or secretary. One of Bob Kelly's cryptic comments comes to mind in this context: 'Tickets are currency.'[28]

In the past Kelly had frequently and openly criticised the SFA secretary's policy of giving or withholding tickets – even to SFA councillors – as if he had the right to do so on a personal basis. Kelly now outlined to Graham that it was the secretary's task only to distribute the tickets as outlined in the rules and bye-laws of the SFA, and in doing so with his characteristic bluntness he made it abundantly clear that Graham was 'a paid servant of the SFA'.

In 1955 George Graham was involved in the most bizarre of ticket fiascos, when Celtic were due to play Clyde in the Scottish Cup final at Hampden Park on 23 April. The BBC were anxious to screen the match, and it would have been the first Scottish Cup final to be televised live. However, the SFA members were reluctant to allow the screening to go ahead, being rightly concerned that the attendance at the climax of the football season might be adversely affected. Bob Kelly was certainly one administrator who consistently opposed the idea of televised matches, feeling that it diluted the atmosphere at the occasion and would harm other clubs throughout the country.

On the morning of the match Gair Henderson, writing in the *Evening Times* (cup final special-edition) stated that

> ... months ago an announcement came out from Carlton Place that the Cup Final would be televised only if 80 per cent of 134,000 tickets were sold exactly a fortnight before 23 April. The deadline expired a fortnight ago and the SFA remained as silent as the tomb. On 9 April nothing like the 108,000[29] ticket quota had gone, and the SFA would have been perfectly justified in coming out with an announcement banning the BBC cameras at Hampden. (23 April 1955)

Henderson later added that the decision to allow the telecast seemed to have been a last-minute one as:

---

[28] Bob Kelly was a most generous man and distributed many complimentary tickets to a wide circle of acquaintances, including the clergy. To his immense credit he was personally responsible for reimbursing the club for many of these tickets. When his nephew Kevin Kelly took over as chairman he was astonished at the numbers involved and, as a married man with four children, he was simply unable to continue the practice at the same level.

[29] Henderson is slightly out in his figure; eighty per cent of 134,000 is 107,200.

The Hampden scene did, after all, go out on the television screen, but you would be astounded at the number of people who were absolutely furious that no 'TV or not TV' decision was taken before Celtic and Clyde came running out on to the field today. One or two of us who keep an ear pretty close to the SFA ground had a fair idea of what was happening ten days ago, but some able-bodied folk could not make up their minds whether to join the Hampden trek or risk staying at home and seeing nothing when the sets were switched on in the afternoon.

Assuming that Celtic would romp to victory against their local rivals, most football men realised that this final had little genuine appeal to the neutrals. Ticket sales had been sluggish and tickets were still on sale at the SFA headquarters up to noon on the actual day of the fixture but the *Evening Times* reported that 'four hours before kick-off there was not the slightest sign of cup final excitement in the centre of Glasgow.'

However, permission was given – presumably by the secretary – that transmission could start, and the first Scottish Cup final to be televised live came on air at 2:50, or ten minutes before the kick-off. No doubt briefed by Sir George Graham, the *Evening Times* journalist credited the go-ahead to the SFA having 'a thought or two for the very old, for the unfortunate football fans who spent today in a hospital bed.'

The attendance at the Celtic–Clyde cup final on 23 April was later announced as 106,234, a significant drop in the numbers anticipated, based on the SFA forecast. The authorities, when confronted with the discrepancy in the figures, suggested at first that a surprisingly large number had bought tickets but had simply failed to turn up.

The mystery was cleared up some months later when a batch of tickets – 10,000 in all – was found under lock and key at the SFA headquarters, left there for safekeeping by the secretary and apparently forgotten about. Sir George apologised for this oversight but, as a result of this 'accident', the financial records of the SFA had to be amended and, among other things, both finalists (Celtic and Clyde) were ordered to return a portion of the gate-money they had already received.

What exactly had happened? Nothing could be proved for certain but it would have been a major embarrassment for the SFA not to have allowed TV coverage of the match: much organisational work would have been wasted, and the SFA would not have collected a fee for allowing the coverage to proceed.

Many reporters, and other football men, assumed that the misplacing of the 10,000 tickets was a most predictable accident. Was Graham at fault here, or was he working to instructions? Given his autocratic style, it is more likely that any decision was his alone and no doubt he felt that he was acting in the best interests of the SFA.

In fact, that autocratic style at last earned him an official rebuke from his employers only a month or so later during Scotland's continental tour. One SFA Council member (Hugh McMillan of Dunfermline Athletic) was told by the secretary in no uncertain terms: 'I put you on the Selection Committee and I can put you off.' The President of the Scottish League, William Waters of St Mirren, was so incensed that 'a paid servant' could treat a committee member with such contempt that, upon the party's return to Scotland, he moved that Sir George be severely reprimanded and warned about his future conduct.

At the SFA meeting on 5 December it was revealed, after an enquiry into the complaint, that Mr. McMillan's charge 'had been proven beyond doubt'. Despite that conclusion, Mr. Waters' motion of censure was narrowly defeated by thirteen votes to eleven with several abstentions playing a part in the outcome.

Although he had escaped an official censure, it was the clearest indication yet that the Secretary's grip on the council chamber was loosening. This suspicion was verified by his abrupt departure from the SFA in 1957. He retired suddenly – apparently without any prior warning – and his resignation was accepted equally promptly by the SFA. The newspapers were surprisingly reticent about the development of the SFA's most prominent bureaucrat after almost thirty years in the role.

Shortly afterwards, on 16 September 1957, the SFA Council voted for 'the withdrawal of certain privileges awarded to the recently retired secretary'. The nominal cause of the Council's last action was its disapproval of the contents of a series of articles in the *Sunday Express* provided by Sir George. The articles, for which he presumably was paid handsomely, purported to provide revelations about the workings of the SFA, and were relatively bland, but the opportunity to further discredit the former secretary was taken by the Council.

However, Bob Kelly may have had something more to contribute to the background of the 'resignation' of the SFA secretary. As an office-bearer, Bob Kelly was becoming more and more aware of some of the dubious activities of the SFA secretary and it seemed to Kelly that Graham was abusing his position of authority to profit directly and indirectly at the expense of the SFA.

Over the years Kelly had had several run-ins with Graham over his running of the SFA bureaucracy, and had slowly gathered a following among those (especially in the Scottish League) who had felt affronted at the secretary's high-handedness. Rumours had been rife for years, particularly about irregularities in the distribution of tickets but, because of intimidation by the autocratic secretary and fear of the consequences, nobody had dared to complain at an official level.

However, the situation had changed somewhat by 1957 and several members of the Council approached Bob Kelly with their suspicions. He investigated further and gathered evidence enough to convince him that the secretary had indeed abused his position of trust and had been profiting personally in the transactions. With typical directness he confronted Sir George Graham about the allegations, and after receiving what he considered an unsatisfactory explanation, told him bluntly that this matter would not be swept under the carpet. Above all, Kelly was a man of a man of the highest personal standards in morality, an administrator of undoubted principle and integrity, and Graham knew that the Celtic chairman's threats would be carried out.

It was to be a simple choice: an immediate resignation tendered by the secretary, or the police would be called in to investigate the alleged fraud.

No doubt Kelly's mind flickered back to the grim days in 1952 when George Graham, at the height of his influence at the SFA, seemed intent on humiliating Celtic, or closing them down. Thus, there was little sympathy emanating from Celtic's chairman in the direction of the SFA secretary, and certainly there would have been a grim personal satisfaction at the gradual turnaround in fortunes.

For Bob Kelly it was not a matter for compromise or negotiation and, for once, the secretary's networking skills would not be enough. Sir George Graham, secretary of the SFA since 1928, chose to resign. His downfall was galling for a man who had manipulated the running of Scottish football for so long, and particularly as it was due primarily to his nemesis, Bob Kelly, a man noted for his integrity and determination.

It was scarcely a secret in football circles that the secretary of the SFA had resigned in mysterious circumstances but the actual details were never revealed in any public forum. Bob Kelly, aware of the harm that such a scandal would do to the SFA's image, kept a discreet silence on the affair but let it be known privately among some trusted family members that George Graham had had little choice but to resign.

No doubt Bob Kelly would have been justified in taking a certain satisfaction at the outcome and the part he had played in the drama.

CHAPTER SIX

The Shameful Treatment of Jim Callaghan

It would be accurate to state that the treatment meted out to the Glasgow referee James Callaghan in 1969 represented the antithesis of what had happened to A.B. Gebbie (Hamilton) almost exactly twenty years after the Cox–Tully incident. Gebbie had been reprimanded by the SFA for 'a possible error of judgement' but advised that 'because of his previous good record no further action would be taken against him.' Callaghan, for a similar, and perhaps even less reprehensible error, was suspended for two months, his reputation tarnished and his career as a referee effectively diminished.

For many Celtic followers the essential difference in the two cases arose from the fact that Gebbie's decision favoured Rangers, while Callaghan's favoured Celtic.

The suspension rose out of a complaint lodged by Rangers in the wake of Jim Callaghan's handling of a League Cup-tie between the Old Firm at Celtic Park on 20 August 1969.

It was a mirror image of the events of 1949 and reflected no credit on the Ibrox club. By this time Rangers were the underdogs, struggling hard for a breakthrough against Jock Stein's apparently invincible Celtic side. In the earlier incident at Ibrox Park serious crowd trouble had broken out almost immediately afterwards, but in the latter case at Celtic Park the spectators had remained well behaved.

The events leading up to the fateful match were similar; the outsiders, Rangers, had beaten Celtic 2–1 at Ibrox Park in the sectional play to encourage hopes that a revival was underway. R.H. Davidson (Airdrie) refereed that encounter, and it appeared to be a typical Old Firm clash as this excerpt from the *Daily Express* indicated: 'Celtic may feel they were harshly treated. They were denied a penalty when a Gemmell shot struck a defender. They can look back on the last Ibrox meeting between the two when Rangers won the game by a penalty granted in exactly similar circumstances' (14 August 1969).

The stage was set for an epic clash in the return match a week later with Rangers still needing a draw or a win at Parkhead to ensure advancing to the quarter-final stage, while Celtic were more determined than ever to recover from the setback at Ibrox. The official appointed for the fixture was J. Callaghan (Glasgow), a FIFA referee generally recognised as among the best in Scotland, having been honoured with the Rangers–Celtic Cup Final on 26 April 1969, and due to officiate in the Fairs Cities cup-tie between Glentoran and Arsenal on 29 September.

That Scottish Cup final might be the best starting-point for the unfolding events. Celtic won the trophy by thrashing Rangers 4–0, but it was a ferociously fought clash. The *Glasgow Herald* reporters condemned the rough tactics adopted by both sides, and chose to spread the blame relatively evenly between the teams. *The Scotsman* was more forthright, with its chief reporter (John Rafferty) reserving much of his criticism for Willie Johnston, Rangers' winger: ' ... who instead attacked the Celtic defence physically. It is no exaggeration to say that on three occasions he could conceivably have been ordered off.' Johnston, of course, had the reputation of being a fiery competitor and, by the end of his career, had fully earned the 'distinction' of being one of Scotland's worst-disciplined players.

The broadsheets were mildly critical of Callaghan's refereeing, while acknowledging that the actions of warring players had made his task infinitely more difficult: 'The referee would have been quite justified in sending off a couple of players from either side.' (*Glasgow Herald*) and 'There was some deplorable foul play and the referee, Mr. Callaghan, tackled it tolerantly like an English referee – and I can think of nothing more disparaging to say' (*The Scotsman*).

Upon reading these match reports, it is clear that Mr. Callaghan was a referee reluctant to distort a football match by ordering players off; he was an official who preferred to allow the game to proceed and trust that early rough play – if treated impartially – would evolve into more acceptable practices.[30] Unfortunately, Old Firm matches do not always follow that pattern, but it is commendable that this referee managed to complete a most difficult assignment without resorting to orderings-off as a method of control. The Scottish Cup final was refereed fairly and, if anything, the losers were given more of the breaks.

Rangers, however, did have one legitimate grievance against Callaghan. On the opening day of the 1968/69 season Celtic went to Ibrox in a League Cup tie and won fairly convincingly by 2–0, but near the end Jimmy Johnstone, objecting to a late tackle by a Rangers defender (Dave Smith), retaliated by kicking him on the ankle. Most observers, including the author, feel that Johnstone was extremely fortunate to escape punishment for the incident. David White, Rangers' manager, was irate at the referee's tolerance and condemned the non-decision as 'Disgraceful!' and he was, of course, later censured by the SFA for his remarks.

However, in this vital League Cup-tie on 20 August 1969 at half time the

---

[30] Mr. J. McCluskey (Stewarton) would be the one referee in recent times who resembled Callaghan in approach and style. Although often involved in controversy for his *laissez-faire* attitude, McCluskey enjoyed the respect of most Scottish players until his retirement at the end of 1999/2000.

score was still 0–0, and the contest evenly contested. In the accepted manner of Old Firm cup-ties it had evolved into a war of attrition and neither side was giving an inch of territory without a fierce resistance. Mr. Callaghan, keeping a tight control over the situation, by the interval had booked three players, two Celtic and one Rangers.

The one controversial moment came only seconds after the second-half kick-off when John Hughes of Celtic and Willie Johnston of Rangers clashed, with the ball far away. Johnston, so lucky to avoid being ordered off in the last Cup Final, fell to the ground after the incident; the linesman's flag shot up and remained so until Callaghan, who was upfield, noticed it. The referee halted play, made his way to his linesman, spoke at length with his assistant, and walked over to Hughes. Surprisingly – and to vastly differing reactions from both sets of supporters – he confined his actions to lecturing the Celtic player. Hughes, of course, had been booked in the first half and, if guilty of any further serious infraction of the rules, should have been dismissed immediately.

On 12 October 1969 the TV programme *Sports Arena* covered the match and its aftermath in complete detail, including footage of the incident between the two players, seconds after the restart of the tie, and it showed the events in the off-the-ball clash in isolated slow-motion. Ian Wooldridge, the com-

mentator for London Weekend TV, was unequivocal about the incident: 'This clearly shows Johnston of Rangers fouling Hughes.' Later in the programme Wooldridge defended the match official, pointing out that 'Callaghan, a world-class referee, did not see the incident ... and Johnston had been provoking Hughes throughout the game.'

Peter Burns, a Celtic historian, was at the match and had a clear view of the incident and suggests that Johnston had initially fouled Hughes from behind and that the Celtic player had over-reacted and retaliated. Robert McElroy, a Rangers historian, was also at the match and remembers the jubilation among his fellow supporters as the official made his way towards the

John Hughes in action against Airdrie in a Scottish Cup semi-final

linesman. However, he recalls thinking that the discussion between Callaghan and his assistant was lasting too long, that some doubt was existing or forming in the referee's mind.

As a writer, I have always been reluctant to include anecdotes without some corroboration but I have been given the following account of the 'conversation' between referee and linesman from a minor Celtic official who was within earshot.

Callaghan: What's up?
Linesman: Hughes and Johnston, right after the kick-off. Hughes retaliated.
Callaghan: Right. What are you suggesting I do then?
Linesman: The rules are clear. You don't have much choice; he [Hughes] has to go.
Callaghan: Are you really sure about that? You are going to be the man running this line for the rest of this game.
Linesman: Remarks were inaudible.

In the Scottish Cup final back in May, won 4–0 by Celtic, Rangers supporters had come over the retaining wall in their hundreds, but this was probably in order to effect a quick retreat from Hampden after Chalmers had scored Celtic's fourth goal with fifteen minutes left. At Celtic Park – and in 1969 there were few stewards available – the only barrier between the spectators and the pitch was easily surmountable. Given the tense atmosphere inside the ground that night, Callaghan's concerns for the safety of his linesman – and the players – were probably legitimate.

But the referee had made a mistake: Johnston should have been cautioned for his part in the incident, and Hughes, already booked, should have been dismissed for his retaliation. Celtic had clearly been given the benefit of that doubt and – characteristically of Celtic sides coached by Jock Stein – capitalised on the 'break' by eking out the narrowest of 1–0 wins through a goal headed in by Gemmell, after Rangers' goalkeeper had spilled a shot.

In hindsight, the non-action of Jim Callaghan in the Hughes–Johnston clash may have been a decisive factor in the outcome, but many at the match admitted later that the incident had passed them by. *The Scotsman* referred to the clash which was to provoke the controversy but only in passing; the *Glasgow Herald* did not mention it at all in Glyn Edwards' match report. Willie Waddell, who had starred with Rangers just after the war and who would shortly become the Ibrox club's manager, was writing a column for the *Daily Express* at that time, and his lengthy comments on this particular match made no mention of the Hughes–Johnston incident, his overall opinion being that Rangers were on the way back to parity with Celtic.

In fact, the subsequent coverage by the *Daily Express* in the wake of the Ibrox club's defeat at Celtic Park failed to mention the particular incident in any way, directly or indirectly, until 1 September.

On that date the newspaper went into commendable detail about a further development, quoting 'an Ibrox spokesman' who said: 'In conjunction with the normal report on the match referee we sent a letter making an observation on the clash between Hughes and Johnston. This is not an unusual procedure. We did not ask for an inquiry. Any further move is up to the SFA.'

The secretary of the SFA, Willie Allan, quibbled slightly with Rangers' position: 'It [sending a letter] does not happen very often. However Rangers describe their letter, it expressed dissatisfaction and it was sent presumably in the hope that some action would be taken. I should point out that the SFA do not get a referee's report on a league game – only a report of action taken against a player. Since no action was taken against John Hughes for this incident there was no report, and therefore no official information.'[31]

The *Daily Express* summed up Rangers' action in writing their letter, and the SFA's knee-jerk response in conducting an inquiry: 'Whatever the authorities do the result stands, there can be no delayed punishment to the player and the only possible sufferer is the referee who, by edict of the SFA, must remain silent' (1 September 1969).

However, the SFA Referee Supervisor, J.A. Mowat, entered the controversy somewhat indirectly. Mowat, once a highly respected official, wrote for a Sunday newspaper and his task was to answer questions about the Rules of the Game. He chose to respond to a query about the incident: 'I wasn't present and cannot judge. One must assume that the referee did not see or have a clear view of the incident and therefore consulted the linesman who had raised his flag. You state that he [Hughes] had already been cautioned which means that any further misconduct should incur an ordering-off. If the game was re-started with a free kick to Rangers, one would believe that the Celtic player was the offender.'

This raises the issue of the linesman's input. Mr. Callaghan did eventually notice the upraised flag, and stopped play: either he was not completely convinced by the linesman's version of events, or he felt that his own action was sufficient under the circumstances. The latter scenario does fit in exactly with the events during the rest of the contest, as described in the newspapers. A bruising cup-tie that was threatening to get out of hand settled down into a hard, evenly contested match.

Rangers, irate at the circumstances of their knock-out from the League Cup, had pursued the matter further by writing to the SFA and the Scottish League, complaining about the refereeing in this particular match. In doing so, the Ibrox club were contravening one of Scottish football's traditions.

Referees have been criticised in the past by clubs, and downgraded as a result of that criticism, but the demotion has come at the end of the season and is based on a comprehensive evaluation of the comments made by all the clubs they have refereed that season. It was simply unprecedented that one complaint from one club in the early stages of a season should endanger the career of a referee till then highly regarded by his association and recognised by FIFA as one of the best officials in Scotland.

---

[31] The match was a League Cup-tie and, accordingly, a matter for the Scottish League.

On 15 September 1969 the SFA announced the suspension of Jim Callaghan for two months, during which time he could not referee any football matches, including the Glentoran vs. Arsenal European tie for which he had been already nominated by the SFA. Ironically the Glasgow Referees' Association had chosen Mr. Callaghan as the recipient of the Charlie Faultless Trophy – awarded to the previous season's best referee – and the presentation was made on 11 October, only three days after the suspension was ratified. Mr. Callaghan was given a standing ovation by his fellow-referees as he accepted the trophy.

It would be too simplistic to state that the action taken by the SFA's Referee Committee in response to Rangers' complaint was due to the club's eminent position in the game and its influence within the SFA but, at the risk of raising the question of Celtic's alleged paranoia, how far would Celtic have got had they ever taken a similar course of action? Consider the response Celtic received from the SFA in the aftermath of the Cox–Tully affair.

Rangers refused to comment on the outcome of their 'observation', but Celtic, although they were in Switzerland preparing for a European Cup-tie, were forthright in their condemnation.

Bob Kelly may have had faults as Celtic's chairman but he could never be criticised for his moral judgements; he was aghast at the suspension and, as an administrator, wondered about the long-term implications: 'In all my years in football this is the worst decision I have ever known. Can a referee ever again feel that he has solid authority backed by the game's governing body?' Jock Stein delivered a double blast against Rangers and the SFA: 'I would hate to think we would ever stoop low enough to make an official protest that could possibly result in a decision like this.' He went on to admit that referees did make mistakes and 'made decisions which have sometimes cost us the game. But, however wrong they may have been in our eyes – and we concede that we are not always justified in protesting – we accepted their decisions.'

Bob Kelly continued to fret about the treatment meted out to the beleaguered referee, and asked for an inquiry to rectify the situation. He objected in principle to the idea that a single letter condemning a referee's performance in a single match could result in the man's public humiliation and suspension. It was unfortunate for Kelly that his complaint concerned the action of Celtic's greatest rivals, Rangers.[32] Too many officials from other clubs

---

[32] Ironically, in view of their current stance in the Hughes–Johnston clash, Rangers had been involved in a dispute with the SFA over their striker Colin Stein who had missed the cup final through suspension. Stein, bought from Hibernian in 1968 for the first £100,000 fee between two Scottish clubs, had been ordered off three times that season (1968/69) in all, twice with Rangers. On the last occasion (against Clyde at Ibrox Park on 15 March) Rangers claimed unsuccessfully that Mulherron, the Clyde player, had provoked the incident and Stein was being punished for 'mere retaliation' – a lesser offence in their eyes.

assumed that the matter was a continuation of Old Firm antipathy – and that weakened Kelly's argument on behalf of the referee within the SFA.

Kelly's appeal was rejected out of hand, and the SFA detailed the case against Mr. Callaghan as summarised by the *Daily Record* of 8 October 1969:

1. Mr. Callaghan is a Class 1 referee and on the FIFA list. More is expected of him than of others

2. experienced referees are expected to set an example to younger colleagues;

3. if this type of laxity is allowed, it could result in deep malaise which could permeate the whole referee movement. Discipline would cease. Why should some court unpopularity by sending players off while another gets away with it?

4. it was a grave error of judgement. Referees should be desirably perfect in the atmosphere of a Celtic-Rangers match. And Mr. Callaghan was not involved alone;

5. the linesman [J.M. Wilson (Bishopbriggs)] was also involved, and the committee are not prepared to sacrifice him to save the face of Mr. Callaghan.

It is not difficult to conclude that Mr. Callaghan had few friends among the officials of the SFA and the club representatives who comprised the various committees. One member of the committee leaked the 'information' to the press that 'Callaghan did not send off Hughes because it might produce an explosive situation with the crowd.'[33] And it has been noted in Callaghan's defence that the behaviour by both sets of players did improve after the incident, an indication that his authority was not impaired by his defusing a difficult situation.

Ironically, the one man who could have contributed most meaningfully to the discussion was not able to provide any help at all. The Referee Supervisor, George Mitchell (Falkirk), had forgotten his Celtic pass and was refused admission by Celtic's doorman, who stubbornly denied him entry although Mitchell had been a regular at Celtic Park as a referee and SFA official for more than twenty years.[34]

It proved a public relations disaster for the SFA.

---

[33] This seems to substantiate in part the alleged conversation between Callaghan and his linesman as reported earlier in the chapter.

[34] The doorman (Bill Peacock) had a well-deserved reputation for being a martinet. He had been instructed by Desmond White in particular to crack down on the number of gatecrashers at Celtic home games, and he carried out his duties with apparent enthusiasm. Among his 'victims' over the years were John Toshack (Liverpool) and Billy McNeill's wife, Liz.

In fact, Celtic were one club who sent the match official a card, asking him to bring it with him as confirmation; some years earlier the same George Mitchell, due to referee at Celtic Park that day, was denied entry by Peacock because he had misplaced the card. The referee was rightly irritated and told the doorman to inform his chairman that he had been refused entry, and set off towards London Road. Peacock had to pursue Mr. Mitchell for some distance down the street in an effort to rectify the situation.

Celtic's chairman Bob Kelly – by now Sir Robert Kelly – resigned from the SFA Referee Committee in protest at the handling of the affair. He handed in a letter of resignation, and commented briefly to the press: 'I felt I could no longer serve on the committee as it would be an embarrassment to the chairman [George Fox of Dundee United] whose views I oppose.'

The print media were sympathetic to Jim Callaghan at his personal humiliation, but the more perceptive among the journalists saw the wider issue clearly. John Fairgrieve quoted the Minister of Sport, Denis Howell: 'Referees never make mistakes. Their decisions are always right whatever people think about them. The biggest need in the game today is the acceptance of referees' decisions by players, managers, directors and fans. Without this, there is no satisfactory basis for conducting sport.'

Fairgrieve used the last sentence in Howell's speech as his theme throughout his column:

> Consider these last ten words, simple, uncompromising. They are words with that quality of obviousness which so often distinguishes truth. I would commend them to the Scottish Football Association for study and for action. The SFA have given what purported to be an explanation of the Callaghan suspension. If they are now congratulating themselves on the assumption that this particular controversy has fizzled out, they assume too much. What the appointed spokesman of the SFA did was to ignore – or fail to recognise – the deep and basic issue. He detailed the mistake made by Mr. Callaghan in that Old Firm match, although nobody had ever disputed the fact of the mistake. It did not matter whether Mr. Callaghan was right or wrong. What mattered was the public destruction of a principle – the principle which shores up 'the satisfactory basis for conducting sport.' If a referee makes a mistake significant to the result of a match, *and if that mistake is officially admitted by the ruling body*, does not the losing club have a case – and possibly a legal case – for compensation? What happens then to the structure of the game? You see now what Mr. Howell means when he says a referee is always right? (*Daily Mail*, 10 October 1969)

Referees had been suspended before, but never in the full glare of publicity. If Jim Callaghan had been a poor referee, his match reports would have indicated that and any demotion would have been justified at the end of the season, and should have been handled in private after consultation with him and the SFA Referee Supervisors. But to be suspended for two months – after failing to take action on an incident which took place behind his back – was an unprecedented action against a referee who had established himself within his avocation.

Recently, I spoke to two prominent Referee Supervisors (separately) and mentioned the treatment accorded Jim Callaghan. Both were sympathetic and spoke highly of Callaghan's abilities and integrity, but one made a most significant comment: 'Jim's face just didn't fit the new regime. He was a good referee, highly respected by players, but he didn't really look in good shape and had an awkward, shambling sort of run. The deciding factor might have been a social thing: Jim worked as a storage supervisor in a factory, and he lived in Easterhouse – not quite what the SFA wanted'. In its coverage the *Daily Record* thoughtfully printed his full postal address.

Both Referee Supervisors, who were on the active list in 1969, mentioned the consternation the suspension had aroused within the refereeing fraternity; one suggested that the possibility of 'strike action' by the officials had been raised, but that did not materialise. He shook his head sadly, when speaking about Callaghan's punishment: 'A referee cannot make a comeback after a public suspension; everybody remembers it and he cannot referee a match effectively again – and that is what makes it unfair. And who was involved in the incident? Willie Johnston ... enough said.'

It was widely believed that Mr. Callaghan's career ended with this suspension. However, the official was of a resilient character, resuming his duties after the suspension and continuing to referee at the highest level within Scotland for another six seasons. In fact, he was the referee at Celtic Park on 1 May 1971 when the club paraded the Lisbon Lions for the last time in a fixture against Clyde. But the finger-pointing and whispered comments continued – and this was manifestly unfair.

Celtic supporters were convinced that the suspension was imposed because Jim Callaghan was believed to be a Catholic, and that he had favoured Celtic in a match against Rangers. Those supporters wondered about the probable outcome for a referee who was Protestant, and who had favoured Rangers in a match against Celtic. And those same supporters were not hesitant about giving specific examples to illustrate the latter scenario.

The Hughes–Johnston incident had occurred in an important match, a cup-tie between Celtic and Rangers. Of course, Old Firm matches are notoriously different as Willie Syme, who had recently retired as a referee, indicated in an interview:

> After refereeing one of these games on a Saturday, I used to head for home, get the phone off the hook, and settle down in the house. If I left the phone as it was, then we were plagued with anonymous calls. Threats, insults – you name it – we had it on that phone. And going to work in the town I had to change from my normal route. Normally I went along Argyle Street around the same time every morning but after an Old Firm game I was down on the Broomielaw. That game can bring out the worst in people, fans, and players. It's the one game where no one can be influenced even slightly by the crowd ... because you just don't hear anything at all. The noise is so great and so constant that eventually it's like refereeing a game in total silence. (*Daily Record*, 19 September 1969)

Mr. Callaghan was also a victim of changing circumstances.

Prior to the 1969/70 season, any player receiving three cautions automatically faced disciplinary action from the SFA, and was routinely suspended, usually for a two-week period. It should also be noted that referees were more reluctant to caution a player in those days, and that the players themselves were generally better disciplined. Remarkably, the nature of the caution was not taken into consideration and minor offences (such as entering the field of play as a substitute without formal permission from the referee) carried as much weight as major ones (such as foul play). [35]

Naturally, players were upset at this discrepancy and had agitated for some change in the SFA's position.

Back in April 1969 the Council of the SFA had ratified a recommendation of the Referee Committee dealing with cautions. Firstly, from the start of the new season (1969/70) – and of primary importance in the Hughes-Johnston affair – a player was to be sent off if he persisted in misconduct after receiving a caution earlier in the game.

The rationale for the change was simple: previously, referees – especially older officials approaching the end of their careers – had considered a caution as a punishment in its own right, and a punishment which acted as a deterrent. However, noting a recent increase in rough play and other unacceptable conduct among players, the authorities were starting to consider that a caution was no longer a significant deterrent and felt it should be used as a step towards the ultimate field-punishment – the ordering-off.

However, the SFA had made a fatal mistake in its administration procedures: it had decided that it should no longer deal immediately with a player who had collected three cautions (although the number of cautions accumulated by the player would be considered if a player were to appear before the committee on an ordering-off charge).

The Council had made a critical error in this latter endorsement and there was considerable confusion even in the days just prior to the new season as a statement by Ernie Walker, the assistant-secretary of the SFA, would indicate: 'No player will be called before the committee to answer for cautions.' He added gloomily:

> The committee will have no authority to call players – a player could have a caution in every game but he would not be answerable for them. There is a possibility that the committee will decide that, if a player is ordered off, then his record of cautions will be taken into consideration when passing sentence on him, but no firm decision has yet been made about that. We will continue to record cautions for the sake of the statistics, and to know the behaviour patterns. (*Glasgow Herald*, 8 August 1999)

The Scottish League – the most visible and important of all the organisations under the aegis of the SFA – was nonplussed. According to Fred Denovan, the

---

[35] Jimmy Johnstone missed the Scottish Cup final against Rangers because of suspension. He was the last player to miss a cup final because of his three cautions. Colin Stein of Rangers also missed the same match, as a consequence of being ordered off and receiving a five-week ban. This sentence was considered harsh but Stein had been ordered off three times during the season. The chairman of Morton (Mr. J.S. Thomson) became involved in the controversy by offering to pay for an appeal against the suspension in the courts: 'The action will go ahead at the instigation of Colin Stein and sponsored by me.' Fortunately, Stein was persuaded, perhaps by his club, to drop the appeal.

secretary: 'We were campaigning so that the seriousness of the offences should be taken into account but, to our utter surprise, the SFA eliminated the whole regulation dealing with cautions.'

Of course, the onus fell on the referees, the men charged with enforcing the new regulations and it was anticipated that the number of orderings-off would increase dramatically.

This might well have placed a burden on referees like Mr. Callaghan, who preferred to keep a player on the field if possible. His behaviour in the Scottish Cup final in April and in the League Cup-tie in August was perfectly consistent with that interpretation. Johnston of Rangers should have been sent off at Hampden, and Hughes of Celtic should have been dismissed at Parkhead. When Mr. Callaghan himself appeared before the Referee Committee, no doubt he would have been questioned about not applying the new SFA edict concerning cautions at the League Cup-tie of 20 August.

It has been asserted earlier that there were similarities between the Cox–Tully incident in 1949 and the Hughes–Johnston clash in 1969. Some differences were immediately more apparent. In 1949 Rangers were the superior team and organisation, and Celtic were making considerable efforts to catch up while, in 1969, Celtic, with Jock Stein in control, were in the ascendancy and Rangers were desperate to regain their traditional supremacy.[36] Gebbie was an average referee, neither outstandingly good nor bad, while Callaghan was recognised as among the best in Scotland. Gebbie made a mistake in not consulting a linesman, if indeed he had been unsighted at Ibrox, while Callaghan did listen to the linesman and apparently decided to overrule his contribution by only lecturing Hughes.

Furthermore, at Ibrox Park, Cox's action had taken place in the full view of the Celtic support and play had been allowed to continue; this had led directly to violent scenes on the Celtic terracing and a cessation of play for some minutes while the police and ambulance men dealt with an explosive situation. At Celtic Park, Hughes' action had occurred some distance from the massed Rangers support although they were instantly aware of it and, given their collective conviction that Hughes should have been sent off, it reflects well on them that their behaviour was within acceptable bounds.

Both clubs felt that the referees' decisions had cost them the match, and the probability of advancing to the next stage of the League Cup at the direct

---

[36] As an organisation Rangers were so sensitive about Celtic's superiority that their manager, David White, in August 1969 was critical of comedian Lex McLean's variety act. McLean, a lifetime Rangers' fan, was asked by White to stop poking fun at his team because 'it was ruining morale'. A sample of McLean's patter which had annoyed Rangers, and was cited in the *Daily Record*, ran as follows: 'A gang of thieves broke into Celtic Park and Ibrox on the same night, making off with the silverware. Later, they discovered that they obtained £2,000 more from the haul at Ibrox because they were all antiques.'

expense of their most bitter rivals. Celtic, back in 1949, were angry at the incident and rightly dreaded the consequences of their fans' misbehaviour. In fact, they were fearful that Celtic Park might be closed for a period as a punishment. Rangers in 1969 were similarly outraged at a referee's perceived lapse of judgement, but they had no anxieties regarding the conduct of their supporters. In calling for an independent inquiry Celtic had wanted justice in 1949, while Rangers were now demanding immediate revenge on a referee who, they felt, had wronged them.

Back in 1949 the football authorities, when dealing with a referee who had erred, bent over backwards to protect the official almost automatically, but in 1969 there was to be no similar cover-up for a referee who had made arguably a less harmful wrong decision.

At the end of the day, some Celtic supporters and officials felt that Gebbie had been treated leniently by the authorities because his decision had favoured Rangers and Callaghan harshly because his had favoured Celtic.

And the more cynical felt that Mr. Callaghan's religion had been a factor in the punishment inflicted upon him.

MEDIA COVERAGE

Celtic vs. Rangers
Scottish Cup Final: 26 April 1969

Bluntly the first half was a disgrace to football. Tackles were intimidating, even brutal. Man went for man. Tripping, kicking, hacking, and jersey-pulling were rife. How on earth can the management of both sides raise their hands piously in horror against the hooliganism among their supporters when the players themselves indulge in the orgy of crudeness which made this so unpalatable a spectacle. The pattern of viciousness was set within the first minute when McNeill rose from a tackle badly shaken and needing treatment to his face. Thereafter foul came upon foul. Players faced up to each other angrily at all points. Murdoch was twice fouled within the space of a few minutes, Brogan was booked after three abrasive tackles in quick succession, Ferguson was given a stern warning, another went to Chalmers, still another to McKinnon ... and so it went on. For such violent fronts as these war correspondents should be employed and not sports writers. (*Glasgow Herald*, 29 April 1969)

Many a beaten team have come off Hampden Park to applause and to find there can be glory in defeat. Rangers came off with nothing they can be proud of. Celtic had provocation enough to turn this final into a brawl but they didn't ... not one Celtic player lost his temper and one exceptional aspect of the final was when Murdoch was butted in the face. Many would have been sorely tempted to retaliate but not Murdoch. An expression of surprise crossed his face, but he ignored it and ran to take up his position in defence. That was true professionalism. (*The Scotsman*, 29 April 1969)

Celtic vs. Rangers
League Cup: 20 August 1969

It was a hard game in which the tackling by several players was less than scrupulous but it was great entertainment for the 70,000 crowd, even though the proceedings were marred by the booking of Murdoch, Hughes and McKinnon. (*Glasgow Herald*, 21 August 1969)

In the first minute of the second half Hughes was involved in an incident with Johnston when the ball was far away. A linesman reported it, but the referee did no more than administer a long, stern warning. Hughes was lucky he stayed on the field. That altercation seemed to do some good as the viciousness went out of the tackling. (*The Scotsman*, 21 August 1969)

The match was often bad-tempered, sometimes ruthless, and always nerve-wracking. And John Hughes was the luckiest man in the world in a sensational outburst just one minute after the interval when he downed Willie Johnston with the play 50 yards away and the referee's back turned. Jim Callaghan called Hughes, already booked, towards him and the big winger looked a certainty to be sent off. The flashpoint and the hushed silence that followed while the referee spoke to Hughes seemed to calm tempers all round – and a match that always simmered never quite boiled over. (*Daily Express*, 21 August 1969)

CHAPTER SEVEN

Personality Clash: Jock Stein and R.H. Davidson

During the research required for another book on football, I interviewed one former Celtic player who made a most interesting statement: 'For years we got absolutely nothing from referees. When Stein arrived back at Celtic Park as manager, we got our share of penalty kicks – even against Rangers.'

This man had played throughout the period of 'the Kelly Kids' and also under Stein, and his claim, delivered without too much passion or resentment, echoes the words of a former Celtic director: 'Jock Stein cowed referees into fairness.'

The indictment merited some examination, and I decided to check the statistics for domestic matches played by Celtic for a period of five seasons, between 1962/63 and 1966/67 – in other words, the periods immediately prior to Stein's arrival and immediately after it.

In 1962/63 Celtic were awarded eight penalty kicks in fifty-one competitive matches; in 1963/64 nine penalties in forty-nine matches; in 1965/66 thirteen penalties in fifty-two matches; in 1966/67 fifteen penalties in fifty-three matches.

Jock Stein's first match in charge was at Airdrie on 10 March 1965 and the findings for that 1964/65 season are significant, to say the least. Celtic, under Jimmy McGrory played thirty-eight matches and were awarded six penalty kicks; with Jock Stein in charge for the remaining fifteen fixtures they were awarded another six.

The overall statistics for these five seasons are equally revealing: Jimmy McGrory was Celtic's manager for 138 matches and Celtic were awarded twenty-three penalty kicks; Jock Stein was manager for 120 matches and Celtic were awarded thirty-four penalty kicks. Statistics may be used for a variety of reasons but there is no escaping the conclusion that McGrory's Celtic teams got one penalty kick every 6.0 matches, and Stein's sides got one spot kick every 3.5 matches.[37]

---

[37] It might be fair to indicate that the research was not entirely exhaustive. I knew of four books that covered Celtic matches during this period and which listed goalscorers for each game, and checked them. One of these books (*The Celtic Football Companion*: David Docherty, Edinburgh, 1986) also frequently indicated when Celtic players had missed penalty kicks, and therefore was of most value, but it may not have been fully inclusive.

Some might argue that the latter Celtic sides were much more attack-minded, and this would account for the apparent discrepancy, but the youthful Celtic sides prior to Jock Stein's arrival as manager were even more positive – or hare-brained – in their attacking approach. One famous Celt, a member of the Lisbon Lions, told the author: 'We used to attack even more under Jimmy McGrory, but Jock Stein taught us how and when to attack.'

One obvious conclusion is that Celtic got a better deal from referees with Jock Stein as manager, and that Stein's powerful personality had played some part in it. One present-day Referee Supervisor told me of his own dealings as a referee with Celtic's manager, and summed it up: 'Jock Stein was a master of psychology ... although I doubt if he had ever studied the subject formally.'

An equally valid conclusion is that referees **can** be influenced (despite their claims of objectivity).

However, one referee appeared to be immune to the strong will of the Celtic manager and his wiles. R.H. Davidson (Airdrie) was considered to be Scotland's best official, and indeed was widely believed to be on the short-list for the World Cup final in Germany in 1974, and Jock Stein was considered to be Scotland's best manager. Both were Lanarkshire men, and shared a traditional Lanarkshire stubbornness; both were strong-willed, assertive, and totally convinced of the rightness of their actions. It was perhaps inevitable that they should clash on and off the football pitch – and they did. Repeatedly Jock Stein crossed swords with Bobby Davidson, and often to Jock Stein's financial loss in a long-running personal feud.

The author asked two (older) members of the Edinburgh No.1 Celtic Supporters' Club for their recollections of Mr. Davidson. Both are usually temperate in their opinions on football but the first man was almost apoplectic with rage, even thirty years later: 'R. H. Davidson (Airdrie). The most biased bastard of a referee I've ever seen in my life! I used to think "Airdrie" was his last name.' The other supporter considered matters more carefully: 'An officious type, tending to be fussy and overbearing. Arrogant. Over the years, I don't remember him ever giving us a single thing.'

The most infamous match, refereed by Davidson and involving Celtic, was the Aberdeen vs. Celtic Cup Final played before a crowd of 108,434 at Hampden Park on 11 April 1970. Aberdeen won the match against a Celtic side, already League champions and in the European Cup semi-final again, who started the game as odds-on favourites. Police were to report afterwards that more than a hundred people had been arrested: thirty-two inside Hampden Park for breaches of the peace, thirty-nine outside for similar offences, and thirty-one elsewhere for public mischief – and this was during a period when Celtic, with Bob Kelly as Chairman and Jock Stein as Manager, could very often praise the club's followers for exemplary behaviour.

It would be too easy to say that Celtic supporters were reacting badly to an unexpected defeat but ...

> The unsatisfactory aspect of the Cup Final was that Aberdeen will never be given full cred-it for their win because of the refereeing. Eventually and inevitably this match will be remembered as Bobby Davidson's final. Never on such a big occasion can any referee have aroused so much controversy in so many instances – and my view is that he had a right bad day. If he has one as bad in Mexico during the World Cup, then I hope I am many miles away. (*The Scotsman*, 13 April 1970)

Every other newspaper was virtually in total agreement with the forceful views expressed in *The Scotsman*; one example is Hugh Taylor's report in the *Daily Record*: 'The highly arguable decisions of the referee, however, were shattering for Celtic's morale and there is no doubt they had an effect on their play afterwards' (13 April, 1970).

In another column in the same newspaper a young and bombastic Alec Cameron, after examining the controversial moments in the match and ruling against the referee, proclaimed: 'There will, of course, be no SFA inquiry into the Cup Final refereeing of Bobby Davidson. Decisions of a match official must be final. There is no case for another Callaghan Affair. Chaos would be the only result.'

Having protested in vain about the public humiliation of Jim Callaghan in 1969, Celtic were scarcely in a position to demand any persecution of a ref-eree or demand any form of inquiry.

In fact, Celtic had even more pressing concerns to deal with; only four days after that Scottish Cup final, Celtic were due to face Leeds United in the second leg of the European Cup semi-final and that massive fixture took pri-ority. But considerable anger simmered away within Celtic Park and among the supporters at Davidson's officiating.

Celtic's anger stemmed from three incidents within a ten-minute period in the first half during which Aberdeen were awarded a penalty kick (converted coolly by Harper), a Celtic 'goal' by Lennox was disallowed, and a strong appeal for a penalty kick was dismissed by Mr. Davidson.[38]

The referee, of course, had been a frequent adversary of Celtic's manager down the years. Stein often had run-ins with referees and they were usually confined to barbed comments inside the privacy of the dressing room areas, but his disagreements with Davidson were often public, as was the case after the Cup Final defeat:

> Jock Stein's denunciation of the match official started at the top of the stairs inside Hampden's crowded foyer and did not stop until he had reached the bottom, where he hinted to waiting pressmen that there ought to be an investigation into Davidson's handling of the match. It was an ugly end to the day's sport. Johnstone and Gemmell were cautioned for

---

[38] These incidents are covered in more detail in the Media Coverage at the end of this chapter.

dissent and the Celtic players made numerous suggestions to Mr. Davidson on the track as he and they watched the Aberdeen players bound up the stairs two at a time to the winners' rostrum, the least aggressive of which was that the referee should go up and get a medal for himself, considering all he had done for Aberdeen. Stein himself was later fined £10 by the SFA for his outburst, an amount so small as to encourage the notion that there were people in high places not unsympathetic to his reasons. (Hugh Keevins and Kevin McCarra: *100 Cups*, Edinburgh, 1985)

Given the frequency of Jock Stein's outbursts, this official's handling of other important Celtic matches, therefore, bears closer examination.

He refereed the League Cup final of 1967, won 5–3 at Hampden Park by Celtic over Dundee just prior to the Parkhead club's departure for South America to participate in the ill-fated World Club Championship Cup against Racing Club of the Argentine. There seemed to be nothing untoward about the referee's performance in that League Cup final, and similarly his officiating at the 1974 League Cup final between the same two teams. This time Dundee won by 1–0 and Celtic did have a loud appeal for a penalty kick in the last minute turned down by the referee.

Most critics claimed that the match should never have been allowed to start, so treacherous were the underfoot conditions as heavy rain and sleet swept and soaked a Hampden surface already bone-hard and icy in patches. The miserable crowd of 27,974 who turned up that 15 December were short-changed in the football sense, and the objections of both teams and their managers were known to the referee before he made the controversial decision to continue with the fixture.

On 2 January 1968, when Celtic faced Rangers in a vital league match at Parkhead, Rangers led the table by two points over a Celtic side, not yet fully recovered from the trauma of South America – and R.H. Davidson (Airdrie) was the referee. Inevitably it turned out to be a hard, physical encounter and Rangers left Celtic Park still two points ahead – and clear favourites for the title, thanks to two grotesque errors by Celtic's back-up goalkeeper John Fallon.

Irritated at the loss of a point in the 2–2 draw, Stein was furious at the treatment meted out to Jimmy Johnstone, who had been literally a marked man. Stein's complaint about this match was a valid one: a skilful player repeatedly hacked to the ground by larger and heavier opponents intent on stopping him is entitled to the full protection of the match official, and the mere awarding of a series of free kicks for such treatment is not acceptable refereeing.

Davidson also refereed the Celtic vs. Dunfermline Athletic Scottish Cup-tie on 27 January – little more than three weeks later – at Celtic Park, won 2-0 by the Fifers who had started the match as 7–1 outsiders. After the match Jock Stein berated the official for his handling of the tie, and was subsequently fined £100 for his criticism. Some astute observers of Jock Stein have suggested that the manager was quite prepared to risk a fine from the SFA over his comments, and indeed welcomed it and the attendant publicity, as the attention would focus more attention on the referee's handling of his next Celtic match. The main point of contention in this cup-tie was a goal disallowed in the first half with the score 0–0 at the time; Jim Brogan's fierce shot from long range had beaten Bent Martin in Dunfermline's goal but another Celtic player, apparently, out on the wing and not interfering with play, had strayed into an offside position.

Some of Stein's frustration undoubtedly stemmed from the fact that the Celtic side which won the European Cup in Lisbon back in May 1967 had been struggling: eliminated by Dynamo Kiev in the first round of the next European Cup, battered physically and emotionally by Racing Club (Argentina) in the ill-fated and unofficial 'World Club Championship', and contending with a resurgent Rangers side determined to regain supremacy in Scotland.

If possible, Stein was even angrier at the next Celtic vs. Rangers match handled by Davidson. This was another league fixture on 14 September 1968, again at Celtic Park and won deservedly by Rangers, this time by 4–2 after an epic encounter. After the game Stein made several barbed remarks to a linesman, and the Celtic manager's conduct was included in Mr. Davidson's report. Subsequently, Stein was fined again by the SFA.

The *Celtic View* was adamant that Celtic had been treated badly yet again: 'Why should the goal [by Lennox] be cancelled and the Rangers first goal allowed to stand when two Rangers players were practically standing on the goal-line at the time Persson scored?' (18 September 1968).

More significantly, Hugh Taylor of the *Daily Record* also felt Celtic had been given a raw deal by Mr. Davidson:

> They played on Saturday without Murdoch, had what seemed a valid goal disallowed, and at least one penalty claim turned down. And what would have happened had the Bobby Lennox goal been allowed to stand no one can say. The jet-paced forward is being sorely punished for his lightning reflexes, and I am not impressed with the impetuousness of linesmen who instinctively raise their flags when they see a flash of Lennox in the clear. Was it a goal? I had no doubt that it was. (16 September 1968)

Celtic met Dundee in the quarter-final of the League Cup in 1972, and R.H. Davidson (Airdrie) was appointed to officiate at both legs. It was noted in the newspapers, perhaps alerted by Stein, that the referee had not been assigned a Celtic match for some considerable time, despite his stature as a FIFA official.

The first leg was played at Dens Park on 11 October, resulting in a 1–0 win for the home side, who had already defeated Celtic in the league programme by 2–0. The match, splendidly contested at pace throughout, was a fine advertisement for Scottish football and afterwards Jock Stein summed it up: 'You don't mind losing a game like that.' The return match was played at

Celtic Park on 1 November and ended in a 3–2 victory for Celtic, and thirty minutes of extra time failed to produce another goal.

This game was marked by a controversial performance by the referee, one which incurred the wrath of Celtic's manager during and after the match.

> Long after the end of this League Cup quarter-final police stood on duty outside Parkhead's main doors. Their task surely must have been to ensure the continuing good health of the Airdrie referee, Bobby Davidson. The replay will be at Hampden on November 20th and 39,000 of Celtic's supporters will surely hope that Mr. Davidson is elsewhere on that Monday night. For Mr. Davidson this quarter-final was his first appointment with Celtic for over two seasons. There have been complaints about this World Cup referee before – and they will surely break out all over again.

> At the end of ninety minutes – as both teams lay gasping with breath – Jock Stein strode briskly out on to his Parkhead pitch and, ignoring the players, made straight for the three officials standing aloof in the centre circle. He queried a point about a Dundee goal and the Parkhead crowd rose to applaud him chanting his name through the night air as he walked back to the touchline. It had been the gesture of a baffled manager. (*Glasgow Herald*, 2 November 1972)

A replay was necessary and took place on 20 November and Celtic ran out comfortable winners by 4–1 at a neutral Hampden Park before a crowd of 36,483. Things went better for Davidson in the play-off:

Jock Stein and Jimmy Johnstone on their way to a disciplinary hearing at the SFA.

> While the Celtic fans had been waging a cruel and occasionally obscene war with a referee that they did not want, Dundee hit the crossbar and then took the lead [in 18 minutes]. Mr. Davidson, it should be mentioned here, went on to have a fine game, booking Celtic's Jimmy Johnstone and Dundee's George Stewart to show that he held no fear nor was swayed by any bias. On a satisfactory night all round this was a major cause for joy. (*Glasgow Herald*, 21 November 1972)

However, there was considerable trouble on and off the pitch at Celtic Park on 17 March 1973 when Celtic faced Aberdeen in the quarter-final of the Scottish Cup. Eighteen arrests were made inside the ground, mainly for breach of the peace; supporters spilled on to the track near the tunnel; beer cans rained on to the pitch after Jimmy Johnstone was ordered off. The Celtic winger had become involved in a tussle with an Aberdeen defender and a linesman raised his flag; the referee consulted him, and ordered

Johnstone off to the general disbelief of the Celtic support. Mr. R.H. Davidson (Airdrie) again required police protection when he later left the ground after the match, which ended 0–0.

John Rafferty was one of the few journalists to be candid about Davidson's stormy relationship with Celtic and their manager:

> What made the matter more disturbing was that, after their experiences with the referee over the years, there were so many among the 40,000 present forecasting that such a thing would happen. Of course, that was nonsensical talk. But, when the ridiculous is forecast and then happens, what does one say? They forecast equally disturbing happenings on Wednesday night [for the replay]. Bobby Davidson must not referee that replay at Pittodrie. It is ridiculous to imagine that he could control the game dispassionately after the further controversy and abuse he heaped upon himself on Saturday with a stiff and pedantic piece of refereeing. It is equally ridiculous to expect at least half of the players to have confidence in him – something which could also be true of a great number of those on the terracing. He thus cannot fulfil the full requirement of acceptability – so he must withdraw or be withdrawn. Over the years there have been increasing suggestions of a feud and, right or wrong, that must be stopped. (*The Scotsman*, 19 March 1973)

Hugh Taylor in the *Daily Record* examined the incident in detail – the part after the raising of the linesman's flag – and considered that Johnstone had to be sent off. The journalist felt that Davidson was forced to accept the word of his linesman especially in view of what had happened to Jim Callaghan only three years earlier. A Mr. J. McGarigan from Kilsyth wrote to the newspaper on 24 March, disagreeing with this rationale: 'You use the Jim Callaghan case as his reason for acting on a linesman's decision. Who do you think you are kidding when you suggest Davidson would meet Mr. Callaghan's fate if he hadn't taken action after his talk with the linesman?' (24 March, 1973).

Rather surprisingly, the *Glasgow Herald's* match report of the Celtic-Aberdeen cup-tie on 17 March (written by columnist Willie Hunter) did not comment on Mr. Davidson's performance at all, and the reader would be hard-pressed to realise that any trouble had broken out at the match. However, in the days before the replay at Pittodrie on the 21 March, the newspaper referred to the first match as 'controversial' and afterwards damned Mr. Davidson's officiating at Aberdeen with faint praise: 'The referee kept a firm grip of the game, and deserves credit for a competent performance' (*Glasgow Herald*, 22 March 1973).

It was near the end of his match report in *The Scotsman* on 19 March that Rafferty made the most telling point of all: 'I think that Davidson is the best referee we have in Scotland and I have been convinced of that after watching him work at the highest level. But I have to write that I have never seen him at his best when refereeing Celtic or Rangers. It would be better were he kept away from them in the Cup as he apparently is in the League.'

Celtic supporters could list many matches in which this official appeared to have a bias against the Parkhead club, and many would have assumed that his decisions in general favoured Rangers, and would have read that into

Rafferty's comments. But, could Rangers have been discriminated against as well?

Back in 1958, Davidson had refereed a Scottish Cup semi-final between Rangers and Hibernian at Hampden Park and awarded Rangers an equalising 'goal' although the ball had been punched out of the Hibernian goalkeeper's hands by Brand. The Edinburgh players protested furiously and persuaded him to consult a linesman and the goal was disallowed. Photographs (and TV coverage) indicated that the linesman had been correct in helping to change the referee's mind. It is also a reminder that Mr. Davidson was an official who was prepared to consult his linesmen when necessary.

However, it is more probable that John Rafferty was hinting that Mr. Davidson's decisions frequently favoured Rangers, rather than hurt them. In fact, only two weeks before this infamous match between Celtic and Aberdeen, Davidson had officiated at Easter Road in a Scottish Cup replay between Hibernian and Rangers. The following excerpts were taken from *The Scotsman* of 1 March, 1973 (and were not penned by Rafferty):

> Rangers took the lead in 6 minutes. Parlane pushed the ball behind Schaedler to McLean who looked in a suspiciously offside position. There was no flag though. The winger ran on, rounded Herriot, and slipped the ball home. Back came Hibs, however, and they had a strong appeal for a penalty turned down when a Rangers player appeared to handle in the box. Minutes after Duncan equalised, Parlane was pulled down by Schaedler. Referee Davidson consulted the linesman before making the award, and McLean neatly slipped the ball past Herriot from the spot.

Ian Archer, writing in the *Glasgow Herald*, made no mention of the dubiety of Rangers' first goal and wrote about the late winner: 'Mr. Davidson was well behind the play but went straight to his linesman who suggested that Rangers be awarded the penalty' (2 March 1973).

Robert McElroy, editor of *The Rangers Historian*, and author of several highly readable books on the Ibrox club, was asked by me about Davidson and Rangers: 'He was never a particular favourite at Ibrox, and I don't recall too many instances in which he gave us too much.'

In October 1999, I asked a contemporary referee of Davidson's to name the five best Scottish referees and his list was as follows: Mowat, Mitchell, Wharton, Phillips ... and Davidson. Knowing that I was a Celtic follower, he smiled when he gave the last name, adding the jocular comment: 'A man who is hated by Celtic, Rangers, and Hearts fans must be doing something right.' The possibility also exists that the official might be doing something wrong on a fairly consistent basis.

The mention of Hearts in this context rang an immediate bell and sent me to the newspapers to look up the Hearts vs. Celtic Scottish Cup-tie at Tynecastle in February, 1962 and won 4–3 by Celtic. The match had been an old-fashioned thriller with five goals coming in the last nineteen minutes, and

Hearts felt more aggrieved at the officiating. They claimed reasonably enough that one Celtic goal was scored from an offside position, but their major complaint was over Crerand's penalty-kick winner scored in the eighty-sixth minute. Crerand missed with his original attempt, but was permitted to retake the kick apparently because Mr. Davidson had not signalled for it, nor had he yet positioned himself properly.

However, this Referee Supervisor did point out to me one aspect of Davidson's refereeing previously ignored:

> Bobby Davidson was always on the fast-track as a referee, and he was a Class 1 official by the time he was twenty-three. That's very rapid promotion. I used to wonder if he ran into trouble at times later on because he was too high-handed, and a man who did not want to have his authority ever questioned by players or managers. You can get very defensive and stubborn when you have been at the top rung for such a long time.

Was this his Achilles' Heel as a referee? Everything seems to suggest that R. H. Davidson (Airdrie) was a competent official, but one with a reputation to sustain. He was considered a strong official, and not a man to take liberties with. Weak referees are often considered 'homers', but Davidson often seemed to favour the away team, or the less-supported side. It is a brave man – or a stubborn one – who disallows goals for Rangers and Celtic against provincials like Hibernian and Aberdeen in Scottish Cup-ties! The 'fact' that he was hated by the followers of Celtic, Rangers and Hearts, the three best-supported clubs in Scotland, might be significant in any analysis of a referee known to be 'a thrawn character'.

As all good referees must, he valued his independence. Like every other official in Scotland, he knew Jock Stein and had had dealings with him over the years. He also knew of Stein's legendary reputation for manipulation, if not outright intimidation. Davidson, when refereeing matches involving Britain's first European Cup winners, before vast crowds of fanatical supporters, and with Jock Stein in charge, seemed a man too determined not to be overawed nor intimidated. Of course, these are admirable traits but can lead to a certain contrariness which can be fatal in a referee. Unfortunately, judgement can be flawed in such instances and, rightly or wrongly, the impression of being unfair is created.

Celtic, on occasion, were treated badly by this official. There should be no doubt this was almost certainly due to genuine mistakes by the referee; any 'motivation' was perhaps more personal and understandable, rather than actuated by any form of religious animosity as has been so often charged by Celtic zealots.

Similarly, Jock Stein was a man equally determined never to be bested in a contest of wills and the feud between the two men was a fascinating, but sometimes depressing, insight into the dynamics of Scottish football.

At the end of the day, neither man had backed down nor perhaps was capable of doing so; the result was inconclusive in a scrappy, untidy battle of heavyweights. Stein was fined several times by the SFA for his part in a public squabble, and Davidson's reputation for impartiality was often questioned.

Stein, in going public with his complaints, came close to pandering to the persecution complex cherished among many Celtic supporters, leaving Davidson, forced to remain silent under SFA edict, struggling to maintain his reputation as a competent and fair referee.

MEDIA COVERAGE

Celtic vs. Rangers
Scottish League: 2 January 1968

Greig's answer to the tricks of Johnstone was to sweep the feet from under him, and there were numerous free kicks just outside and to the right of Rangers' penalty area. (*The Scotsman*, 3 January 1968)

The winger [Johnstone] was brought down by Rangers defenders almost on a rota system and the referee might have given him more protection than he did. Auld's shot was deflected by Jardine into his own net with Sorensen stranded out of range – a quick and savage retribution paid by the wing-half for having conceded the kick with his foul on Johnstone. Jardine's offence was typical of Rangers' play at that stage. (*Glasgow Herald*, 3 January 1968)

Celtic vs. Dunfermline
Scottish Cup: 27 January 1968

Celtic looked to have drawn first blood when in 39 minutes Brogan drove a glorious knee-high shot through Dunfermline's defensive wall and in at Martin's left-hand post. A splendid goal it seemed and one which gave the Dunfermline players not the slightest cause for protest. But a linesman had evidently spotted an infringement and instead of a goal the referee awarded a free kick to Dunfermline, presumably for offside against Wallace. (*Glasgow Herald,* 29 January 1968)

They [Dunfermline] were fortunate that a goal was not allowed when Brogan shot to the net from 25 yards in the first half. A linesman's flag had been raised for an obscure offside when the ball was away over on the left and before it came near Brogan. (*The Scotsman*, 29 January 1968)

Celtic vs. Aberdeen
Scottish Cup Final: 11 April 1970

The three principal incidents were crowded into ten minutes around the half-hour. They left Celtic a goal down, and with two men booked, and their composure shattered. The first involved the award of a penalty kick.

The facts are that, when McKay crossed hard into goal, Murdoch was poised alert with arms and legs spread, and the ball struck his arm. The referee has some discretion in such a situation and Mr. Davidson used this to award a penalty kick but it is safe to say that few referees indeed would have decreed intent against Murdoch. The next incident came as a result of the Aberdeen goalkeeper being unable to clear the ball with his left foot. This is surely a vital failing in a goalkeeper with pretensions to international standing. Celtic's forwards seemed to have been briefed on this and covered his right foot when he had the ball in hand and so put him on his bad foot. Shortly after the penalty kick Lennox trapped Clark with the ball in hand and, when the goalkeeper became flustered and tried to work round to the right, he dropped the ball. We are not allowed to quote players but the best available evidence is that Clark knocked the ball against Lennox's chest and dropped it but, after Lennox put the ball in the net for what seemed a good goal, Mr. Davidson vetoed the score.

Then Lennox was going through and Buchan slid in to tackle. He missed the ball but got Lennox's feet and he went down. There seemed no clearer penalty kick but Mr. Davidson was not impressed. (*The Scotsman*, 13 April 1970)

Three highly debatable decisions by the referee all went against Celtic who, in their frustration, failed to respond and pick up their normal game against Aberdeen: a penalty kick which was fiercely contested along with the disallowing of a Bobby Lennox goal and the rejection of a penalty claim when the same player went headlong near goal in a tackle with an opponent.

Accidental or otherwise, a Celtic hand undoubtedly touched Derek McKay's cross which threatened no danger in 27 minutes. The referee had no hesitation with his award, and from the cheap penalty Joe Harper scored the opening goal.

I would disagree with the official's judgment in the other two instances. Bobby Clark, who had a nervous match, should have been punished for his habit of standing defiantly with the ball instead of clearing it. Lennox challenged him and, without any physical contact being made, Clark dropped the ball which the Celtic player hit into the net. The official and his linesman seemed to be the only people who saw any infringement. It seemed harsh on Lennox again when his appeal for a penalty was denied, the referee signalling that he had dived after the tackle by Martin Buchan. (*Glasgow Herald*, 13 April 1970)

Here is the inside information.
VERDICT Aberdeen were awarded the penalty because Bobby Murdoch was said to have played the ball with his arm about shoulder-high. A careful study of TV film appeared to confirm that Murdoch, off-balance, had tried to head or bodily smother the ball with his arms outstretched. The nearest Aberdeen player Derek McKay clearly thought that a free kick was being awarded against the Dons.
VERDICT Lennox's back was to the referee but his view was supported by a linesman that the player had knocked the ball down with his left hand. From the TV gallery there was absolutely no sign of this, and the goal looked a good one.
VERDICT Slow-motion film showed that Buchan tackled much too late to get the ball. It was 5 or 6 yards away when Buchan stuck in his foot. A good penalty. (*Daily Record*, 13 April 1970)

Celtic vs. Dundee
League Cup: 1 November 1972

The refereeing of Bobby Davidson was again in question. After previous 'trouble' he has not refereed a Celtic match for three years – until this tie. He had another night of controversy and Jock Stein was seen to speak to him in midfield before extra time started. This was much to the liking of the crowd, and much more could be heard of this.

From a corner melee Scott hooked the ball off the byline. A linesman raised his flag apparently signalling that it was over. In the confused crush in the goalmouth Wallace shot into the net and by that time the flag was down and Celtic were left lamenting. And then in the 32nd minute it was Dundee's turn to be displeased. Callaghan shot hard through the crowd in the penalty area. Macari let the ball glance off his chest and it went into the net. There were appeals that a hand had been used and when Stewart protested forcibly his name was taken. (*The Scotsman*, 2 November 1972)

Celtic and Dundee queried a goal apiece and there can be no suggestion of bias levelled at the official. But, with an ominous certainty, this tie slipped increasingly out of his control. As his relationship with his linesmen deteriorated, as one eccentric decision followed another ... a replay became more certain with every blast on the whistle rather than every kick of the ball. The teams did not want an argument with each other; this was never a vicious or even ill-tempered tie (although Hay, Stewart and Houston were booked for dissent) but somehow the referee lost control.

Stein later questioned the goal because Jocky Scott seemed over the byline when he turned a corner kick back into the path of Wallace who edged it over the line. The linesman's flag was briefly raised, and the protests duly mounted. But the goal stood – and the erosion of authority started in earnest.

When Celtic took the lead, the Dundee defenders appealed strongly that the striker (Macari) had handled the ball, but Mr. Davidson pointed to his chest.

Police carried away spectators when Macari did get the ball in the net shortly afterwards only to be pulled back for offside. Normal time ended – and an unspoken truce seemed to have been declared for the overtime period. (*Glasgow Herald*, 2 November 1972)

Celtic vs. Aberdeen
Scottish Cup: 17 March 1973

I was fortunate in that I was watching the play off the ball as Celtic broke, through Lennox. Immediately, Johnstone scampered up the right wing thirty or forty yards from the play. Jim Hermiston saw the danger of allowing him to race into an open position and he ran alongside, holding the Celtic player's left arm while Johnstone struggled to free himself. In the struggle he swung round, went off balance, and swung a boot at Hermiston – and all this unseen by the referee.

The linesman (Jim Renton) had signalled for an infraction, and the referee noticed the raised flag eventually.

He went over to hear his tale, called over Johnstone and Hermiston, booked the Aberdeen player and sent the Celtic winger from the field. It was a trivial incident and I am certain, had the referee actually witnessed it, then he would not have taken the action he did. I am convinced of that for, almost immediately afterwards, he booked Arthur Graham for kicking down Danny McGrain – a much more violent offence than that of Johnstone. It is seldom I have hard words to write about referees, and less seldom do I take the part of ordered-off players. But in this instance I am certain that I am right, and in this I have the advantage over Davidson: I saw what took place and he did not. (*The Scotsman*, 19 March 1973)

Not long after Johnstone's dismissal, Danny McGrain was sent flying after a wild tackle by Arthur Graham. It looked nasty but Graham did not suffer the same punishment as Johnstone while Celtic fans chanted for him to be sent off. Instead, Davidson only booked him. (*Daily Record*, 19 March 1973)

CHAPTER EIGHT

Fergus McCann vs. Jim Farry

During his five turbulent years at Celtic Park, Fergus McCann found himself under unprecedented scrutiny from the media. It was an attention he did not want and it seems clear that he was unprepared for it. The problems were not hard to seek at Celtic Football Club: a run-down stadium, out-of-date and unsafe by modern standards; a mountainous debt run up by the Board in recent years in desperate attempts to turn things round; a mediocre, dispirited squad of players; an unpopular manager; and a support that expected miracles in short order.

The press did not know what to make of McCann: on the one hand, the romantic notion that he was a Celtic supporter who had struck it rich abroad and had come back like a diminutive John Wayne and the US Cavalry to save the day; or the cynical thinking that he was simply a hard-headed, pragmatic businessman who saw an opportunity and had the means to realise it. The truth lay somewhere in between these extremes: he was a Celtic supporter, he had the money, he wanted to save the club, he worked hard to get control, risking a lot in financial terms to do so, and he worked even harder to safeguard his investment, refusing to stray too far from his five-year plan.

In image, he was unprepossessing; apparently slightly built, middle-aged, balding and with an unfortunate squint. In reality, he was much more dynamic – vigorous in manner, brisk in speech, neat in appearance and, for his age, relatively fit and healthy. The journalists, in the main, never did quite make up their minds about him and resorted to cliché and stereotype; their approach was understandable, but distorting.

One of the more perceptive members of the corps assessed the situation:

> First of all, we saw him as a fan, who had got lucky in Canada or the States, and came back to fulfil a childhood dream, a fantasy. We were waiting for 'the wee man with the bunnet' to fall flat on his face, to lose his millions, and see Celtic as badly-off as ever. It would have been a human-interest story, the lottery-winner who squanders it all.
>
> We were wrong, totally wrong. We resented the fact that this outsider could come in and see immediately the things that were bad about the set-up of Scottish football, we resented the fact that he wanted to change things too quickly, we resented the fact that he worked so hard in the minutiae of running a football club, instead of cavorting with the players, we resented the fact – even though we were journalists in need of stories – that he kept providing us with the raw material of the revolution in football.

It was a brief honeymoon.

Only three months after the McCann takeover on 4 March 1994, Celtic's

Fergus McCann, wearing his trademark fedora, in the Director's Box at Celtic Park.

manager Lou Macari was released, and Tommy Burns, presently at Kilmarnock, became an immediate target among others including Kenny Dalglish, Ivan Golac and Bobby Robson. Unfortunately, the emerging front-runners Burns and his assistant, Billy Stark, still had two years left to run on their contracts and were highly regarded at Rugby Park; another complication was the fact that they were also still registered as players with Kilmarnock.

On 11 July Tommy Burns quit Kilmarnock, and was paraded as Celtic's new manager the following day amid scenes of celebration among the supporters outside Celtic Park. Kilmarnock were far from happy at the situation and lodged a complaint about the 'tapping' of their player-manager. McCann was unrepentant, and insistent that he would not be paying any form of compensation to the Ayrshire club for the loss of Burns, adding: 'Tommy has resigned from that post and he is retiring as a player, and Celtic have no intention of registering him as a player.'

However, the Scottish League stated that a formal complaint had been received from Kilmarnock as Peter Donald, the League's secretary, confirmed: 'Kilmarnock's letter details circumstances which they believe put Celtic in breach of Scottish League rules, and we will examine their claims and take the matter up with Celtic.' The Ayrshire club had already initiated court action against both Burns and Stark but this was called off only minutes before the action was due to be heard in Edinburgh; Kilmarnock were prepared to accept the verdict of the Scottish League on Celtic's alleged transgressions.

On the 18 August Celtic were fined £100,000 for their illegal approach to the player(s). The Scottish League's management committee deemed the offence to be 'a serious and blatant breach of the rules', and the committee's verdict was reported to be unanimous. Fergus McCann refused to accept this decision gracefully, and with characteristic stubbornness decided to appeal against the verdict. A special General Meeting was held on 29 September to consider the appeal and it proved to be heated at times, before Celtic's appeal was thrown out by a resounding vote of sixty-nine to one. The media dutifully and gleefully reported that the vote would have been unanimous but for the fact that a representative of a lower division club had 'got mixed up' and voted wrongly. Shortly afterwards, at the same meeting, Celtic's next appeal – against the size of the fine imposed – was also rejected by the decisive vote of sixty-five to five.

The amount of the fine was a sore point with McCann who pointed out that it was twenty times heavier than any previous fine levied for a comparable offence. When asked why Rangers had been fined only £5,000 for an illegal approach to Duncan Ferguson of Dundee United, Peter Donald asserted that 'this case was more complicated' but he did not expand on the complexities. McCann was acidic about the outcome and the fine: 'I would anticipate a fine of that severity in a court of law for a serious offence with a death involved, and it's an alternative to five years in prison.' It took several weeks before he announced that Celtic would pay the fine rather than engage in a further appeal.

Meanwhile, the SFA had become involved in the affair: Tommy Burns and Billy Stark were fined £2,000 for breach of contract as Kilmarnock players, and suspended from playing any football in the future; Celtic and Kilmarnock were given a further three weeks to resolve the matter of compensation, or the SFA would do so. Jim Farry, the Chief Executive of the SFA, in his statement suggested that, if no solution could be found by that date, then Burns and Stark would not be allowed to continue their managerial responsibilities at Celtic Park.

The SFA also on 12 October 1994 endorsed the Scottish League's decisions and Jim Farry described them as 'final and binding' in view of the fact that Celtic could not resort to a court of law, given the SFA's power to expel a club from all organised football world-wide. McCann, already characterised as tireless in his determination, saw this as a challenge to the autonomy of the successful clubs and proposed at the SFA's next AGM, held in May 1995, that clubs should have a recourse to law if they were not fully satisfied with the verdict of an SFA tribunal. The motion was seconded by Rangers, but was heavily defeated by a show of hands. Clearly, McCann was warming up for the next confrontation and preparing the ground for it because, on 22 May, Celtic were ordered by such a tribunal to pay Kilmarnock £200,000 for obtaining Burns and Stark.

It was an unpleasant wrangle which did not reflect much credit on Celtic: it badly affected hitherto cordial relations between Celtic and Kilmarnock, and their chairmen Fergus McCann and Bob Fleeting; it soured relations between Celtic and the Scottish League over the size of the fine; it raised the spectre of the Old Firm as powerful comrades-in-arms locked in an ongoing dispute with the SFA.

It also confirmed the perception of Fergus McCann as a maverick outsider, increasingly a loner in the Byzantine world of Scottish football.

McCann saw the situation as highly ironic as well as frustrating; he felt that almost certainly the majority of the representatives at the Scottish League's meeting which had imposed the original fine had also been privy to similar dealings in the past. He was not alone in this view: 'Tapping of players and managers may be against the rules, yet there cannot be a club so pious as to plead that they have never indulged in it. Most take the precaution of employing middlemen as, at the risk of blowing his cover, a venerable colleague in journalism would testify. He has tapped more managers and players than a shipyard worker has rivets' (*Daily Mail*, 29 April 1995).

While Jim Farry acted perfectly correctly in this instance, his demeanour had not endeared him to Fergus McCann, and it was not long before the two men were in further disagreement.

Frankly, neither of the two principal combatants would have won a popularity contest with most football supporters or journalists.

Fergus McCann was considered an outsider, brash and irreverent towards traditional approaches, rude and overbearing towards his employees and, despite his wealth, mean. Farry, like most bureaucrats, appeared meticulous to the point of exasperation, annoying in his air of condescension towards his nominal employers, out-of-touch with what supporters (and chairmen) wanted and, for an ex-gardener, vastly overpaid at an estimated £110,000 per year.

The truth was different from the popular belief about the two men, although the above were recognisable caricatures.

Jim Farry, in a frustrated reply to unfair criticism in the media, said in November, 1995: 'Myths have grown that I was a landscape gardener and that rugby was my first love. Being a landscaper would have been job promotion. I drove the dumper truck and shovelled soil. I was labouring but that's character-forming. I played football before I did rugby and only switched when I realised there was more chance of getting a regular game in a 15-man side than one of 11.'

Of course, these myths were totally irrelevant in any evaluation of Farry as an administrator and he was considered most capable, but they do hint at his undoubted unpopularity.

Born in 1954 in the East End of Glasgow, Farry considered that his parents were the greatest influence on his life, stressing that they had imbued him

Jim Farry, former Chief Executive of the SFA

with traditional Scottish values among which he numbered ' ... to speak up for yourself, and not hide your light under a bushel.' It would be fair to say that he did have a high, and perhaps justified, opinion of his own abilities. He is on record as having said: 'I consider myself one of the best administrators in Europe.'

The latter trait in his character might have been a factor in his downfall. Like Sir George Graham before him (and other SFA secretaries), Farry was 'the paid servant' of an organisation whose members he could dance around intellectually in the vast majority of instances. According to his critics within the SFA, he did little to hide his shrewd mind and quick intelligence. One journalist described him as similar to 'the know-all swot at school'. Farry attempted to rationalise his unpopularity as a mark of his competence: 'If other people, clubs or public or the greater football audience don't like it, sometimes that is a testimony that you are doing it quite well. If they liked you, it could be a problem.'

Fergus McCann saw the rebuilding of Celtic Park as a priority and the work was a major undertaking. He was advised by the SFA that, in the interests of safety, a switch to another stadium would be the best way of dealing with the situation while the first phase of reconstruction was being completed at Celtic Park. It emerged later that McCann was furious about this 'advice' or instruction, stating later (in 1996):

We went to the Scottish Stadia Committee – which is basically a group of SFA nominees – and they said: 'Guess what? We have a very good stadium on the south side of Glasgow to rent.' That was a complete outrage not fully appreciated by the public. The Stadia Committee quango should never have been delegated such powers by the Scottish Office and then have its buddies at the SFA and Queen's Park profit by renting Hampden ... a clear conflict of interest.[39]

At first sight Hampden Park did not seem to be a poor choice to stage Celtic's home fixtures, but it proved to be a ground almost entirely devoid of the passionate atmosphere that often animates Celtic Park.

However, any lack of atmosphere surely remains more a criticism of Celtic's poorish performances or their fans' apathy throughout that season (1994/1995). In fact, it is difficult to sympathise too much with McCann's complaints of being 'duped' in this particular instance. While the massive 26,000-capacity new stand was being built during that season, Celtic Park was largely a building site. It could well have been dangerous for spectators within any degree of proximity and Celtic's flitting to nearby Hampden Park was a necessary evil. It would have been difficult to shoehorn that season's average home gate of 23,467 into the old ground under the circumstances.

What McCann may have been more annoyed by was the terms imposed by the landlords: a basic rent of £600,000 for the season, and with no opportunity to recoup any of that through sales of programmes and food concessions; and the definite feeling of being barely tolerated as tenants, as any attempts to have the temporary quarters decorated in Celtic's colours were rebuffed.

In fact, Hampden Park – or the National Stadium – was to be a *leitmotif* in the running battle between Fergus McCann and Jim Farry, and understandably so.

McCann wanted Celtic Park to be the mecca for Celtic supporters, and a ground with money-making potential outside ticket sales for football; considerable effort was put into expanding the Celtic Shop on-site and in providing fast-food outlets within the ground. He also wanted to capitalise on the availability of Celtic Park for major events within Scottish football: the staging of cup finals and/or international matches with Celtic collecting a healthy percentage of the gate as a reward. The completed Celtic Park, the largest football ground in Scotland with its all-seated capacity of 60,832, has been a dramatic and fitting venue for such show-games.

Farry, on the other hand, was the principal promoter of the rebuilt Hampden Park. As Chief Executive of the SFA he stated: 'I would hope to do many things after Hampden has been completely rebuilt, but it is doubtful if

---

[39] McCann also pointed out that five clubs in England had obtained some relief from the imposition of the terms of the Taylor Report but Celtic had received none from the SFA although the mandates of the Taylor Report did not extend into Scotland.

anything will give me greater satisfaction than that project.' To give Farry credit, it often is the responsibility of the SFA, who represent all levels of football within Scotland, to stand up to the powerful clubs – and in promoting Hampden Park the Chief Executive was striking a blow for the Association's independence. According to *Rothman's Football Yearbook (1995/96)*, the SFA were responsible for 6,148 clubs and 135,474 players.

As a businessman with a vested interest in the issue, Fergus McCann simply could not see the need for a revamped Hampden Park, dismissing the completed National Stadium contemptuously as 'the third best ground in Glasgow.' A spectator there on three occasions in 1999, I can vouch for the fact that the distant view from behind the goal leaves much to be desired, as do the limited toilet facilities and refreshment kiosks. But what McCann was objecting to was the cost, which kept escalating. He pointed out that the costs, now estimated at more than £60 million, could have done a lot to help clubs struggling to survive as well as to develop football within the amateur and juvenile ranks. Of course, the infighting involved in the completion of the stadium has also detracted from its appeal to football fans.

As adversaries in the debate over the National Stadium, Fergus McCann and Jim Farry were constantly at loggerheads. Many felt that the SFA's Chief Executive was describing Fergus McCann (as well as David Murray) when he went on record as saying: 'New people with an entrepreneurial approach bring innovative thinking. They have a contribution to make, but how many of them are committee animals? Most are self-made, have flown by the seat of their pants, and are not used to working by committee. It is anathema to ask them to work in the SFA Council. They do their own thing and, if it works for their clubs, that is fine.'

The departure of John Collins from Celtic Park also caused some animosity between the club and the SFA. The stylish midfielder was the first British player of any real quality to join a continental club at the termination of his contract without a transfer fee being exacted. This development was in consequence of the result of the test case involving Jean-Marc Bosman and UEFA – a ruling that greatly benefited players and their freedom of movement. Collins eventually joined Monaco of the French League and settled down admirably in the Mediterranean tax haven. However, it was pointed out to Fergus McCann that, while Monaco did play in the French League, the principality was not a member of the European Union. Thus, it appeared as if Celtic still might be able to obtain a transfer fee for the player, a sum estimated to be in the region of £2.5 million.

Despite the obvious merit of his legal argument, McCann received more derision from the media when he drew attention to the situation; and, when he sought assistance and advice from the SFA, it appears as if he were not given too much encouragement to continue his struggle. However, he was undeterred by this and the case dragged on through various international bodies before being dismissed in 2000. As an indication of the man's tenacity, however, McCann was prepared to continue the legal battle even after he had left Celtic Park in an official capacity.

It marked one of Fergus McCann's few defeats in the legal arena, and it seemed that he resented the low level of support from the SFA. Some attributed the SFA's lack of enthusiasm as an unwillingness to cause any trouble for itself within UEFA or FIFA. McCann went so far as to accuse the SFA of prejudicing Celtic's case by forwarding the fee required to lodge an appeal to FIFA after the due date; however, FIFA leaked the information that it was the basic legal argument, and not the administrative error, which caused that appeal to fail.

Some commentators feel that, as a small country, it would not be too prudent for Scotland to cause waves on the world or European scene. The historical anomaly of having all four national bodies within the United Kingdom represented in the international legislative bodies may have come into this equation. International politics had come into the picture.[40] As one perceptive, or cynical, observer commented: 'There are a lot of people at Park Gardens who would like to have the perks enjoyed by Charles Dempsey [the New Zealand official, whose 'voting' in the ballot for the 2006 World Cup venue caused such controversy]'.

However, the climax in the on-going battles between McCann and Farry came in the aftermath of the Jorge Cadete transfer to Celtic in 1995. Let us examine the basic issue as objectively as possible.

In 1995/96 Celtic, with Tommy Burns as their manager, were locked in a fierce contest with Rangers for the League Championship and also for the Scottish Cup; it was going to be a close-run thing in both competitions. Celtic's need was for a top-class striker, if necessary 'a poacher', and the target was Jorge Cadete, the unsettled Portuguese goalscorer of Sporting Lisbon.

As with all international transfers, the negotiations were not simple, and in such cases the advice and assistance of the national association is of great help. Celtic thought that the administrative work had been completed by 26 February 1996 when they submitted a registration form and 'a contractual agreement' (between the club and Cadete) to the SFA. At that time no objection seems to have been made by the SFA to the content of the form and/or agreement. Because the player had been registered with the Portuguese Football Association, an international clearance certificate was required under FIFA reg-

---

[40] Hearts may have had a similar complaint with the assistance extended to them by the SFA in the aftermath of their UEFA Cup tie with Real Mallorca. In the second leg at Palma, Hearts reluctantly went on to complete the fixture despite the fact that the crossbar at one goal obviously was lower than the required eight feet.

The flamboyant Jorge Cadete celebrates after scoring at Celtic Park.

ulations. A copy of this International Transfer Certificate (ITC) was sent by fax from the Portuguese Football Association (PFA) and received on 7 March; Celtic confirmed this by fax to the SFA on the following day.

Once more there was no indication of any concern on the part of the SFA about the procedures.

On 12 March the original of the ITC was received by Celtic in the mail; it was, of course, identical to the fax received on 7 March. On the same day FIFA had sent a fax to the SFA advising it that the ITC had been issued by the PFA under the instructions of FIFA so that the player could be registered in Scotland – and eligible to turn out for Celtic.

The normal procedure would have been to process the registration and then to allow it to be in effect from 26 February, the date that Celtic sent the registration and contract to the SFA. However, the SFA failed to process the registration of Jorge Cadete, the Chief Executive of the SFA, regarding the ITC of 12 March (and 7 March) as being invalid. Jim Farry felt that he could not register the player until Celtic resolved a dispute over compensation with Sporting Lisbon and until some conditions attached to the ITC were removed. Celtic claimed later that they had received no communication from the SFA advising them exactly why the SFA regarded the ITC as invalid.

The situation became more complicated with the revelations about the player's dealings with both clubs involved, although Celtic and Sporting Lisbon had reached an understanding. Apparently, Cadete had separately entered into another agreement with the Portuguese club. As a consequence of that, Celtic had to devise a new agreement with the player and, of course, submit it to the SFA, and new registration papers and a revised player agreement were submitted on 23 March.

On 27 March the SFA faxed Celtic to inform the club that Cadete would still not be registered on the basis of the application forms submitted on 23 March, the SFA alleging that a clause has been included in the player agreement to which they took exception. Upon receiving this fax, Celtic re-examined the player agreements of 23 March and also those of 26 February, and found that the same clause – or one in substantially identical terms – was included in both agreements. The club was concerned that the SFA had made no objections to it until that day (27 March).

On 29 March the SFA received a fax from FIFA, advising it that the ITC had been valid from 7 March onwards, and that the issue of a contractual dispute regarding the player's status with Sporting Lisbon was irrelevant to that document. The SFA Executive Committee met and deemed that the international clearance had been granted, but now required the player agreement submitted on 23 March to be further amended by deleting the clause objected to on 27 March and a further two clauses not previously objected to.

Celtic, at the later Inquiry, were to claim they were given no opportunity to make representation to the SFA Executive Committee regarding the position at, or prior to, the meeting on 29 March.

The club also would claim that, during a telephone conversation between 'an officer of the club' and Jim Farry, Celtic were advised that they would be required to submit a third application form and player agreement with those clauses deleted. According to Celtic's evidence, an agreement was also reached during that phone conversation that the registration of Jorge Cadete as a player would be given effect to on 22 March on the basis of the third form – and the normal procedure of the SFA in backdating such forms. Celtic, accordingly, resubmitted that revised form either later on that day (29 March) or on the 30th.

Jim Farry, however, would later dispute that version of events, and denied the existence of such an agreement.

So far in this summary I have concentrated on the bureaucratic workings of this transfer, but for Celtic supporters, and the management, the time factor was becoming more and more critical in football terms.

Cadete, who had resumed full training, could not be fielded against Rangers in the Scottish Cup semi-final at Hampden Park on 7 April unless he had been registered by 23 March. Unfortunately, it does not appear that the SFA Executive Committee were made aware of this circumstance officially at their meeting of 29 March, although anybody reading the sports pages would have known this. For the record the office-bearers were as follows: vice-presidents John McBeth (Clyde) and Chris Robinson (Hearts), treasurer George Peat (Airdrie) and the SFA president, Jack McGinn, who took no part in the discussions because of his previous Celtic connection. It seems inconceivable that these men, active in football, should have been unaware of the need for urgency – or that Celtic had expressed such concerns.

Celtic submitted the papers for a third time on 30 March. Once again the SFA (or Jim Farry) refused to register Cadete with effect from 22 March, and insisted on further amendments to the third player agreement. Celtic complied with that request within hours, but the SFA proceeded to effect the registration from 30 March, leaving Celtic unable to play the striker against Rangers in the vital Scottish Cup fixture on 7 April.

Reluctantly, Celtic felt obliged to accept the SFA position because the Scottish Football League registration deadline was due to expire on 31 March and, if Celtic continued to appeal and the SFA to object, Cadete would not have been available for any of the remaining six league fixtures in the run-in for the championship.

In football terms, consider the difference that Jorge Cadete might have made in the semi-final which was lost narrowly by 2–1 to Rangers on 7 April; apart from his goal-scoring ability, Cadete would have provided an enormous boost to Celtic's morale on that occasion. When he did make his debut as a substitute against Aberdeen at Celtic Park in the league campaign on 1 April, he received a tremendous ovation from the rain-soaked crowd and scored within thirty seconds! Cadete, an outstanding striker, was to make a similarly immediate impact on the Scottish football scene: in the six games for which he was eligible that season, Cadete managed to score five goals. In the following season (1996/97) he netted thirty-three goals in forty-three games – a remarkable scoring record.

The outline of the obstacles presented above might well have taxed the tolerance of a saint, and Celtic's managing director was not noted for his patience.

Given the bureaucratic run-around he was subjected to, a less stubborn man would have given in but Fergus McCann, 'Celtic's terrier of a chairman', was determined to win a contest of wills with the SFA and/or its Chief Executive, Jim Farry. It was a long-drawn-out struggle, and unnecessarily so.

One of the aims of the SFA is to provide service to football clubs, and the registration of players is a principal area within that remit; clubs should expect assistance and expertise from the SFA secretariat especially in dealing with players transferring from other jurisdictions. This help did not seem to be forthcoming in the Jorge Cadete affair.

When I showed the table of contents for this book to a former Celtic chairman, and he spotted that one chapter was devoted to the conflict between McCann and Farry, he commented: 'Almost the same as Bob Kelly and George Graham, isn't it?' The one thing that should be made unreservedly clear is that nobody at Celtic Park has ever considered that Jim Farry, either personally or in his capacity as the SFA Chief Executive, acted out of religious bigotry – unlike one of his predecessors, Sir George Graham.

Indeed, there were some similarities: Kelly and McCann were both Celtic spokesmen and frequently locked in conflicts with the SFA and its secretaries, Graham and Farry.[41] These were struggles that lasted for several years and in both cases the SFA men had the upper hand at the start, but the tide eventually turned. At the end George Graham and Jim Farry left the SFA after years of service but somewhat under a cloud, and the opposition of the Celtic chairmen was the principal factor in their downfalls.

Perhaps the main difference in the two instances is the fact that, for Bob Kelly, discrimination against Celtic, on the basis of the Siamese-twin issue of religion or nationality, was considered rightly as the key factor while, for Fergus McCann, competence and any administrative or bureaucratic procedures that delayed things were the issues.

---

[41] In this chapter the terms 'SFA Secretary' and 'SFA Chief Executive' are to be regarded as interchangeable.

During the early skirmishes which were 'won' by Farry the disapproval of the press was reserved almost exclusively for Fergus McCann. In fact, he was frequently ridiculed for his attempts to contest decisions of the SFA. One journalist (Alan Davidson of the *Evening Times*) summed up McCann's efforts: 'He must recognise the rules of the game were not established to be so blatantly disregarded by a man who knows virtually nothing of the structure of Scottish football.' Most journalists tended to underestimate McCann's abilities and his determination, preferring to dismiss him as eccentric.

Throughout these skirmishes between McCann and Farry at first nobody seemed to be on McCann's side. There was a tacit agreement that, while the SFA was a clannish, secretive organisation and prone to error, McCann should be regarded as the outsider. One journalist reminded his readers that, at the time when Celtic (or McCann) was fined a record £100,000 by the Scottish League, the club's managing director had been involved in Scottish football for less than 200 days.

Time had appeared to be on Farry's side. Since the original dispute over Cadete's registration, three years had passed, as McCann's complaints passed through the various channels within the SFA. Perhaps the fact that Celtic's managing director had always insisted that he would be leaving football after five years was enough to instil a false sense of confidence.

That body seemed in no particular hurry to settle the matter, and indeed from Celtic's point of view strictly as a football matter the issue was dead. However, McCann had become irritated and wanted a satisfactory resolution. At any rate, two internal inquiries at Park Gardens, held to determine the facts in the case, had taken place, and in each case Jim Farry's stance had been fully vindicated, and, after the verdict of each hearing, Fergus McCann came in for further ridicule and criticism in the media.

However, Fergus McCann simply refused to give in because he believed that he and his club had been denied justice, and would be able to achieve that in any court of law or independent inquiry. Eventually such an inquiry was scheduled for the first week of March in 1999. The *Glasgow Herald* mused admiringly (?) about how 'a man [McCann] who is about to turn his back on it all has the stamina and resilience to hang on in there battling for the cause with only weeks of his tenure to run.'

On 2 March Jim Farry was suspended on full pay when the SFA abruptly halted the Independent Inquiry before one of the country's foremost arbitration experts, Lord Dervaid. Rod MacKenzie of Harper MacLeod, the Glasgow-based legal firm representing Celtic, had spent a full day cross-examining Farry but, before he could resume his questioning, the SFA intimated that it wanted to abandon its defence against Celtic's case.

It was a complete capitulation: a letter of apology was conveyed to Celtic from the SFA spelling out everything that the club wanted to hear. Celtic had initially claimed substantial compensation, but accepted £100,000 and their considerable legal expenses.

What had happened during the inquiry? Rod MacKenzie, in preparing for the inquiry, always felt confident that Celtic had a very strong case in law, and so it proved as the event proceeded; Kevin Sweeney gave evidence on Celtic's behalf, and Jim Farry for the SFA. Under the weight of cumulative questioning by Mr. MacKenzie, Farry's answers increasingly dismayed the SFA councillors, and they asked their legal team to call a halt, with Mr. MacKenzie due to question two of Farry's assistants and also the SFA Vice-President John McBeth (Clyde).

According to some accounts, Mr. Farry's performance, admittedly under stressful circumstances, was considered to be 'poor'. Fergus McCann was widely reported as saying: 'I was there when he was giving evidence and his position, which was quite amazing, was that he was right, his executive committee were wrong, FIFA were wrong. He did not agree with his own assistants and he maintained that black was white. If I had been his counsel, I would have done the same thing, brought it to an end as soon as possible.'

It was not the best of times for the SFA. Bob Crampsey, writing in *The Scotsman*, examined the situation the day after the suspension was announced:

> Willie Allan, Ernie Walker and, it is fair to say, Jim Farry, have hitherto been distinguished for their meticulous administration. If they have appeared 'pompous' or 'stuffy' or 'outdated', three of the favourite critical adjectives directed at them, it is because their role in the game is largely custodial. The fact that they have each been deeply unpopular at various times in their stewardship is not necessarily to their discredit. The President and Council will change in personnel, the secretary will normally long outstay them. Because of that, the secretary can acquire, if not great power, at least considerable influence. He conveys the decisions of Council and committees and is, therefore, a fairly frequent conveyor of bad tidings. There will be folks with long memories. (2 March, 1999)

Frankly, the decision to suspend Jim Farry did seem excessive if the trouble over the Jorge Cadete transfer was a simple administrative error, and a very rare one on the Chief Executive's part. Crampsey raised the point in his article: 'Does the suspension hint at something darker: the deliberate obstructionism at which Celtic themselves have seemed to point?'

Certainly, the office-bearers of the SFA, Jim Farry's employers, should also have borne some of the responsibility for the delays in effecting Cadete's transfer, and in bringing the matter of Celtic's complaints to a satisfactory conclusion much sooner. For example, how could internal inquiries within the SFA have cleared Farry when Celtic's case, when presented at an independent hearing, proved too strong to continue defending? Several prominent journalists felt that the decision to suspend Jim Farry was 'hypocritical in the extreme'.

Following the abandoning of the independent tribunal on 1 March 1999,

Farry was suspended on full pay. His reaction was couched in typical language, known to some irreverent journalists as 'Farry-Speak':

> I have received notification from my employer that the SFA may require to carry out an additional investigation of certain issues arising out of the dispute between Celtic and the SFA. I indicated I would be pleased to co-operate with any such additional investigation, which will be the third review since the player was registered for Celtic on March 30th 1996. It is normal, I understand – although it is a first for me – that, when an employer notifies you of a suspension pending the outcome of a proposed investigation, it is prudent to comply.

The normal corollary to a suspension is dismissal and during the following week it appeared clear that the Chief Executive's position was, in Fergus McCann's word, increasingly 'untenable'. McCann was adamant that the SFA's Chief Executive should go: 'In the overall interest of Scottish football, and to maintain its reputation for fairness and justice, this case demonstrates clearly that Mr. Farry cannot be allowed to hold and exercise such powerful authority' – and he had the SFA's fulsome letter of apology to back up his argument.

Jim Farry, on the other hand, continued to express his bemusement at the turn of events: 'No one has yet informed me of what I am supposed to have done wrong. [My employers] have not elaborated in any way on their decision to abandon the hearing before it had been completed. I find it strange that certain witnesses were not called.'

Farry's attempts to retrieve the situation, however, gave the impression that he was merely preparing to negotiate an equitable settlement. Despite the public humiliation of the suspension, Farry was still in a strong bargaining position with the SFA. It would be awkward for his employers now to dismiss him, after having proclaimed him innocent of wrongdoing in two separate internal inquiries. Any settlement was likely to be costly as Farry was already receiving a salary estimated at £110,000, and was still at the relatively young age of forty-four.

In the week between the suspension and dismissal of Jim Farry other people entered the lists. Perhaps predictably, and appropriately, Donald Findlay QC appeared on the side of the defence: 'Mr. Farry is entitled to full and fair notice of what he has done, time to prepare a response, and the chance to present it.'

Archie Macpherson, in his column in *The Herald*, wrote: 'We simply do not know the degree of incompetence, or malfeasance, or bloody-minded obduracy, or whatever else your imagination cares to light on for we are bogged down by conjecture. So, although we know what the outcome was, what is the actual depth of Farry's alleged culpability?' (6 March, 2000).

On 8 March 1999 the SFA announced: 'The decision has been taken to dismiss Mr. Farry for gross misconduct.'

The suspension, and subsequent firing, of a capable administrator was not a matter for celebration or jubilation because the affair probably raised more questions about the running of the SFA than it provided answers. Jim Farry may well have made mistakes, or failed to act correctly, but he was far from alone in doing so.

It seemed that the consequences would continue to dominate the headlines for some time. Ken Gallagher, also of *The Herald*, immediately took up the matter. In a well-prepared article in the newspaper he virtually presented the defence that Farry might have offered had the opportunity arisen at the independent inquiry. There did appear to be some new information, but the whole situation was resolved more with a whimper than a bang.[42] Jim Farry was quoted as saying: 'The view of my family is that I should just get the hell out. The last thing they would want is for me to become an obsessive old man with long fingernails worrying my life away about the outcome of a long-drawn-out court case.'

The last word perhaps should remain with Fergus McCann: 'I cannot see a rational explanation for his actions. I am not claiming there was any malice, but there was intent. This was not a mistake; it was a failure to administer the rules correctly.'

James MacMillan in his speech referred to the previously universal criticism of McCann's actions: 'Remember the sports press's fury at Fergus McCann in his terrier-like determination to face down Jim Farry in the court case to prove that the SFA had deliberately and unjustifiably delayed the registration of Jorge Cadete ...' and the composer added somewhat gratuitously about the consequences: 'The snarling jibes about Catholic paranoia were for once brought to a sudden gob-smacked silence.'

However, there was no way that Jim Farry, unpopular as he might have been, could be ousted by Celtic, or any other club, acting on their own. It is not in the interests of the Scottish Premier League for the SFA to have a capable and powerful Chief Executive, and it seems clear that Farry had little support from that area. Hearts, for one, could still have been seething over the controversy at Mallorca, and Chris Robinson was a member of that SFA Executive Committee which largely decided his fate.

The general football public also had grievances: in 1997 Falkirk were due to play Kilmarnock at Ibrox Park in an unfashionable Scottish Cup final, but the event grew in anticipatory popularity as it was dubbed 'the People's Final'. The match itself was entertaining, and both sets of supporters, although unused to the occasion, enjoyed themselves thoroughly and behaved impeccably. Prior to the match, however, Farry had issued a detailed set of

---

[42] In the recent past Jim Farry has written a column about football for *The Herald*, and rumours that he received a handsome 'golden handshake' from his former employers remain unconfirmed.

instructions to the players and officials of both clubs outlining the proper etiquette, thus preventing harmless and spontaneous actions. He was, of course, rightly criticised for his directions, and roundly booed by both sets of fans at the match.

Farry was also widely criticised – and almost certainly unfairly – because he insisted that the Scotland–Belarus match should have been played, as arranged, on 2 September 1997, the day of the Princess of Wales' funeral. His argument that the match would start at 3 p.m. – four hours after the funeral – and at a location in Aberdeen several hundred miles away from London met with strong resistance from a hysterical media and a sentimental public.[43] To Farry's genuine puzzlement the fixture was eventually postponed until 7 September.

An exceptional administrator, Jim Farry remained an unpopular figure and, increasingly, many of the clubs' representatives resented his attitude. An indication of this is surely the fact that, when the SFA secretariat recommended for themselves a handsome bonus when Scotland managed to qualify for the 1998 World Cup finals in France, the recommendation was promptly turned down.

But there is no doubt that Fergus McCann's reluctance to accept an unfair decision about the registration of Jorge Cadete as final was the major factor in Jim Farry's removal from office.

* * *

Unfortunately, it was not the first time Celtic and the SFA had been at loggerheads over the registration of players and Celtic, as a club, have a long memory.

Back in 1947 Celtic had watched Paddy Buckley, a bustling young centre forward play for the junior side Bo'ness United, and immediately snapped him up by signing him on a provisional form. For the rest of the season he was allowed to play for the junior side in order to gain further experience, but Celtic paid him throughout this period.

For some unknown reason Celtic chose not to send his registration forms into the SFA, delaying that step until late in June, 1948. At the same time they amended the original provisional form by changing the date to 28 June 1948. Meanwhile, unknown to Celtic and in the very recent past, Buckley had signed another form with another senior club, St Johnstone. Both clubs sent in the registration forms to the SFA, and St. Johnstone's arrived one day earlier than Celtic's.

---

[43] Three Rangers players in the Scottish squad [Andy Goram, Ally McCoist, and Gordon Durie] threatened to withdraw out of respect for the late Princess – and one cynical observer felt that Farry was lucky that the Celtic players had not withdrawn as a mark of respect for Mother Theresa.

The secretariat of the SFA was bemused by the arrival of the two forms, and investigated further. George Graham pointed out, accurately enough, that Buckley had signed for Celtic earlier but the date on Celtic's registration form had been altered by the club without the player's knowledge and consent. According to Graham's interpretation of the bye-laws, Buckley, although he had been paid wages by Celtic for almost a season, and was generally recognised as Celtic's 'property', was free to make other arrangements because Celtic had not registered him for the 1947/48 season.

Upon the completion of the investigation the results were announced as follows: the player should be considered as having signed for St. Johnstone in time for the 1948/49 season. St. Johnstone, Bo'ness United, and Buckley were exonerated of any wrongdoing, although both Buckley, directly, and Bo'ness United indirectly, had received moneys after the youngster had signed the original provisional form for Celtic. On the other hand, for having doctored the form, Celtic were fined £50 and censured by the SFA, and Jimmy McGrory, their manager, was fined £100 and censured also.

Frankly, it did not seem a fair outcome to an episode in which Celtic's only fault lay simply in changing the date on the provisional form before sending it in to the SFA for endorsement. The censures were embarrassing and the fines fairly substantial for 1948, but more importantly Celtic had lost the services of a promising player, who went on to become a prolific goalscorer with St Johnstone and Aberdeen.

The panel who ruled against Celtic on the Paddy Buckley case met on 21 July 1948, and also had to make a decision on the resolution of another Celtic signing, a teenager from Pollok Juniors named Bobby Collins.

Bob Kelly had seen this youngster play for his junior side and was highly impressed. Despite his small stature, Collins had every requisite for an inside forward, and Kelly was determined to sign him in the face of opposition from other interested clubs, including Everton. In fact, Collins had gone as far as to accept an invitation to travel to Goodison Park along with his father and an official from Pollok, but, upon their arrival in Liverpool and also at the ground, they found nobody there to welcome them nor to discuss any offers. Accordingly, they returned to Glasgow slightly disillusioned.

Celtic moved quickly to sign up the promising youngster, but Everton claimed that he belonged to them, and asked the SFA to rule on the matter. The same SFA/Scottish League committee that had decided the Buckley case earlier that day now turned their attention to Bobby Collins.

Once again, the outcome did not favour Celtic: Collins was to be considered an Everton player, mainly on the basis of alleged correspondence between officials of Everton and Pollok Juniors; the transfer of Collins to Everton should be completed forthwith; new registration forms were to be completed by Pollok; and any form completed before April 1948 was to be considered cancelled, thus invalidating Collins' signing for Celtic.

Celtic were furious about this decision, and determined to fight on, invoking the aid of all the other parties (except, of course, Everton). Bobby Collins and his father testified that neither of them had ever received any written offers from Everton, and that neither had received any money as an inducement to sign on. Pollok Juniors, and the Scottish Junior Football Association became involved on Celtic's side, as did the Players' Union.

Everton, upon hearing from Collins that he would refuse to travel south to join them, eventually withdrew from the legal wranglings leaving the player free to sign for Celtic. It had been a long-drawn out affair, and Kelly commented acidly: 'It was a dispute during which we at Celtic Park believed that our club

Bobby Collins, the subject of a transfer dispute between Celtic and Everton. Bob Kelly, Celtic's chairman, argued that the SFA did little to help the club resolve the matter.

had a harder task than others in getting support from Scotland's football legislators.'

It was worth the struggle, however, as Bobby Collins played for Celtic for more than nine seasons, after being pitched in at the deep end on the opening day of the 1949/50 season on the right wing against Rangers. The diminutive winger (only 5 ft 4 ins) won the hearts of the Celtic support that day by his courageous performance against Rangers' captain, the hard-tackling 'Tiger' Shaw, and helped the side to a 3–2 win. As a more experienced campaigner he was switched to inside forward, and became a regular in the Scottish side.

In September 1958 he was transferred to Everton for the very substantial fee of £23,500 and was an immediate success at Goodison, if a belated one. Four years later he was targeted and captured by Leeds United, whose manager Don Revie made him the linchpin of his emerging side.

However, it can be seen clearly that Celtic were treated shabbily and inconsistently by the SFA in the matter of these two signings. The protracted struggle to capture Jorge Cadete years later served to bring back memories of previous 'injustices'.

CHAPTER NINE

Celtic and Scotland

Another area in which some Celtic supporters feel persecuted lies in the treatment of the club's players in relation to Scotland's international side.

It is an honour to be chosen to represent Scotland and every player is aware of that recognition, and welcomes it up to a point. During the course of a long season a conflict often arises between the demands of club and country and for clubs such as Celtic and Rangers, invariably in the running for the honours, the selection of players for the national side is a mixed blessing. Players are reminded about who pays their wages, and to recognise their primary responsibility to their clubs. [44]

Many Celtic followers, conscious of the fact that Celtic have been under-represented in the past, feel more outraged in view of the impression that some Rangers players, even after preferential treatment, seemed almost reluctant to represent their country except on specific occasions. Bob McPhail is frequently cited in this regard, along with a number of modern-day players, who have called off with assorted ailments from representing Scotland. It would be more difficult to find a similar number of Celtic players behaving in this manner, although some have expressed a wish not to be selected in the first place.

I would submit, however, that the situation with regard to Celtic players has improved considerably in the past fifteen years, and that it no longer represents a major problem.

However, it was felt for a long time that Celtic, despite their prominence, had been under-represented in Scotland sides, and that some players had been singled out for exclusion by the selectors and/or 'the treatment' from the Scottish fans. This, of course, would be in line with the feeling that some segments of Scottish society have never really accepted the existence of a foot-

---

[44] In recent seasons Rangers pointed out to the SFA that Colin Hendry's proposed transfer to Derby County might be jeopardised if he played for Scotland with an injured knee. In fact, Rangers lodged a compensation claim of £100,000 because Hendry was unavailable to play for them after being injured playing for Scotland against Bosnia – an ironic claim as Hendry was no longer a regular first-team choice at Ibrox.

Similarly, Rangers objected to possible painkilling injections to enable Barry Ferguson to play for Scotland against England in a qualifying match for the European Nations Championship in 2000. Again the complaint seemed odd because the player apparently had been already receiving such injections before club games (and at half time) and was suffering by his own account because he had been given no chance to rest between fixtures by Rangers.

ball club in Glasgow so clearly identified with an alien country. In fact, some Celtic players have been barracked by sections of the Scottish support when representing other countries, and even former Celtic players have been accorded similar treatment.[45]

I asked several 'Celtic men', among them two former directors of the club, to name those players they felt were most badly treated by the Scottish selectors, supporters and media. The final list included the following: Jimmy McGrory, Bobby Hogg, George Paterson, Bobby Evans, Billy McNeill, Bobby Lennox, Jimmy Johnstone, David Hay and Kenny Dalglish. I approached the subject with an open mind, and I would suggest that some of the conclusions might surprise die-hard Celtic supporters.

It should always be remembered that the selection and fielding of international sides has been the sole prerogative of the SFA, and the original purpose was for the Scottish players to demonstrate the arts and crafts of the game in exhibition matches significantly called friendlies.[46] Only in relatively recent times has there been real pressure on Scottish international sides to get a result in order to qualify for an important world-wide or European competition.

For decades the normal practice was to play three internationals against the other home countries: Wales, Northern Ireland and England. The latter fixture was regarded as the highlight of the season, the other two matches being somewhat downplayed. In fact, several players – respectable, hard-working and competent – may have been given international caps against Wales and/or Ireland as a reward for services to football and not strictly on merit.

An SFA Selection Committee, normally consisting of seven of the Scottish game's legislators and called together by the Secretary, chose the national side. It was not unknown for some of these men to put forward the names of their own club's best players as candidates for caps; nor was it

---

[45] Before and during the pre-World Cup friendly on the 28 March 1990 between Scotland and Argentina, both Brian McClair (Manchester United) and Roy Aitken (Newcastle United) were singled out for barracking by sizeable sections of the Hampden crowd. Both players, of course, had been Celtic stalwarts. Anton Rogan, the Celtic full-back, was a victim of barracking by Northern Ireland fans whenever he was chosen to represent his country. It is not clear if the barracking was due to the fact that he was a Catholic, or because he represented Celtic. Two Polish players, Darius Dziekanowski and Darius Wdowczyk were booed repeatedly when representing Poland against Scotland at Hampden on 19 May 1990.

[46] It is widely believed that the SFA (or more accurately its secretariat under George Graham) preferred Scotland's participation in friendly internationals rather than competitive fixtures. Scotland, along with England, received an invitation to the World Cup held in 1950 in Brazil but declined to accept it saying that they would go only as unofficial British champions and, of course, lost to England by 1–0 at Hampden Park. Another major factor in Scotland's isolationism was an ongoing feud between Graham and Sir Stanley Rous of the FA.

unusual for a certain amount of horse-trading to be done in private. Thus, one selector might add his support to another's nomination, and the favour would be reciprocated at some time in the future. In such negotiations the input of the Secretary would be invaluable.

Until the World Cup of 1954 in Switzerland, Scotland did not have a manager and, in fact, the first manager (Andy Beattie) quit abruptly halfway through that tournament and returned home to leave the thirteen players to fend for themselves. The squad went to Switzerland without a backup goalkeeper and at the first training session one player, noting that the players had been forced to practise in their club strips, commented: 'We look like liquorice all-sorts.' The expedition turned out to be a thoroughly amateurish exercise, leading inevitably to a 0–1 defeat by Austria and a humiliation from Uruguay by 0–7. Among the criticisms later levelled was the accusation that more SFA officials were present on the jaunt than players. Neil Mochan, the Celtic centre forward, was chosen for the event and commented later: 'It was treated more like an end-of-season tour than anything else.'

Later advertisements for the position of manager suggested that the SFA had still not wakened up to the reality of the modern age as they suggested the post could be carried out successfully 'on a part-time basis'. The early 'managers' still had to deal with the members of the Selection Committee, who were most reluctant to give up any of their power or influence. Ian McColl (ex-Rangers) apparently was unable to announce his side for one match until the selectors had voted between Willie Henderson and Alec Scott, both of Rangers. The latter had been a regular for Scotland at outside right, but had recently lost his place in Rangers' team to the newcomer Henderson. Rangers were able to solve that particular dilemma by transferring Scott to Everton and retaining Henderson.

It is generally believed that the first Scottish manager to insist on his right to pick the side was Jock Stein, when he took over for a few months in 1965 to help the SFA out in a crisis situation.

Thus, if any bias was shown against Celtic players, the blame lay for years with an unwieldy committee, and later by individual Scottish managers. Some Celtic supporters insist that such a bias has continued and exists even at the present. Perhaps it is time to examine the facts objectively.

The most obvious example of the existence of such discrimination lies in the shabby treatment of a genuine Celtic hero, Jimmy McGrory. Signed by Celtic from St. Roch Juniors in 1921, McGrory, a shy youngster, took some time to adjust to the senior game and was farmed out to Clydebank in 1923 but, after returning to Celtic Park for the start of the 1924/25 season, he embarked upon a magnificent career as a centre forward.

He was a one-club man, a jersey player, totally loyal to Celtic and their supporters, who personally resisted efforts by the club to sell him to Arsenal for a British record transfer fee in 1928. In the 1920s and 30s football was much more physical than at present, and the stocky McGrory, although on the short side for the spearhead of the attack, was frequently the target of crude tackles and rough treatment. Despite that, and the inevitable toll of injuries, he played for Celtic until 1937 averaging almost a goal a game for fifteen years. He ended up with the amazing total of 410 goals in 408 league matches, a figure which includes twelve goals for Clydebank, and the overall tally of 550 goals in the top flight of senior football. It was truly an incredible career as, during many of those seasons, Celtic were an inconsistent side and McGrory frequently lacked genuine support up-front.

Jimmy McGrory, Celtic centre forward and the greatest goalscorer in the history of Scottish football, in a game against Queen's Park.

The major surprise lies in the meagre number of caps won by this legendary performer. Jimmy McGrory played only seven times for Scotland, despite smashing almost every scoring record in British football, and in those seven games he scored six times.

The issue was clear-cut to partisan Celtic followers; they argued that there was a bias against McGrory simply because he was a Celtic player. On the other hand, apologists for the SFA committee which chose Scotland international sides could argue that McGrory was unlucky to be a near-contemporary of Hughie Gallacher.

This latter argument is worth considering in some detail.

Hughie Gallacher was undoubtedly one of the most gifted strikers ever to play for Scotland. After his start with the strong Airdrie side of the early 1920s Gallagher's career flourished following his move to England and his appearances with Newcastle United, Chelsea, and Derby County. In fact, he was a member of the most famous of all Scottish sides, the Wembley Wizards who thrashed England by 5–1 in 1928. The 'Anglo' also had the advantage of being the man in possession, having won his first cap in 1924, at the time when McGrory's career was just starting with Celtic. Gallacher, a prolific scorer at international level, went on to make twenty appearances for his country.

I would have to agree reluctantly with the SFA's position with regard to the dilemma posed by having two such gifted players competing for the same position. In addition, this was a time when international matches were rationed, the three fixtures against the other home countries being the norm. Gallacher, a man who had never let Scotland down, was still at his prime at the period when Jimmy McGrory was emerging as a star in Scottish football and deserved to be chosen more frequently than the Celt.

However, consider what happened when the veteran Gallacher's talents began to erode with age and the contributory factor of a dissolute lifestyle. Gallacher made a further five appearances for Scotland during the 1930s, four in the home internationals and one cap against France awarded in an unimportant European tour. Such loyalty by the selectors was understandable and commendable.

By the early 1930s Jimmy McGrory was at the height of his powers. He scored two goals to help win the replayed Scottish Cup final against Motherwell in 1931, having inspired Celtic to an unlikely recovery in the first match. He scored the only goal of the 1933 final also against Motherwell, despite losing two teeth in the opening minutes of the match. And, most notably, in a rare appearance against England at Hampden Park in 1933 McGrory scored both Scottish goals in a 2–1 victory; the second, when he crashed the ball past Harry Hibbs, being generally recognised as the start of the famous 'Hampden Roar' as 134,170 Scots celebrated.

Despite his outstanding form for Celtic (and Scotland), McGrory, the logical successor and heir-apparent to Gallacher, was capped only six times in the 1930s and had to share the representative honours with a variety of men: Jimmy Fleming (Rangers) who played against England in 1930; Benny Yorston (Aberdeen) chosen against Northern Ireland in 1931; Barney Battles (Hearts) fielded against Wales in 1931; Neil Dewar (Third Lanark), who played against England in 1932 and Wales in 1933; Willie McFadyen (Motherwell), selected against Wales in 1934; Jimmy Smith (Rangers), chosen against Northern Ireland in 1935; Matt Armstrong (Aberdeen), fielded against Northern Ireland and Wales in 1936; and Dave McCulloch (Hearts and Brentford) who was preferred in 1935 against Wales and in 1936 against England. McCulloch's appearance against England must have been a particularly bitter blow for the veteran McGrory as it meant that the greatest goalscorer in British football was denied a last chance to play at Wembley Stadium – and during a season in which the Celtic player had scored fifty league goals!

The purpose of the above paragraphs is not to disparage the other players chosen for the internationals: for example, Neil Dewar was a prolific scorer at club level for Third Lanark; Jimmy Smith ended up as Rangers' all-time highest scorer in league matches with 225 (excluding the war-games); Jimmy Fleming, a versatile player who often played as a winger, ended up with a tally of 177 league goals for Rangers; and Willie McFadyen, as a member of a classic Motherwell side, still holds the Scottish record of fifty-two goals in a single season.

However, any objective historian of football would have to admit that none of the men who shared the representative honours with McGrory during those seasons was the equal of the Celtic player in terms of ability, effort and achievement.

Only one other argument in favour of the selectors might be forwarded: the fixtures against Wales and Northern Ireland were regarded as relatively unimportant, and were frequently used to reward players and clubs. Sometimes the selectors – usually seven in number and drawn from various parts of Scotland – were capable of 'regional voting' to encourage local interest throughout the country. This might well have accounted in part for the selection of the two Aberdeen players (Yorston and Armstrong) in preference to McGrory. As the selectors met infrequently and probably saw only those fixtures in which their own clubs were involved, a disproportionate influence was exerted by the SFA secretary. George Graham was appointed to the post in 1928 and no doubt saw the advantage in 'regional voting' as a sure-fire method of promoting his own career within Scottish football.

One outstanding – and influential – player who championed McGrory's cause was the Rangers inside forward Bob McPhail. He played against McGrory in many Old Firm clashes, and alongside him in several internationals; it was his pass that provided the chance for one of McGrory's goals against England in 1933. McPhail was critical of the selectors' repeated failure to chose McGrory, and it was rumoured that he had gone as far as to withdraw from one international 'through injury' as a protest.

In view of the oft-repeated claims that Rangers are 'a Scottish club' and Celtic are 'an Irish club', it is ironic to note McPhail's own admission in his excellent autobiography *Legend: Sixty Years at Ibrox* (Edinburgh, 1988) that he was actively encouraged by his club manager to withdraw from the national side in order to conserve his energy for important Rangers matches: 'Bill Struth made sure I suffered no financial loss any time I had to pull out of an international squad.'

McGrory himself, of course, was a shy, retiring type of personality and a genuinely modest individual; he would never have resorted to complaining about his treatment at the hands of the selectors. Perhaps this diffidence contributed to the meagre total of caps won by this most whole-hearted of all players although he was hurt, as this excerpt from his own autobiography *A Lifetime in Paradise* (London, 1975) suggests: 'Despite my goal-scoring feats the SFA overlooked me for the game against England at Wembley – my last chance to play on that famous ground which had always eluded me. But, as I've said, we Celts were used to being overlooked in those days, unfair as it was. It is very refreshing in these modern times [1975] to see the club so well represented in the Scottish team whose jersey I was always proud to wear.'

'Jaymak', a columnist for the *Evening Times*, pointed out on 1 April 1936 that McGrory's surprise omission 'has brought me many expressions of indignation' and cited one letter as an example: ' ... up till last weekend he was a certainty. What went wrong? There is no doubt that he is showing as good, if not better, form than any of the players chosen. It seems to me that the selectors are determined McGrory shall never play at Wembley.'

Some apologists for the SFA had suggested that McGrory, by then in the veteran stage, had been rejected this time on account of his age and 'Onlooker' attempted to refute this argument in the *Glasgow Observer* of 4 April 1936: 'Age becomes a decided handicap, especially in soccer, when one is playing against such youthful talent as [Bob] McPhail, who played with Airdrie who won the 1923/24 Scottish Cup final. Seems this handicapping according to age only applies if those concerned wear the green-and-white jerseys, for McGrory didn't become a Celt until the following year.' The columnist's argument is weakened somewhat by the fact that Jimmy McGrory was eighteen months older than Bob McPhail, although the latter had indeed broken through as a senior earlier.

It is interesting to note that Bob McPhail also never played at Wembley. The Ranger played five times against England at Hampden Park and it is believed that he was encouraged to withdraw from some international matches against England because the stamina-draining effects of the famous Wembley turf might have reduced his efficiency for Rangers in forthcoming Scottish Cup final appearances (in 1930, 1932, 1934 and 1936).

Nothing can convince older Celtic supporters that Jimmy McGrory was not treated shabbily by the Scottish selectors, and that the neglect was due solely to the fact that he played for Celtic. The *Evening Times* printed an anonymous poem submitted to its 'Gossip and Grumbles' column on 6 April 1936:

If he hadn't played for Celtic and he'd worn the jersey blue,
I'm sure he'd be at Wembley to the delight of me and you.
But, because a good man's Irish, sure it's always been a sin.
Why! They wouldn't give us credit for our champion Jimmy Quinn.
Long life to you, McGrory, you're the best we've ever seen.
You're the finest centre forward who wore the white-and-green.

Two other Celtic players who were frequently overlooked in the late 1930s were Bobby Hogg and George Paterson, both members of the team that won the Empire Exhibition Trophy in 1938 by beating the best sides in Britain in an invitational tournament.

Bobby Hogg was an exceptional right-back, and at one time was the youngest signed professional footballer in Scotland; he made his debut at the age of eighteen against Queen's Park in 1932. Fast, and sure-footed in his tackling and in the clearing of his lines, he was considered one of the cleanest and most sporting of opponents. As a Celtic player, Hogg won medals in the League Championship in 1936 and 1938, and in the Scottish Cup in 1933 and 1937 in addition to the triumph in 1938 in the Empire Exhibition Trophy. Despite that impressive haul, he was chosen only once to play for Scotland – against Czechoslovakia in Prague in 1937.

Some Celtic followers felt that Hogg was simply overlooked by the selectors through bias, but this might be too simplistic an explanation. Scotland was well-served by right-backs in the 1930s and the competition was fierce for the position in the national team. Prior to Hogg's arrival on the scene the struggle was among the following: Nibloe (Kilmarnock) with eleven caps, Gray (Rangers) with ten, Crapnell (Airdrie) with nine, and Carabine (Third Lanark) with three. All of these players were highly competent professionals, worthy of international appearances. As Hogg started to make an impression and to be considered for Scotland, the main obstacle was Andy Anderson (Hearts) and he could not be ousted from the Scottish side; the highly competent Anderson earned all of his twenty-three caps between 1933 and 1939, the outbreak of World War II.

I would submit that Bobby Hogg was unlucky to be in direct competition with such a redoubtable defender, but his ability could have been recognised more often with honours against the likes of Wales and Ireland. Nobody doubted the Celtic man's ability nor temperament; in fact, he was chosen as 'travelling reserve' so often that he was able to furnish a wartime Scotland side with their ten outfield strips for one fixture during the clothes rationing.[47]

George Paterson made his Celtic debut late in 1933, and became estab-

---

[47] The idea of a Scottish 'squad' is a relatively new one. Previously, one other player was chosen in addition to the starting eleven, and frequently this travelling reserve was a versatile player.

lished as a member of a highly effective halfback line of Geatons, Lyon and Paterson at the start of the 1935/36 season. Not the tallest player in the Scottish game at 5 feet, 7 inches, the solidly-built Paterson was a tireless worker and a superb distributor of the ball; he was also a crack shot as his low drive from thirty yards to win the 1944 Ne'erday clash with Rangers at Ibrox would testify.

However, George Paterson only received one cap for Scotland, a solitary appearance against Northern Ireland in 1938/39, although he did receive a number of unofficial wartime honours for Scotland while he was serving with the RAF. Inexplicably, he was dropped from the Scottish side to face England in the 'Victory International' at Hampden Park despite being the man in possession during the 1945/46 season. Admittedly, his replacement, Jackie Husband of Partick Thistle, played well and contributed to the leading-up play for Delaney's last-minute winner.

The man who kept Paterson out of the Scottish line-up for so long was George Brown of Rangers whose international career started in 1930/31 and ended in 1937/38. Certainly, George Brown was an outstanding wing-half but, during the late 1930s when he was a veteran player, he was not immeasurably superior to Paterson who, like Hogg, was a key member of an outstanding Celtic eleven .

The case of Bobby Evans in the 1950s was just as interesting.

Evans, a red-headed teenager with boundless energy, had joined Celtic from St Anthony's in 1944 and was used primarily as a utility forward, before he was chosen to play at right-half in the so-called 'relegation battle' at Dens Park in April 1948. He played well that day and Celtic's manager decided that Evans would benefit from an extended run in the position; the player himself was reluctant to do so and protested. However, McGrory insisted and, under the tutelage of the new coach Jimmy Hogan, Evans' play improved dramatically.

Like many other forwards fielded as a wing-half, he benefited from gaining the extra split-second afforded to those who play facing the ball. In fact, Evans was a revelation: good in the air, strong in the tackle, industrious in defence and eager in attack. He developed skills in passing hitherto missing, but his greatest gift was an uncanny sense of anticipation, allied to a magnificent fighting spirit.

Within a couple of months of his move backwards he had won the first of his forty-eight caps for Scotland and in his home debut for his country at Hampden Park he was the inspiration behind a remarkable comeback against Northern Ireland. Scotland had given up two early goals but Evans was playing magnificently: he mastered his immediate opponent, the talented Peter Doherty; he steadied the defence when it was still reeling; and gradually he urged on the forwards, plying his more experienced right-wing colleagues

Waddell (Rangers) and Mason (Third Lanark) with a stream of precise passes. At the end the youthful Evans was acclaimed as a Scottish hero in a memorable 3–2 victory.

Evans' development as a player was all the more remarkable as he played in a poor Celtic side for much of his early career. On the field Bobby Evans was a most sporting player, and was booked only three times in a long career, but he could be touchy about what he perceived as unfair criticism. On one occasion he actually went to the home of a man in Paisley to 'discuss' with him face-to-face the contents of a letter written to a newspaper in which Evans' sportsmanship in a recent match against St. Mirren had been questioned. The affair ended amicably enough, but it remains a clear indication of the player's attitude. Later in his career, in the days preceding the 1957 League Cup final against Rangers, Evans and Charlie Tully came to blows at training over another newspaper article, ghost-written for Tully. Once more, Evans felt that his talents and performance had been undervalued.

Evans was convinced that an orchestrated campaign would swing into operation in the week or two prior to a meeting of the Scottish selectors. Long after his retirement he was quoted as saying: 'I still believe to this day [1988] that if I had played for any other club but Celtic I would have won far more international caps than I did, perhaps as many as twenty more. There were times when players I knew were inferior to me were picked and often from the most obscure places while I was under the noses of the Selection Committee and recognised as playing well.'

This might well be construed as paranoid thinking on Evans' part, but the player received some unsolicited support in 1960 from a most reputable journalist, John Rafferty of *The Scotsman*: 'A rash of vicious criticism of Evans breaks out just as the Scottish selectors prepare to pick a team. The general theme is that Evans, Celtic's centre-half and Scotland's captain, must go. He is too old; he is slow on the turn; and never was a great player anyway. It is amusing to remember that, except when the selectors are about to gather, Evans is wonderful.'

Any newspaper criticism of Evans in the early 1950s, and which apparently remained a constant, although intermittent, factor throughout his career, was generally unfair. Evans was the supreme Scottish wing half of the period and for many seasons in his prime he was invariably the best performer on the pitch week after week. Had he been playing in the present time, he would have been exhausted carrying home the 'Man of the Match' awards.

However, Evans, over-sensitive as ever off the field, had not helped his cause by writing a letter to the SFA in 1950 advising that organisation that he 'would prefer not to be chosen for international matches at the present time'. In his letter Evans had expressed his displeasure at the attitude of some selectors but he had also assured them that, if selected in the future, he 'would naturally

Bobby Evans. Despite winning forty-eight caps for Scotland he believed that being a Celtic player cost him many more international honours.

turn up and give of my best as always.' Bob Kelly, Celtic's chairman, advised Evans not to send the letter, but the player persisted in his action. No doubt, some of his subsequent omissions were due to the SFA selectors' natural resentment at his action. However, Evans was eventually restored to his rightful place in the Scotland line-up as a wing-half.

Again it is a valid exercise to examine the facts of the case. Evans had claimed that 'inferior' players were chosen ahead of him, and the men who most frequently challenged him for the Scotland berth were Ian McColl (Rangers), Jimmy Scoular (Portsmouth), and Tommy Docherty (Preston North End). Let us examine this situation more objectively, player by player and in chronological order.

Jimmy Scoular was an Anglo-Scot, and sometimes that fact can sway the wavering opinion of the Scottish selectors. Nobody would ever accuse Scoular of being a polished wing half, his forte being ball-winning and some of his performances for Scotland, if not Portsmouth, bordered on the crude and intimidating. At a time when international matches were viewed as showpiece games arranged to demonstrate the best of Scottish football, Jimmy Scoular was no advertisement for skill and sportsmanship. Despite that, he was selected to play for Scotland on nine occasions between 1951 and 1953 at a time when Evans was playing at his best.

Tommy Docherty won twenty-five caps for Scotland, starting in 1951 and ending in 1959. Ironically, before moving south, Tommy Docherty had been a fringe player with Celtic making only nine appearances in two or three different positions. Neither Celtic nor he could see any prospects for Docherty replacing Evans at right half, as he admits in his 1960 autobiography: ' ... that magnificent player, Bobby Evans ... there was no hope of displacing him.' Accordingly, Docherty was transferred to Preston North End in 1949, and later to Arsenal.

Like Scoular, he was a combative right half and, like his fellow Anglo-Scot, he was often criticised for his uncompromising style. Even his most ardent admirer would find it difficult to consider him superior to Evans as a

wing half, although Stanley Matthews regarded him highly: ' ... a tough, tena-
cious tackler who would leave inside forwards of delicate constitution as rat-
tled as a shutter in a cyclone ... once he had won the ball, however, as he
invariably did, he would use it intelligently and to good effect. Very rarely did
I see him give the ball away ... his physical demeanour belied a clever and cal-
culating football brain.'

Ian McColl, signed from Queen's Park in 1945, played in a highly successful Rangers side and was a key figure in the vaunted Ibrox 'Iron Curtain'
team. He was an efficient, rather than showy, wing half and noted more for
his defensive qualities than attacking skills. As a member of a settled team
(Rangers) he could concentrate on his own responsibilities almost exclusively.
Again, it is dubious if too many objective football men would consider him
the equal of Bobby Evans, although he was awarded fourteen caps.

Is there any merit in Evans' claim that he was discriminated against as a
Scotland player?

Evans made forty-eight appearances for Scotland and the combined total
of his three main 'rivals' also comes to forty-eight. On the surface, that does
not appear to be an unduly unfair distribution of the honours. However, two
things should be remembered within this context: after replacing George
Young of Rangers as Scotland's pivot in 1957, Evans went on to make more
than twenty appearances for Scotland as centre half rather than as right-half.
Accordingly, the validity of Evans' accusation is enhanced by the amended
statistics. Another factor which should be considered is the fact that Evans'
international career was a long one, stretching from 1949 to 1960 because he
was exceptionally fit and a remarkably consistent player not prone to losses
of form. It would appear that, whenever Evans was dropped, the selectors had
judged that his replacement was the better player and the omission was not
due to any injury suffered by Evans nor to loss of form.[48] The problem was
complicated by Evans' ill-judged action in sending his letter of complaint to
the SFA; undoubtedly, that impulsive action caused him to lose several
appearances for his country, and not surprisingly. [49]

Several Celtic-minded men have suggested that Billy McNeill was another
victim of prejudice in the matter of international honours.

No possible doubt exists that McNeill, Celtic's captain and on-field
leader, was one of the country's outstanding footballers. Certainly, he was one
of the most successful with a considerable tally of medals: nine League

[48] Evans' only major spell out through injury occurred between September and December 1958 when
he suffered back problems after the opening league fixture at Shawfield.

[49] George Young may also have contributed to his replacement by Evans because he had announced
that he would be making his last appearance for Scotland against Spain at Madrid in 1957; incensed
at this presumption the selectors promptly made the decision to drop Young from the Scotland team.

Championships, seven Scottish Cups, six League Cups – and one winning European Cup. As a defender he was unbeatable in the air, and solid on the ground; he could organise a defence around him, and his sorties into attack for set-pieces were feared by the opposition, as goals in three different Scottish Cup finals would indicate: against Dunfermline Athletic in 1965, Rangers in 1969, and Hibernian in 1972.

McNeill was honoured twenty-nine times for his country, and that seems at first sight to be an acceptable total, but Celtic zealots point out that his principal rivals, Ian Ure of Dundee and Arsenal (with eleven caps) and Ronnie McKinnon of Rangers (with twenty-eight) were simply not in the same class as McNeill.

Again, it is important to examine the facts. Billy McNeill made his international debut against England at Wembley Stadium in 1961 and Scotland lost by 9–3, a national humiliation. However, McNeill was one of the few Scots to be given pass-marks that day and was able to retain his position in the side.

The great Billy McNeill, captain of the first British team to win the European Cup. Celtic supporters are convinced he was not given the recognition he merited by his country

In 1961/62, and for the following two seasons, he shared the role of centre half in the Scottish side with Ian Ure; the ex-Dundee pivot won ten of his eleven honours during this period, while McNeill picked up a further nine. It could be argued that McNeill was superior in every department to Ure, but the critics could point out reasonably enough that McNeill's Celtic side, known mockingly as the 'Kelly Kids', were too inconsistent. Ure, on the other hand, had managed to lead the unfancied Dundee side to a league championship in 1961/62 but it should be pointed out that Celtic's defence, marshalled by McNeill, conceded nine goals fewer than Dundee that season.

Eventually, McNeill, by now established as Celtic's pivot and experienced despite his relative youth, saw off Ure's challenge and was recognised as Scotland's first choice for the position.

His qualities were, by now, widely recognised and in 1965 he was named Player of the Year by Scottish sports journalists.

However, McNeill had to withdraw from the Scottish side to play Italy in a World Cup qualifier on 9 November 1965 and his place was taken by the steady Ron McKinnon of Rangers. McKinnon was outstanding in a thrilling 1–0 victory over the Italians at Hampden, and rightly praised by the media; McNeill, who had played in Scotland's two previous matches (a 2–3 loss to Northern Ireland and a 1–2 loss to Poland) found his position under threat.

Jock Stein, although working full-time at Celtic Park, had taken over as Scotland's part-time manager and was in an awkward position. His dilemma was solved when McNeill picked up another injury which kept him out of the Celtic side from 27 November 1965 till 26 January 1966, when he returned for a vital match against Dynamo Kiev. Between 1965 and 1971, the period of their rivalry, Billy McNeill was selected thirteen times for Scotland, and Ronnie McKinnon on twenty-eight occasions. Normally it is futile to compare two players exactly, as both were outstanding performers, but McNeill's admirers do have some valid points to make.

McNeill's credentials had already been established, and he was adding lustre to his career season by season under Jock Stein's management. He had led Celtic to domestic success and European glory; McKinnon, on the other hand, had tasted little success with Rangers, either at home or on the Continent. It seemed foolish of the selectors, or manager, not to use the proven talents of a winner, a leader and the better player, in the opinion of most. The verdict of history seems to confirm this view: Billy McNeill has since been voted Glasgow's most outstanding sportsman; and in December 2000 he was picked for the greatest ever Scotland team by readers of the *Daily Record,* the country's largest circulation newspaper.

Bobby Lennox was yet another Celtic player frequently overlooked by successive Scottish managers despite his record as goalscorer with the Parkhead club during its greatest era. In all, Lennox was capped only ten times starting on 16 November 1966 with an appearance against Northern Ireland at Hampden Park; he scored one of Scotland's goals in a 2–1 win, Bobby Murdoch netting the other. Later in the same season, he outdid Jimmy McGrory by playing at Wembley and scored again in a famous Scottish victory by 3–2 over the reigning World Champions. However, he was not a regular choice for his country except for the 1968/69 season during which he made four appearances.

Generally, the preference was for Willie Johnston of Rangers, who won twenty-two caps, and it is hard to argue the case that the Ibrox man was not a very dangerous forward. Was he better than Lennox? Both were fast and direct, both could terrorise defences with the threat of their pace, both could finish off moves with a clinical efficiency. It would also not be fair to compare the two players directly as they were different types: Johnston was a winger and confined himself to that role while Lennox could be employed as a winger, inside forward, and as a striker. In other words, while their effectiveness might be similar, Lennox offered many more options for a manager. Under the circumstances, it is hard to escape the conclusion that the services of Bobby Lennox were shamefully underused by the national side.

In addition, Johnston was a player hounded by controversy. Many defenders played on the fact that his temper had a short fuse and provoked him into foolish retaliatory acts and Willie Johnston paid the penalty throughout his career, amassing a record total of orderings-off with his various clubs – but more frequently he was the aggressor. When I spoke to a Referee Supervisor about the Hughes–Johnston incident, the official at first could not recall the Rangers player involved and, when I reminded him, he smiled ruefully and said: 'Willie Johnston? Well, to be frank, I would be most reluctant to order off anybody for a foul on him especially if I hadn't seen it myself. His record speaks for itself.'

The argument that some members of the media put forward to explain the relatively low number of caps for Jimmy Johnstone of Celtic was not applied in the case of Willie Johnston of Rangers. If Jimmy Johnstone's temperament was considered unsound, surely Willie Johnston's was even more so? Lennox, on the other hand, was a model professional, seldom in trouble with referees and it came as a complete surprise that he was sent off in the World Club Championship in Montevideo in November, 1967. In fact, Stein ordered him back on to the pitch, telling him the match official had sent off the wrong man, and Bobby went back and forth before being escorted off the pitch by an armed policeman. Predictably, Lennox was 'totally exonerated' later on by the SFA, that announcement coming after due process on 4 March 1968.

Like Johnston, Lennox was singled out for attention by desperate defenders but he seldom retaliated; his even temper was tested more often by the flag-happy linesmen who found it impossible to believe that it was the player's speed and acceleration that had allowed him to break clear of the defence.

Bobby Charlton was moved to praise him highly after a testimonial match in Liverpool: 'If I'd had Lennox in my team, I could have played for ever.' Tireless and endlessly foraging for the ball, Lennox was a nightmare for defenders. His energy was one weapon the longer the game went on; his pace could never be matched; and he was a striker of the highest quality as 273 goals for Celtic would attest.

Several other Celtic players, honoured by their country, have complained about ill-treatment at the hands of Scotland fans at Hampden Park. Those with justifiable complaints include Jimmy Johnstone, David Hay and perhaps Kenny Dalglish.

In November 1970 a youthful David Hay was making one of his early appearances for Scotland, against Denmark in a European Nations' cup-tie and the youngster was looking forward to the experience. Scotland were expected to win comfortably enough against the Danes, but scraped through only by 1–0. The crowd, perhaps understandably, became disenchanted with the team's pedestrian performance and expressed their irritation vocally.

Unfortunately, this took the form of barracking directed against David Hay – and the disapproval was coming from the traditionally 'Rangers End' of the stadium. A section of the support, congregated there, kept calling for Hay to be replaced by Sandy Jardine, Rangers' right back, who was on the bench.[50] Hay was more than a little disappointed:

> I have learned to shut my ears to most of the variety of terracing expressions. I had been doubtful with 'flu before the game, but I have always considered it an honour to play for Scotland – and that is not the ritual quote every player gives when he is selected. I mean it, so I made an extra effort to be fit. But it was impossible that night not to have heard the fans chanting for my substitution. I would have needed to have stuffed my ears with cotton wool for the whole match.

Finally, Bobby Brown, the Scotland manager, made the move late in the contest partly to appease the crowd but also to take the pressure off the Celtic player. He explained to Hay afterwards that he felt the player's strength was ebbing away due to his illness. Controversy broke out in the press about the rightness of the manager's decision. Hay refused to comment openly, but his disappointment was obvious; Jock Stein, his club manager, was furious about the treatment his player had received from the crowd and expressed his opinions in typically forthright manner. Bobby Brown, a couple of months later, described the barracking as 'nauseating'.

Hay was philosophical about the incident:

> Perhaps the saddest aspect is that it is doubtful if any amount of words from any team boss, or legislator, can change the situation much. Yet, any hopes Scotland has of becoming a world power at international level will always be sunk if the fans cannot give us their support. I know there are team-mates of mine at Celtic who just do not want to know about playing for Scotland. They are entitled to their viewpoint. Mine, as I have said, is that I would still like to be picked. (*Playing for Celtic, No. 31*, London 1971)[51]

Several other Celtic players had received the same treatment as Hay, when representing their country, most notably Jimmy Johnstone.

One problem with Johnstone in particular was that he looked the archetypal Celtic player: small and vulnerable, red-headed and quick-tempered, and more of an individualist than a team player. Johnstone, nicknamed 'Jinky'

---

[50] Jardine was a talented right-back, and some Celtic partisans point out that Danny McGrain of Celtic, superior to him, was frequently chosen for Scotland as left-back, out of his regular position, in order to accommodate the Rangers player.

[51] A similar situation appears to have evolved in Northern Ireland in the cases of Anton Rogan and Neil Lennon. Rogan, admittedly not the most skilful of players, was frequently barracked unmercifully. More recently Lennon, who had made many appearances for his country as a Leicester City player, was forced to consider his position after his first cap as a Celtic player in 2001 brought forth death threats. It appears to be a phenomenon that affects only players in a successful Celtic side; Charlie Tully and Bertie Peacock apparently made many appearances for Northern Ireland without any adverse comment.

because of his dribbling skills, had never made any secret about his love for Celtic and his joy in wearing the green-and-white, and had confided that he 'always tried even harder against Rangers'. So successful was he in this personal quest that Campbell Ogilvie, Rangers' secretary, once confessed to a Celtic director: 'My heart used to sink whenever I saw that wee man take the field against us.'

Another, and more important, problem in Johnstone's early career as a Scottish internationalist was that he was in competition for the right-wing position with Willie Henderson of Rangers. For Johnstone to become an established Scotland player, Henderson had to be displaced – and the Rangers winger was an outstanding performer. Henderson enjoyed some advantages over Johnstone: he had broken into senior football earlier than Johnstone and was the man in possession for Scotland. A skilful dribbler, he was a more direct player than Johnstone, and he had a much better disciplinary record.

Some Celtic partisans, in considering that Willie Henderson gained twenty-nine caps for Scotland, and Jimmy Johnstone only twenty-three, may feel that his greatest advantage was the fact that he played for Rangers, but this is clearly shown to be manifestly unjust if the records are compared in a meaningful way.

Henderson made his first appearance for Scotland against Wales in 1963, and had gained twelve caps in all before Johnstone made his international debut in 1965 against Finland. In fact, Johnstone, despite his undoubted skills, was struggling to hold down a regular place in Celtic's team because of his inconsistency until after Jock Stein's arrival as manager. Stein had his own doubts about the tiny winger's temperament and his name appeared on an early list submitted to the Board as 'possibly available for transfer'. He chose to omit Johnstone from his first Scottish Cup winning side in April 1965 and it was not until the early months of the 1965/66 season that Johnstone could be considered a regular choice for Celtic. By that time, Johnstone had impressed the manager with his attitude and application in training enough to grant him a run in the first team.

So, to be perfectly fair, the only period of legitimate comparison between the claims of Henderson and Johnstone would start in the 1965/66 season, by which time Henderson had already gained sixteen caps, and Johnstone two. Accordingly, in the subsequent seasons – when both players were at their best – Henderson gained another thirteen appearances, and Johnstone twenty-one. I would submit that these figures represent reasonably fair treatment of the Celtic player from the Selection Committee or the Scotland managers in view of the fact that the Ranger was the man in possession at the start of the period.

Scotland were extremely fortunate that it had the luxury of choice between two such outstanding wingers between 1963 and 1975 and, while Johnstone might be considered the better of the two, there seems no evidence that one was preferred unfairly to the other.

What was totally unacceptable, however, was the attitude of a fairly large segment of the Scottish support, particularly in home games at Hampden Park, in which Jimmy Johnstone was unmercifully barracked by 'fans' congregated in the traditionally Rangers end of the ground. Like Hay, Johnstone was incensed at the treatment but he was more vocal in his anger and, in fact, his dissatisfaction might well have cost him a number of caps to which he would have been entitled.

Back in the late 1960s the term 'Tartan Army' had not yet been coined – or at least was not in common usage – and the reputation of Scottish supporters as travellers had not been established in World Cups. The average Scottish side engaged in European Nations or World Cup duty would invariably include players from both Rangers and Celtic as a nucleus, and for fixtures at Hampden Park followers of the Old Firm would turn up to support Scotland.[52] The Celtic supporters were in noticeably fewer numbers; the Rangers fans, or a considerable minority of them, often used these occasions to promote their own agenda particularly when a Celtic player had been fielded in preference to a Ranger. It would be difficult to recall other Scottish supporters abusing a Rangers player representing his country and calling for his substitution by a Celtic player on the bench.

Kenny Dalglish in goalmouth action at Celtic Park.
Incidentally the referee is R.H. Davidson (Airdrie)

Kenny Dalglish was never barracked when playing for Scotland as a

---

[52] One could argue that the fine reputation earned by Scottish fans at international competitions is due to the fact that, in recent times, relatively few of 'the Tartan Army' are supporters of Rangers or Celtic.

Celtic player, but he could express some surprise at the greater level of acceptance he received after his transfer to Liverpool. Previously recognised as a good player, he was almost immediately elevated to the rank of superstar by Scotland supporters and members of the media.

Dalglish seemed to have the most legitimate grounds for complaint when he was dropped from the Scottish side in 1976 for a match against Wales, won 3–1 by Scotland at Hampden. Understandably in view of his array of skills and his attitude, Kenny Dalglish was an automatic choice for Scotland and had been ever since making his debut. Prior to the Wales fixture he had made thirty-three consecutive appearances for his country and was rightly regarded as a key player in Scotland's plans. However, with no great attempts at explanation, he was dropped for this match by the manager, Willie Ormond.

Controversy erupted when it became noticed that, if Dalglish appeared for Scotland on this occasion, the Celtic player would be surpassing the record for consecutive appearances established by Rangers' George Young. Celtic supporters immediately assumed the worst, feeling that Ormond had been instructed by his employers (the SFA) to ensure that this did not happen. The player himself was keenly disappointed, and broke his silence on the matter years later in his autobiography. The SFA did not make any comment on the subject, and the media were not as outraged as one might have expected.

If this had been a shameful attempt by anybody to preserve George Young's admirable record – and the Rangers captain was a credit to the game – it was doomed to failure. Dalglish went on to make a further forty-three consecutive appearances for his country in a most distinguished playing career. One Celtic supporter pointed out to me in a sarcastic tone: 'It didn't matter to anybody then because Dalglish was a Liverpool player by that time.'

The same Celtic enthusiast opened up yet another avenue of exploration when he suggested cryptically that I have a close look at the number of caps won by the members of the Celtic sides that appeared in the European Cup final sides of 1967 and 1970, and compare that with the number gained by the men who represented Rangers in the European Cup-Winners Cup finals of 1967 and 1972. Intrigued, I followed up his advice and the results are as follows.[53]

First of all it would be pertinent to give the line-ups.

The Celtic side that won the European Cup – the first British club to win that most prestigious of trophies – was as follows: Simpson, Craig, Gemmell, Murdoch, McNeill, Clark, Johnstone, Wallace, Chalmers, Auld and Lennox. The side that appeared in the final at Milan three years later read: Williams, Hay, Gemmell, Murdoch, McNeill, Brogan, Johnstone, Lennox, Wallace, Auld (Connelly), Hughes.

The Rangers team that appeared in the European Cup-Winners' Cup final

---

[53] Only caps won when with Celtic or Rangers are considered in this context.

in 1967 was as follows: Martin, Johansen, Provan, Jardine, McKinnon, Greig, Henderson, Smith (A), Hynd, Smith (D), Johnston. The Ibrox side that won the trophy in 1972 read: McCloy, Jardine, Mathieson, Greig, Johnstone, Smith (D), McLean, Conn, Stein, MacDonald, Johnston.

Next, and following the 'reasoning' of the Celtic supporter, consider the number of caps won by these teams.

The Celtic side that won the European Cup in 1967 – almost certainly the greatest feat ever accomplished in Scottish football – earned a total of 114 caps; the team that reached the final in 1970, after beating Leeds United home and away, earned 140.

The Rangers side that reached the final of the European Cup-Winners' Cup in 1967, losing in extra time to Bayern Munich, earned 155 caps; the team that won the trophy in 1972 by beating Dynamo Moscow in Barcelona earned 129. One Rangers player, Kai Johansen, was, of course Danish and therefore ineligible for Scotland.

The members of the two Celtic sides gained a total of 155 caps, and those of the two Rangers teams 193. These totals are significantly different and reinforce the point that this Celtic partisan was making: that is, the Celtic sides were vastly superior to the Rangers ones, as evidenced by their performances both in European football at a higher level, and in the domestic scene in Scotland which they dominated. He points out acidly that the Rangers side which won the European Cup-Winners' Cup qualified for the competition by losing to Celtic in the previous season's Scottish Cup final. The underlying premise in this fan's argument is that Rangers players were given the preference in Scotland sides.

A respected sports editor also reiterated the same point in conversation with me recently, pointing out forcefully that the Celtic side(s) fielded between 1966 and 1970 were recognised as among the most feared in Europe and should have been rewarded with many more caps, especially as they were an all-Scottish team.

I confess to remaining ambivalent about this particular issue, and I would sum up the situation as follows.

No doubt exists that some Rangers supporters – and part-time Scotland followers – have abused Celtic players such as David Hay and Jimmy Johnstone, when these men have been chosen for their country. This type of behaviour on such occasions is distressing but scarcely surprising. What would be disturbing is if this abuse were to affect the thinking of the Scottish team manager in making his selection for vital Scotland matches.[54]

---

[54] Consider the unwarranted abuse heaped upon the Anglo-Scot Gary McAllister in recent times. I also recall that Gordon Smith, the great Hibernian right-winger, was cat-called by sections of the crowd in some international matches, the 'supporters' obviously preferring the more direct approach of Rangers Willie Waddell. The Rangers winger later expressed surprise at his number of caps, given the direct competition of Smith and Delaney (Celtic).

A Scotland manager has to choose a team, and sometimes a player of lesser ability is to be preferred for the balance of the side. The example of selecting both Sandy Jardine and Danny McGrain for the same Scotland side comes to mind as a model of flexibility in selection.

The cases of Jimmy McGrory (in the 1930s) and Billy McNeill and Bobby Lennox (in the 1960s) do suggest clearly that these men were not given the recognition that their performances for Celtic and Scotland merited. The motivation for that on the part of the Selection Committees and/or the Scottish managers remains much less clear. However, Celtic fans are virtually unanimous that the shabby treatment represented a continuing bias against the club and its players.

Bobby Evans and Jimmy Johnstone also deserved better treatment and could have been given more representative honours, but the ultra-sensitive attitude of both players towards criticism may well have been a contributory factor. Bobby Hogg and George Paterson were outstanding players but they were playing in Scotland at a time when there was no shortage of players of quality, and they could be considered unlucky.

I would submit that the uniquely Scottish verdict of 'Not Proven' could well be applied to this charge of bias. But it must be significant that a number of commentators, objective football men and by no means Celtic-minded individuals, agree with the view of Celtic partisans, or have felt that this is (or was) an issue worthy of serious discussion.[55]

---

[55] This type of commentator would also decry the disgraceful neglect of Scottish players outside the Old Firm. One name that springs to mind is the exceptional Raith Rovers full back Willie McNaught, given only five caps for Scotland. McNaught, perhaps discouraged by this turn of events, was said to have advised the youthful Jim Baxter to sign for Rangers; Baxter went on to win thirty-four caps for his country.

CHAPTER TEN

Referees

Between 1995 and 1997 for the first time in my life as a football follower I was tempted to give some credence to the 'Celtic Conspiracy Theory' – the belief maintained by so many Celtic people that referees (and others) conspire to deny Celtic natural justice. It was tempting, but not convincing enough for me till then.

The trouble for Celtic during that period was that Rangers were closing in upon one of the Parkhead club's most treasured records – the famous nine championships in a row won by Celtic under Jock Stein's leadership. Celtic supporters were becoming anxious, if not hysterical, about this issue and often their judgement was clouded by their emotion – but not always.

Celtic had hamstrung themselves for a number of seasons earlier in Rangers' run, and it was proving difficult to turn things around although the improvement was obvious. In May 1995, Celtic had won the Scottish Cup by beating Airdrie at Hampden Park through van Hooijdonk's header early in the match, a boring but nervous final. It was a breakthrough but some discounted it on the grounds that it had been gained unconvincingly, if deservedly, against an unfashionable Airdrie side, but nobody was entirely fooled. Rangers would still start the league campaign in 1995/96 as odds-on favourites to win their eighth successive title, and the realists at Celtic Park conceded that the odds reflected the situation accurately enough. Celtic would improve, it was agreed, and Rangers might decline further but a definite gap in quality or character still existed between the sides.

In a typically ambitious move to seal another championship Rangers had made an important signing during the close season for £4.5 million, and he was the controversial Paul Gascoigne. The troubled Englishman was a player of genuine quality, an exceptional talent, but a man who had only on occasion lived up to his full potential. His career at Tottenham and Lazio had been interrupted by injury, and his temperament was often called into question. Many wondered if he were still fit enough for the more physical Scottish game, or if he would be able to curb his temper when faced with hard-tackling Scottish defenders.

During his three seasons at Ibrox, Paul Gascoigne proved a valuable asset; along with Brian Laudrup, he was perhaps the only genuine world-class player performing in the Scottish League. An outstanding success, he was also more than controversial on and off the field.

The first Old Firm clash took place in the Coca-Cola quarter-final at Celtic Park on 19 September 1995, and Rangers triumphed through a late goal by McCoist from Gascoigne's inch-perfect cross. It had been a splendid match, and a credit to both sides but, before the match, the bookmakers had been accepting bets that Gascoigne would be red-carded, unable to control his temper in the volcanic atmosphere of an Old Firm clash. Nobody would have been surprised, given his reputation and temperament, but during that fiery contest Gascoigne was restrained and well-behaved.

Shortly afterwards, however, all such bets ceased as it had become patently obvious that referees in Scotland were most reluctant – or perhaps even afraid – to discipline the Englishman. Celtic supporters, and those of most other clubs, were incensed that Gascoigne appeared increasingly to be immune from drastic punishment by Scottish referees as his on-field behaviour worsened. The clearest indication of this came in an Ibrox match against Aberdeen with John Rowbotham (Kirkcaldy), a promising young referee, in charge. Gascoigne was at his most irritating; he produced flashes of brilliant football, enough to show that his talent was on an entirely different level from other players, but his behaviour was disgraceful.

He did not accept any form of challenge, fair or not: when in possession he flailed his arms and elbows to create more space, and did so to the physical harm of his opponents; he snarled at his markers, and argued with the referee. Bob Crampsey, who attended the match as a radio commentator and whose judgements are formed by a lifelong devotion to Queen's Park and an admiration for skill and sportsmanship, was aghast: 'That afternoon Gascoigne should have been ordered off on four different occasions.' And he added in the tones of the Scottish headmaster that he once was, 'It would have been better for him if he had been!' In a comment made to *The Absolute Game* in March, 1997 Crampsey was still fuming about the situation: 'The failure of our referees to apply the laws of the game to Paul Gascoigne is a lasting disgrace and an indication of dereliction of duty.'

Nobody had any doubt that the referee had consciously avoided giving Gascoigne the red card; any other player would have been dismissed immediately. Rowbotham was rightly criticised for his handling of the match and it was claimed that he had been effectively downgraded as a consequence although this was never made public by the SFA. I have been assured since by a Rangers official that Mr. Rowbotham left the pitch at Ibrox Park that day reasonably satisfied with his own performance; only later, after reviewing the fixture on tape was he surprised (and reportedly distressed) at the incidents he had missed.

I have seen clips of this match, and Gascoigne certainly should have been dismissed, but an unfortunate pattern had been established. It was going to be increasingly difficult for any Scottish referee to impose 'the ultimate sanction' on the Englishman now – and to be remembered as the first one in the Scottish Premier League to do so.

The match officials seemed in such awe of his prodigious talents that they were prepared to ignore his most flagrant disregard of the rules, especially in his blatant use of the elbows to force his way past opponents. And the bare statistics appear to back up the suspicion that, in Scotland and playing for Rangers, Gascoigne could not be punished as other players; he played 103 competitive matches in Scotland for Rangers, and was ordered off once. Significantly, however, continental referees were more prepared to enforce the rules, as his poor disciplinary record in European matches testifies. He appeared in only fifteen European matches but was ordered-off twice.

The favouritism allegedly extended to the Ibrox club has been a recurring *leitmotif* in Scottish football for decades, and it would be too facile to consider it as sour grapes, or jealousy on the part of their rivals. However, as suggested by the commentary on an official tape-cassette celebrating Rangers' 120th anniversary in 1994, the Govan side were aware of the allegations: there were ' ... mutterings among disenchanted opponents. Some there were to believe that the intimidating atmosphere of Ibrox swayed referees, some felt certain referees were given to handshakes with Rangers directors, and others said that referees were scared of Rangers and their supporters.'

These comments were made in regard to Rangers' remarkable run of success throughout World War II and immediately afterwards. Bobby Brown, Rangers goalkeeper from 1946 onwards, and a later manager of Scotland, took up that theme shortly afterwards on the same tape: 'Queen of the South had never beaten Rangers, and they had a corner on the right very near the end. I asked the referee how much time was left, and he said, "You're alright; it's time-up after this corner." A header by Jim Paterson of the home side found the net, but was promptly disallowed. George Young took the resulting free-kick, and the referee blew the final whistle immediately afterwards.' Brown continued: 'Two years after that, I was privileged to attend a presentation at a lodge for that referee, and in his speech of thanks he said that in his eighteen years of football his proudest boast was that he had never refereed a losing Rangers team.'

Incidentally the two most assiduous of Old Firm historians, Robert McElroy (Rangers) and Pat Woods (Celtic), have been unable to identify the referee from Brown's recollections. Working separately, the two have reached the conclusion that Brown has erred in indicating that Queen of the South were the victims of the referee's bias, or that Palmerston was the venue.[56]

---

[56] However, an extract from *Voices of the Old Firm* contributed by Ian McColl also suggests it was a fixture against QOS: 'George Young was giving the referee a bit of chat; it looked like back-chat, an argument because Queen of the South had a free-kick and they were pushing men forward. As it turned out, the referee was a Rangers supporter and – so they said afterwards – he was telling George that if the goal went in for Queen of the South then he would disallow it!'

However, the match in which Gascoigne was finally sent off took place at Celtic Park on 19 November 1997 and the Rangers player for once could be considered slightly unlucky. The referee was the same John Rowbotham, called in at the last minute when the scheduled official (J. McCluskey) was injured and had to cry off. It was the Kirkcaldy referee's first important match since the infamous Rangers–Aberdeen encounter at Ibrox in 1995, and he ordered off the Rangers midfielder after fifty-eight minutes when he clashed with Celtic's Morten Wieghorst.

Certainly, a hand was raised and there was an attempt at contact, but worse incidents than that had gone unpunished during the match. The indignation – or, more accurately, the fury – this harsh ordering-off provoked among Rangers officials and supporters matched any of the more extreme cases of Celtic paranoia. The opinion most frequently voiced from Rangers men was that the referee had been incapable of acting objectively, given the circumstances of his previous 'demotion'.

Perhaps the furore was more due to a last-minute equaliser for Celtic by Alan Stubbs, a goal that kept Celtic's title hopes alive. However, Paul Gascoigne, ordered off in an Old Firm match, was no longer 'immune' and he picked up a five-match suspension. Accordingly, it came as little surprise that later in the season he was transferred to Middlesbrough.

The treatment accorded Paul Gascoigne was a major source of irritation to Celtic supporters, but they felt convinced more and more that, during the 1995/96 and 1996/97 seasons, referees were making it much harder for Celtic to compete on a level playing field. *The Herald* printed a letter on 13 May 1996 from Mr. John Grieve of Newton Stewart outlining the complaints of Celtic supporters during the 1995/96 season: 'Gascoigne's undeniable talents have won matches, matches he should not have played in had officials not blatantly ignored his vicious assaults on opposing players – he should have been ordered from the field on several occasions. Many of Celtic's drawn matches would have resulted in victories had officials not intervened to deny Celtic. To summarise, Celtic were cheated out of the league championship by bigoted wee men masquerading as referees.'

No doubt Mr. Grieve would have been thinking of the strange ordering-off of Peter Grant at Tynecastle on 23 September when the Celtic midfielder was involved in an off-the-ball incident with John Robertson which the stand-side linesman drew to the referee's attention. The odd thing was that this linesman was more than sixty yards from the clash and the other linesman closer to it – and he was only ten yards away – had decided to ignore the pair's squaring-off!

Or the appropriately-named Mr. Grieve could have been remembering a 0–0 draw at Rugby Park on 21 October when the referee (Martin Clark of Edinburgh) felt that, when John Collins was literally wrestled to the ground inside the penalty area by two Kilmarnock defenders with a few minutes left, the Celtic player had been dispossessed fairly. According to a reliable source, the referee, after seeing the incident on television, had the grace to admit he had 'got it completely wrong'.

Or he might have recalled the incident very late in a 0–0 draw at Brockville on 10 February when Jacky McNamara was the victim of 'a forward's tackle' by Maurice Johnston on the penalty line in the closing stages. Or he could have been thinking of the unlucky McNamara's ordering-off at Ibrox on 17 March in one of the few incidents in a remarkably sporting atmosphere.

Or perhaps he was recalling that on 23 March Mr. Clyde of Bearsden had disallowed a 'goal' by Pierre van Hooijdonk late in the drawn match at Fir Park on the dubious grounds of offside when the Dutch striker netted Paul McStay's rebound off the crossbar. He was not alone in condemning that decision because the referee was reported as having received anonymous phone calls during the next week threatening him with bodily harm.

Mr. Grieve did not mention it in his letter but perhaps the most significant 'injustice' endured by Celtic was the delay in having Jorge Cadete registered to play as the season entered its closing stages.

During the following season (1996/97) things got worse for Celtic, at least in the fraying relationship with referees.

Many of Celtic's grievances arose out of matches with Rangers and it was hard not to sympathise with them for a virtual catalogue of misfortune at Ibrox Stadium on 28 September 1996 when the referee was Mr. W. Young. The flamboyant Italian newcomer Paolo di Canio was denied a stonewall penalty kick early in the match when he was tripped by Rangers' Gough; not only was it a penalty kick but the Rangers captain, as 'the last man', should have been dismissed automatically. 'Tosh' McKinlay was booked twice inside forty-one minutes for two very innocuous offences and was sent off. During the second half a shot from Peter Grant struck the post and ran tantalisingly along Rangers' goal-line. One Celtic supporter, almost apoplectic with suppressed rage, commented: 'Remember that Rangers' goals were scored in the second half when they were faced with ten men. Who scored for them? Albertz took a corner on the left and Gough headed it in. And Albertz again broke away – right after John Hughes struck the bar with a header – and crossed for Gascoigne to head the other goal in the last minute. Think about it – Albertz, Gough, and Gascoigne all should have been ordered off before those goals!'

The radio commentary dwelt on the fact that Jorg Albertz had engaged in an uncharacteristic episode of stamping on the prone Brian O'Neil in the first half and that the linesman, although within a few feet, ignored the offence. The TV coverage, which omitted the Albertz incident, clearly showed Paul Gascoigne later taking a sly kick at Brian O'Neil's ankle, but none of the officials spotted it.

On 2 January 1997 Celtic again experienced controversial officiating at Ibrox. Rangers were below strength for this fixture, but held the interval lead thanks to a stunning free kick from Albertz; Celtic pressed throughout the second half and di Canio equalised. Rangers were reeling under the Celtic onslaught, but Stubbs had to withdraw with fifteen minutes left and a mix-up between McNamara and O'Neil allowed Andersen to put Rangers ahead with only a few minutes left. Once more Celtic took up the attack and Cadete from ten yards out scored what looked like the equaliser, but the linesman's flag had shot up and the 'goal' was disallowed by the referee, Jim McCluskey (Stewarton).

The immediate assumption was that Cadete had strayed into an offside position, but TV coverage showed clearly that he was onside when he gathered the ball to drive it past Goram. The next hypothesis to be offered on behalf of the officials was that Cadete may have handled the ball before shooting for goal. However, the TV reruns did not suggest that a hand had been used; it seemed more probable that Cadete had controlled the awkward ball on his hip.[57] Controversy was in the air and Celtic partisans wondered about the role of the linesman who was positioned perfectly to judge on offside, but who was at least thirty-five yards from an alleged 'handball' which occurred on his blind side. Again the TV coverage suggested that the linesman was the person contributing the vital input into the decision, and during the next week his objectivity was to be called into question.

Newspapers, and the tabloids in particular, were forced to print articles suggesting that the linesman had a strong emotional attachment to Rangers, with several 'witnesses' volunteering the information that he was a keen, if not passionate, Rangers supporter. In the wake of these revelations – and in view of the current mood of hysteria as Rangers closed in on Celtic's record – it was not too surprising that he received malicious phone calls. It was even claimed that his life had been threatened.[58]

---

[57] I spoke to Jim McCluskey in September 2000, after he had retired from refereeing, and he confirmed these details. Cadete had not handled the ball, but had 'deadened' it on his hip; the linesman, in a better position, had indicated offside. McCluskey, noting that there were no protests from Celtic players, had virtually dismissed the incident from his mind – until ten minutes after the match when he was approached by a television commentator asking about the goal. McCluskey, of course, was unable to comment but, after being asked several times, suggested that the commentator should look at the videotape and watch the referee's gestures. The footage shows the official raising his arm to indicate an indirect free kick, and thus confirming that the decision had been made for offside.

[58] During the following season apparently the same linesman was involved in further controversy during a Hearts–Rangers fixture at Tynecastle. The home crowd, incensed at some doubtful offside decisions, hurled abuse and missiles in his direction and the match was halted while the official received medical attention. For the Premier League fixture on 27 August 2000 between Celtic and Rangers some tabloids drew attention to the fact that he was listed as one of the match officials. Ironically, Sutton's goal in the first minute could well have been ruled out for offside.

During that season Celtic's poor discipline became increasingly a matter for debate. The more fanatical of Celtic followers, perhaps already preparing excuses in advance for Rangers winning the title and equalling a proud Parkhead record, assumed that bias on the part of referees had played a significant part. It would be worthwhile examining in some detail the sendings-off before drawing any conclusion. On 10 August at Pittodrie in the first league fixture of the season the new central defender Alan Stubbs was sent off in the second half and 'Tosh' McKinlay was also red-carded as he left the pitch. On 14 September Brian O'Neil was dismissed at Tannadice, as was Peter Grant at Tynecastle in a League Cup quarter-final at Tynecastle only three days later. McKinlay, of course, was sent off at Ibrox on 28 September and Gordon Marshall was ordered off at Celtic Park in the fixture against Motherwell on 12 October. Paolo di Canio was dismissed on 30 November in the home-match against Hearts. On 16 March, Malky McKay was sent off against Rangers, and di Canio was also red-carded for his part in confrontations after the whistle. The manager, Tommy Burns, was fined £3,000 in October for an incident which took place during the previous season.

This list of misdemeanours was embarrassingly lengthy and it would be futile to argue that all of these decisions were wrong, but in some cases Celtic were unlucky. Stubbs gave away a penalty kick at Pittodrie from which Aberdeen equalised and, from the perspective of the referee (H. Dallas), it was the only possible decision. However, the TV evidence from a camera behind the goal shows clearly that Stubbs went for the ball and won it, and that Aberdeen's Duncan Shearer had played for the penalty. Brian O'Neil could be considered a shade unlucky at Tannadice when he tangled with Dundee United's Billy Dodds, as most onlookers felt that Dodds had been the player more at fault. And, of course, McKinlay's dismissal at Ibrox was universally condemned by the media as harsh.

The other orderings-off do not deserve too much sympathy: two of them (McKinlay at Aberdeen and di Canio at Celtic Park against Rangers) took place after the final whistle and involved pointless arguing with opponents. The other offences appeared clear-cut cases of cause and effect, where a serious offence produces a red card automatically.

In fact, it seems clear that Celtic players approached that season with a sense of desperation and discipline was among the first of their attributes to erode. For example, it would be difficult to blame European referees for an ingrained bias against Celtic players, and Celtic's disciplinary record in a brief European run was equally miserable. Simon Donnelly was sent off at Kosice on 6 August, while both John Hughes and Malky McKay were dismissed at Hamburg on 2 September.

It is not my intention to draw attention to individual decisions (or officials) because a referee has a thankless task, even in the most humdrum encounter. He has to make numerous decisions over the course of the ninety minutes: he has to rule on the fairness of every challenge for the ball; he has to consider instantaneously whether to allow the advantage rule; he has to establish a working-relationship with his linesmen; he has to deal with the personalities of twenty-two professional athletes; and he has to control every situation tactfully but firmly. In addition, he is all too aware that one doubtful decision will be the focus of attention rather than the ninety-nine per cent of other decisions which were perfectly correct.

I have every sympathy for referees but, during those two seasons, there were far too many decisions which went against Celtic as they attempted to thwart Rangers in their record-equalling attempt. Too many other Celtic supporters felt that the motivation for this perceived bias against the side was bigotry on the part of the officials – or favouritism towards Rangers.

One school of thought inclines to the view that both Celtic and Rangers, especially when playing at home, do get an edge in the close decisions. Even Tommy Burns subscribes to this way of thinking: 'It's hard to be totally fair when 40,000 fanatics are screaming for a penalty kick. Even if a referee turns down one claim, it makes him think. And, later on in the match if another appeal is made who knows.'

Burns shares this view with most supporters of teams outside the Old Firm, but what happens when Celtic face Rangers?

It would appear beyond dispute that more of the doubtful decisions go Rangers' way and, unfortunately, this does not appear to be a situation that corrects itself over the course of a season or longer. This discrepancy, I would submit, is a cause for concern for Scottish football. I am sure that most referees are not motivated by a sense of religious or racial bias, but the feeling persists that it is much easier to give Rangers the benefit of a doubt than Celtic. A Canadian friend suggested a simpler answer: 'Rangers are usually the best team in Scotland, and think of what happens in a championship boxing match and it is a close thing; a contender has to knock the champion out, because he won't get the decision if it is close; the champion always gets the breaks from the officials.'

The feeling persists also that referees tend to be punished more harshly for making errors that favoured Celtic than for ones that favoured Rangers. It would be impossible to prove, of course, but it remains a constant factor in the equation that constitutes the Old Firm. A letter printed in the *Glasgow Herald* of 25 October 1989 discussed the alleged paranoia of Celtic followers:

> ... these same Celtic fans have recently seen on television [in a documentary] how 20% of the police force are members of a secret organisation, some of whom broke the law of the land to protect and help their fellow members. It was also pointed out that membership of this organisation was proportionally higher in Scotland than in England or Wales. I wonder if any of our referees and linesmen know the existence of this organisation.

Scotland is not the only football country to have some reservations about the calibre of refereeing. In Italy, Lazio issued a veiled threat in 1999 to quit Serie A and join a European Super League following yet another controversial refereeing decision which had left Italian football in turmoil and all but handed the title to Juventus. Parma equalised in the ninetieth minute against Juventus only for referee Massimo de Santis to chalk it off for pushing. 'Evidence' from the television coverage totally disproved this, and Lazio president Sergio Cragnotti was emphatic: 'Our football has to be completely rebuilt. Everybody, whether fans or not, saw what happened in Turin – and no one can explain why that goal wasn't allowed.'

This may seem to be an overreaction to one disallowed goal but the background reveals a familiar pattern. For years it has been widely held that teams from the North of Italy are favoured by referees, and that Juventus (of Turin) gets many more favourable decisions than any other club but, so far, there does not appear to be insinuations of paranoia about the situation. There have been suggestions that referees have been intimidated or influenced, accusations which have encouraged debate on the matter of establishing a cadre of full-time, professional referees.

AS Roma, for example, admitted giving handsome Christmas presents to officials: two top officials of the Italian Referees' Association received £10,000 gold Rolex watches, thirty-six referees were presented with silver Rolexes, while linesmen received more modest versions. When the issue came to light, the club attempted to describe the gifts as 'a traditional practice' and only Juventus among top clubs claimed not to have given presents. The Milan newspaper *Corriere della Sera* reported persistent rumours that the weekly allocation of referees to fixtures was rigged, and public prosecutors launched official investigations both in Turin and Rome. The Turin investigation had been established originally to look into doping accusations in August, 1998 but was widened to investigate the allegations of bribery and fraud.

However, at no time in the controversy in Italy (or England) has the question of possible religious bias been raised as a motivation. It would be pleasant to contemplate such a time in Scotland, when a referee could be labelled as incompetent pure and simple without any thought to the man's alleged religious affiliation, or to categorise a top-ranking official's performance as poor on a particular occasion without being considered paranoid.

Even in England there has been widespread condemnation of match officials, especially in televised fixtures where instant or slow motion reruns indicate errors on their part. Recently, one top referee admitted his mistake in a vital league match and effectively withdrew the red card he had assigned a Liverpool player. The only official in Scotland that I can recall having the maturity openly to admit wrong decisions has been Jim McCluskey, recently retired after sixteen seasons as a Class 1 official. This referee admitted that in an Old Firm match at Ibrox in January 1999 he had erred badly in not giving a penalty kick to Celtic, when Mahe was tackled by Kanchelskis, and, even more significantly, he reversed his decision about ordering off Jacky McNamara in a League Cup semi-final against Kilmarnock when he realised that the Celtic player previously had not been given a yellow card in the match. Such honesty is neither a sign of weakness, nor does it reduce a referee's stature; it earns him more respect from players and spectators alike.

It is generally agreed that referees are only human, and prone to error; it would not be fatal for officialdom to recognise the fact and admit to the occasional unintentional miscarriage of justice by a referee. The attitude of the SFA bureaucracy in 'covering up' for officials is understandable, but perhaps unhelpful. When Celtic played Motherwell at Fir Park on 29 October 2000, a shot from Mjallby was hooked away by a Motherwell defender, and Celtic's appeals for a goal turned down. Afterwards, the SFA refereeing spokesman Donald McVicar 'explained': 'The assistant referee was unable to get a clear view and, having watched the incident on TV, it was not at all clear first time round. You required several replays before you could reach any decision.' No doubt the SFA man was trying to help the match officials but even the most short-sighted person watching the television coverage could see immediately that the ball had crossed the line – and by a considerable distance. Surely it would have been more productive to admit that a serious mistake had been made – and leave it at that?

Paul McStay and Tom Boyd in a frank exchange of views with an official.

Indeed, referees have a thankless task, particularly in the modern era and one has to wonder why anybody would want to become a referee. One Referee Supervisor volunteered various possibilities: as a means of remaining physically fit; as an opportunity to remain involved in football longer; as a method of achieving a personal ambition, or a degree of fame. He discounted the suggestion that some referees were attracted by the money, although the current rate of close to £300 for a Premier League assignment is a reasonable reward. He pointed out that most officials were professional men and not likely to be attracted solely by financial considerations, a feeling endorsed by a former referee: 'There is a terrible snobbery which afflicts refereeing. Basically, the higher your professional standing, the greater your chance of becoming a top referee. If a lawyer and a lorry driver are vying for a place on the FIFA list, you can bet your bottom dollar the man behind the wheel will miss out.'[59]

One factor which makes football rather unique among sports is the fact that all decisions, with the exception of the advantage-rule, have to be instantaneous. Watch a cricket test match and look at the umpire as he considers an appeal; he sometimes takes several seconds re-running the situation over in his mind before giving his decision. Similarly, umpires in American-type football can hold mini-conferences on the gridiron or call for backup information from the cameras to help in the correct decision-making, while rules officials in golf can take ages in deciding what options are available to the player.

The luxury of time is denied to football referees because the nature of the game is different; football is characterised by its fluidity, whereas other sports have a stop-and-start pattern.

Modern players present new and different challenges for referees. As performers on the field, their emphasis is increasingly on pace, and they are much more professional in their training and level of fitness. They are now highly paid athletes and dedicated to maintaining that standard of life, but the financial rewards for success bring out at least one unsavoury aspect of professionalism; more and more nowadays some players readily resort to cheating in order to gain an advantage.

Forwards have developed the art of tumbling down inside the penalty area at the slightest hint of physical contact made by a defender. At its worst the custom is diving or, in the jargon of referees, simulation – an attempt to con the referee into giving a penalty kick, with the added bonus that a fellow-professional is likely to be yellow-carded at least for the challenge.

Referees of an older vintage find this practice difficult to accept. Conditioned to award a penalty kick when an attacker goes down inside the

---

[59] Both Jim McCluskey and Hugh Dallas drive Jaguars with personalised number plates; as a precaution, McCluskey waited until he retired as a referee before getting his number plate fitted.

area, these officials find themselves more and more embarrassed when television replays later show that little or no contact was made, and that the spectacular tumble looks more and more like a theatrical stunt. Some referees simply refuse to rule on such incidents unless they are totally certain of the rightness of their decision. This reaction on the part of referees can rebound heavily on the likes of a Paolo di Canio who was frequently denied stonewall penalty kicks in Scotland (and now with West Ham apparently) because the officials are most reluctant to have to admit later that they were duped.

The most common method employed at the present time to stop a tricky forward is to hold him back by tugging at his shirt, and this can be difficult to detect from the fixed perspective of a referee. Unfortunately for the match official, thousands in the ground can see the offence from their places in the stands. So prevalent has shirt pulling become that most referees tend to ignore all but the most blatant of offences. This mind-set by officials can only harm their effectiveness, and one can only wonder at the non-interference by the assistant-referees (or the fourth official).

These tactics, reflecting no credit on the practitioners, are cynical and calculated but, paradoxically, many players have little self-discipline when expressing dissent either through words or gestures. Despite advice from coaches and managers, players are booked more frequently for dissent than for any other offence, the manager's instructions being simply ignored in the heat of battle.

A word in your ear!
The consequences of further
misdemeanours are made abundantly
clear to Celtic's Bertie Auld

Thus, good man-management – or common sense – is a valuable quality in assessing a referee but it is very difficult for an official to stand mute and apparently helpless, when his decisions, usually correct, are being questioned so openly and disrespectfully in such a public forum. I was impressed with the response given by one present-day supervisor who told me how he dealt with the hot-tempered Jimmy Johnstone: 'If you're fouled and hurt, Jimmy, go down and stay down, and leave me to deal with the player on my own. If you're fouled and feel a red mist coming on, get the hell down the park – and let me handle it. I only want to discipline one player not two.'

Some much-needed support was given recently to beleaguered officials in dealing with the problem of offside. A

162

study conducted by the Free University of Amsterdam suggests that offside decisions are made much more difficult by the perspective of the linesmen because in ninety per cent of cases the linesmen were normally situated one metre beyond the last defender. Raoul Oudejans explains: 'This distorts their perception of the situation drastically; attackers on the far side of defenders would appear from this angle to be in front when they are actually alongside – and therefore onside.'

What is the requirement for a referee in Scotland?

Would-be referees usually start officiating, invariably as linesmen or assistant referees, at a minor level – amateur or juvenile football. The minimum age is sixteen and the maximum is fifty. Prior to that, he (or she) would have taken and passed a twelve-week course with a final written exam; a refresher course is required one year later, and again a pass-mark of eighty per cent is needed.

At the highest level in Scotland – the Grade 1 standard – there are usually slightly more than thirty officials accredited; for the 2000/2001 season there were thirty-six, the highest number so far. Promotion is based on several factors, most importantly assessment by qualified Referee Supervisors, who are usually retired referees themselves. Most referees on the Grade 1 List have reached that pinnacle between the ages of twenty-eight to thirty although there is a present-day emphasis on accelerated promotion at a younger age. This recognises the fact that officials have to be fitter in order to keep up with the pace of the modern game, but it does mean that some higher qualified referees are lacking in experience.

At one time referees were allotted matches by a form of ballot, but the system is more organised and elitist at present; normally, referees know their schedules for the next eight fixtures and the Scottish Premier League (and other highly rated fixtures) are assigned Scotland's FIFA referees, and sometimes another emerging official based on his reports. Scotland automatically is allowed seven qualified FIFA referees who become eligible to officiate at European matches and international matches; thus, the seven most highly rated referees in Scotland are *de facto* FIFA ranked.

I was intrigued by this number and contacted the SFA to ask about it and to find out the numbers for other countries. The SFA spokesman was most reluctant to comment on the subject, citing confidentiality as his reason, but did provide me with FIFA's telephone number. When I contacted FIFA, I was given the information quite readily. The largest number assigned to any one country is ten, and the likes of France, Spain, Italy and Germany were given that number. In 2000/01 England were assigned nine and the FIFA spokesman did not know the reason but suggested that 'perhaps the FA nominated only that number, or FIFA accepted only nine of the ten nominations.' Among the smaller countries both Northern Ireland and Eire have four, while Wales has three. The FIFA spokesman made the significant comment: ' The number of referees allocated depends on the strength of the league.' In other words the number of Scottish referees on the FIFA list is a reflection of the calibre of Scottish teams rather than an assessment of the referee's worth.

It is strange to report that there are as many as twelve regional bodies in such a relatively small country as Scotland. The Class 1 officials come together on a semi-regular basis at meetings under the auspices of the SFA and are usually chaired by George Cumming, the SFA Referee Development Director, and/or Drew Herbison, the Head of the Disciplinary Department.[60]

Referees are a breed apart; they are necessary, but not liked. Being unpopular is part of the job description and, accordingly, there is a camaraderie that exists within the fraternity. Gatherings like the annual conferences held at St. Andrews are essential for morale, but in recent years dissatisfaction appears to have grown. One now-retired referee complained publicly that it was now like going back to school: in 1993, for example, he noted that the referees 'were ordered to wear white teeshirts, while the supervisors wore blue ones of a superior quality'.

He also complained bitterly about the man he held responsible for the needless bureaucracy, George Cumming: 'Yet, when he [Cumming] was a Grade 1 referee in the 80s, his markings weren't high enough to earn him a place on the FIFA list. He never handled a European cup-tie, an international match, he was never given an Old Firm occasion, never officiated at a Scottish or League Cup final – not even a semi-final.'

As has been seen, referees are graded in a hierarchical system and, of course, promotion within that system is valued highly. It is a system that encourages conformity, and many referees have expressed the thought that they are being stifled because a supervisor will criticise them for not applying the letter of the law. A referee deemed guilty of a technical fault is penalised by the deduction of points from his rating; such deductions can quickly lead to the loss of FIFA status or to demotion.

One former referee told me that 'the 18th Law' was the most important – and he was referring to the application of common sense. For example, if a player has to be booked as a calming device, it is better to give the yellow card to a forward; the point has been made, and the chances of awkward ramifications later have been reduced. In some situations common sense should take precedence over the wishes of a bureaucracy, but ... .

I asked the same referee to outline his routine on match-day, and it went as follows:

> I usually arrive at the ground about an hour and a half before the kick-off, if possible, thus by-passing the crowds. I prefer to go straight to the Referee's Room and have a drink, or

---

[60] Mr. Cumming has since taken up an administrative position with FIFA.

more likely a cup of tea and a scone, and watch the TV in the room, chatting with my lines-men. We examine the pitch about an hour before the kick-off, just about the time the first spectators are being allowed into the ground. More than likely, I had parked my car at a hotel about 12:30 for an afternoon kick-off and had been picked up by a club official. After the game, if everything has gone well, I mix a little with the players, and/or officials in their tea room; but, if there has been any controversy or bad feeling in the match, I leave quickly and quietly.

An issue frequently raised is that of the recruiting of referees throughout Scotland. It has been suggested openly by some Celtic partisans that Catholics are discouraged from entering the avocation – or, if admitted, subjected to a more rigorous assessment process than non-Catholics. One former referee, now dead, claimed there was blatant discrimination against Catholics attempting to become referees. He explained his own success in the following way: 'As a Catholic referee you have to be twice as good to be accepted; fortunately that is not too hard.' The consequence of such discouragement in certain areas of the country, and in Lanarkshire in particular, is that some would-be officials simply do not apply and are lost to football.

The case of K.F. O'Donnell (Airdrie) is frequently cited as an example of discrimination practised against a referee who is Catholic and, therefore, perceived to be 'a Celtic supporter'. After more than three seasons as a Grade I official, O'Donnell was downgraded to the rank of linesman and shortly afterwards decided to leave football altogether to concentrate on his full-time career, in which he is now a Head Teacher.

Always enthusiastic about football, O'Donnell took up refereeing when he realised that he had no great skill as a player, and he admits to being inspired by the example of his townsman, R.H. Davidson. He moved up the ranks and without too much controversy or fuss, until he was appointed as a Class I official in 1984 at the age of thirty-four. His progress had been steady, and he recalls with a certain amount of pride that he acted as referee in three Scottish Junior Cup semi-finals, and also as linesman at two Junior Cup finals. The atmosphere in junior football in Scotland, especially cup-ties, can often be more challenging and personally intimidating than at regular fixtures in the Scottish League.

I have been informed that his ratings as a Grade I referee for the three years were as follows: 'tenth or eleventh out of thirty-one', 'nearer the middle out of thirty-one or thirty-two', and 'probably at the bottom out of thirty-one'. These figures were quoted from memory by an SFA official, which accounts for their vagueness, and they suggest an unusual pattern. In his first season, O'Donnell was rated quite highly – higher than sixty-six per cent of his colleagues – but his ratings started to slip in the next two seasons.

The situation worsened dramatically in the aftermath of his handling of a Celtic–Hearts league match at Celtic Park on 12 August 1987, played in heavy underfoot conditions, during which he was involved in two contentious decisions. John Colquhoun, then with Hearts, tumbled in the penalty area after a challenge from a Celtic defender; Mark McGhee clashed with Dave McPherson of Hearts but recovered quickly enough to net the only goal of the match despite protests from the visiting players.

O'Donnell admits that these decisions were difficult to call but, given the fact that his reaction-time was virtually instantaneous, his reasoning seems valid: 'John Colquhoun went down, making a meal of it but the tackle was not that bad,' and 'McGhee and McPherson are both big men, and had been using their weight all through the match. The incident was no worse than several I had permitted by both of them earlier.'

Immediately after the match, O'Donnell, a slightly-built, somewhat diffident man, was verbally abused by some of Hearts' coaching staff in the dugout as he left the pitch, and he heard several insults being hurled back and forth between the two dug-outs. These were typically heat-of-the-moment responses, and O'Donnell was probably wise to ignore them, but the chairman of Hearts (Wallace Mercer) took up the matter of his refereeing at a more official level later.[61] Clearly, Hearts players and representatives felt they had been treated badly by a referee they suspected of having Celtic sympathies. They were reasonably accurate in their assumptions: O'Donnell had always considered himself a Celtic supporter but felt confident that this background was never allowed to influence his decision-making on the field, pointing out with some pride that he had always been able to referee Rangers matches without any problems, even at a period when Graeme Souness' sides were noted for disciplinary problems.[62]

Unfortunately for O'Donnell, the Referee Supervisor agreed with the feelings of the Edinburgh side regarding the two vital decisions: in his opinion, Hearts should have been awarded a penalty, and Celtic's goal should have been disallowed. O'Donnell admits himself that he could have been wrong, but insists that his decisions were made objectively and fairly. As an established Class I official, he deserved to be given the benefit of any doubt.

However, from then on the authorities decided to keep a closer watch on

[61] Wallace Mercer, until he assumed the chairmanship of Heart of Midlothian, considered himself a Rangers supporter. He also stated, upon taking over Hearts: 'The first day I joined the club I was invited to join the Masons. My father was a Mason, and I wouldn't say anything to criticise the organisation, but I decided the moment I took over the mantle of responsibility for Hearts it would be a non-religious, non-political club.'

[62] Several other referees have made claims of similar impartiality; for example, W. Crombie, a self-confessed Hearts supporter in his youth, was the referee in charge of the Dundee–Hearts fixture at Dens Park on 3 May 1986 when the Edinburgh side lost a golden opportunity to win the championship – and he had also handled several Hearts–Hibs derbies over the course of his career. On the same day as the Dundee–Hearts match, A. Waddell (Edinburgh), his fellow-townsman, refereed the St Mirren–Celtic clash at Love Street without much anxiety being expressed by Celtic beforehand.

Mr. O'Donnell and he was under intense surveillance from his superiors, much more so than normal for a referee of three years' experience at the highest level in Scotland. As he points out reasonably enough: 'If I had not been doing well up to that point, why on earth was I entrusted with such an important fixture so early in the season?'

Years later, O'Donnell still remains disturbed about his treatment: 'I felt this surveillance was unfair, and it had an unsettling effect on my level of performance. If you are being watched very closely, it becomes more difficult to concentrate on the game itself, and to make decisions immediately without having to think about all the possible consequences.'

His ratings, based on the reports of the Referee Supervisors, plummeted with shocking suddenness: on 12 August he had been assigned the coveted Celtic–Hearts match; by Christmas he had been warned that he might be downgraded; by February 1988 the SFA had decided to drop him to the rank of linesman. Shockingly, O'Donnell first learned of his actual demotion by having a school colleague hand him a newspaper when he entered the staff room, the news being leaked to the media before the official notification.

Although disappointed and hurt, O'Donnell still felt determined to carry on and, if possible, win back his previous standing but his first experience as a linesman showed him the reality of his new situation:

> I thought about it, and felt I should stick it out and do my best. My first appointment was at Annfield with Stirling Albion and I was determined to do my job as best I could, but there was a Referee Supervisor there – a man who had never refereed at any high level, and I think he had risen in the bureaucracy from the Amateur ranks. At any rate, he spent a great deal of his report alleging that I had allowed two substitute players too near the playing surface when they were warming up. That was the last straw. When I got that report, I decided that I had enough, and so I resigned.

O'Donnell took some consolation from the fact that the first sympathetic letter he received from another referee contained these words: 'Sorry to hear about the way you have been treated, and I am perplexed. A good referee simply does not become a bad one overnight.' Perhaps surprisingly, at least for some diehard Celtic followers, the author of those sentiments was Willie Young.

Was Kevin O'Donnell treated fairly? Was he treated any differently from other referees embroiled in controversy? And was his religion a factor in that treatment?

Apparently, the SFA did pay close attention to the complaint lodged by Hearts' Wallace Mercer, and the decision was made shortly afterwards to have the supervisors keep a close watch on Mr. O'Donnell. While this practice may be unfair, it is a normal state of affairs within bureaucratic organisations. If a man is in a supervisory role, and has been advised to watch somebody closely, it is perfectly understandable that he should assume that the person being assessed is for whatever reason *persona non grata* within the organisation.

Under these circumstances, the supervisor is expected to give lower ratings, and that is what happened in the case of Kevin Francis O'Donnell. Apparently, much the same thing happened to David Syme, a vastly experienced referee, when he was at loggerheads with the SFA as he approached his retirement; Syme's last game was a routine fixture between Dundee United and Kilmarnock, and he received the lowest mark he had ever received from a Referee Supervisor – a fifty per cent mark compared to his previous lifetime low of sixty-three per cent.

Mr. O'Donnell believes that his demotion was due, in part, to the general knowledge that he was a Catholic, and probably a Celtic supporter and some Celtic sympathisers are convinced that the treatment meted out to Mr. K.F. O'Donnell (Airdrie) was in stark contrast to that afforded Mr. R. Tait (East Kilbride).

Nobody doubted the allegiance of Bobby Tait; he was a Lanarkshire man through and through and a Rangers supporter. For many years referees in the Lanarkshire Association trained every Tuesday at Douglas Park, Hamilton (and more recently at Wishaw); according to a referee supervisor, Tait invariably wore his Rangers strip for these training sessions. Every referee has some background in football, and the good referees manage to repress their enthusiasm for one particular team. For most of his career Tait was an acceptable referee and was generally held in high regard by the players. He successfully avoided too much controversy, until the closing months of his last season (1997/1998) when he was due to retire on age grounds.

The most obvious instances involved the three clubs challenging for the championship during that season: Rangers, Hearts and Celtic. Rangers had achieved their ambition of equalling Celtic's accomplishment of nine championships in a row and were determined to surpass that record; Hearts were surprising everybody by holding on in the title race despite being considered the weakest side on paper; Celtic, under a new and pragmatic coach in Wim Jansen, were putting up a very strong challenge to thwart Rangers' bid for further glory. By beating Rangers 2–0 in the traditional Ne'erday clash at Celtic Park, the Parkhead men had moved in front in the race for the title and had become favourites.

A vital match loomed at Tynecastle on 8 February; Hearts still remained in contention for the league title but Rangers had slipped up at Ibrox the previous day with a draw against Dunfermline Athletic. Celtic led at half time with a goal scored by McNamara, and had spurned chances to increase that lead. Wieghorst netted in twelve minutes but the 'goal' was disallowed; Stubbs's low drive struck the bottom of the post; Mahe's shot was touched on to the crossbar; Brattbakk contrived to miss another open goal, and his later 'goal' ten minutes from the end was disallowed on the grounds of offside.

To be strictly accurate, the only complaint that Celtic could have had against Mr. Tait's refereeing was the decision to disallow Wieghorst's goal, which frequent TV reruns suggested had been legitimate. However, after a match which had been played at considerable speed, and one without any appreciable halt for treatment to injured players, the referee chose to add on more than four minutes stoppage-time. Hearts, rarely in the contest until the closing stages, scrambled an undeserved equaliser through Jose Quitongo. Celtic, and their supporters, were gutted at this late blow, and wondered where the extra four minutes had come from. At the end of the day, the two sides contending with Rangers for the championship had each dropped two vital points.

On 28 March he was again scheduled to referee a Celtic–Hearts clash, this time at Parkhead; astonishingly, Hearts still remained in contention for the title and came to Glasgow in a confident mood. One journalist from a quality newspaper remembers clearly being told by another just prior to the kick-off: 'Watch the referee today; Tait is going to do something!' Alerted by the conspiratorial tone, the journalist observed the performance of the match official with particular care.

The match itself was evenly contested, and well-refereed, but the defences remained in control.[63] In the latter stages Hearts had been forced back into defence, and Celtic were pressing hard for the winner, a goal which would have eliminated Hearts from the championship race and almost guaranteed Celtic the title. However, Hearts remained stubborn and held out groggily for a 0–0 draw.

The journalist who had been advised that the referee was 'going to do something' looked at his watch, and calculated that the final whistle had been blown exactly on the ninety-minute mark. He recalled that the match had been hard-fought, with several stoppages for yellow cards and treatment to injured players, most notably to Stephane Mahe with fifteen minutes left. Mahe had gone down in a clash with his compatriot Adam, had received prolonged treatment on the pitch to determine the extent of his injury, and had eventually been stretchered off by the ambulance men.

Once more the result favoured Rangers with both the other contenders dropping two points in another stalemate. Many Celtic supporters felt that the timekeeping had been a factor in these two drawn matches, and I remember feeling uncomfortable in criticising a referee for such a relatively minor matter. However, so many incidents had occurred in recent seasons, and Mr. Tait's attitude to 'injury time' was to be called into question on at least one more occasion that season as he became involved in yet another controversy.

Reports surfaced in a newspaper that he had requested to be given the Rangers–Kilmarnock league match at Ibrox as his 'farewell appearance'. Some journalists, suspicious of Tait's leanings towards Rangers, raised the

---

[63] The only questionable incident was when Neil McCann swept past Stubbs in the second half and was fouled by the defender; Mr. Tait chose to punish Stubbs with a yellow card when it could possibly have been assessed as a red-card offence.

CELTIC'S PARANOIA . . . ALL IN THE MIND?

matter in print, but the SFA attempted to deflect attention from the official by insisting that a referee had no choice in the matter, that he was assigned matches by the authorities. However, the statement of an ex-referee (David Syme) flatly contradicted that statement. Syme, who had ended his own career in dispute with the SFA, spoke bitterly about his latter-day dealings: 'It has always been the custom to allow a retiring referee the match of his choice. I chose to go to the new Hampden, where I had never worked, or to Ibrox, which would have guaranteed ending my career in front of a big crowd. They offered me Firhill instead – I elected to go on holiday.'

On 2 May, the second last Saturday of the league schedule, Mr. R. Tait did officiate at Ibrox Park for the last time as a Class 1 referee, and apparently at his own request. Another referee (J. McGillvray of Edinburgh) who had 'retired' unexpectedly and in controversial circumstances in mid-season pointed out gratuitously that 'Tait's allegiance to Rangers is well known'.[64] Celtic supporters, trying to cope with the strain of a tight championship race, were accused of paranoia when they subsequently raised the matter of this potential conflict of interest.

As Celtic were not due to play Dunfermline Athletic till Sunday, I listened to the second half of the Rangers–Kilmarnock match on radio. Kilmarnock, still hopeful of a place in Europe, came to Ibrox prepared to defend; Rangers had to win to keep in touch with Celtic at the top of the league. At half time the score was 0–0 in a disappointing encounter and the radio commentator pointed out that several minutes of injury time had been played, and expressed surprise at the need for this. The second half was tense: Rangers pressed forward, but without too much imagination and Kilmarnock increasingly broke out of defence. Early in the second-half stoppage time Mitchell scored the winning goal for Kilmarnock to the delight of Celtic followers everywhere. Those listening supporters must have suffered agonies as almost four minutes of injury-time was added on. However, Kilmarnock survived, and Celtic were now odds-on favourites for the title with only one week left in the campaign.

But, once again, Mr. Tait's timekeeping had been called into question with Celtic supporters feeling that some sort of poetic justice had been rendered with Mitchell's injury-time goal. One Celtic man, a former manager of the club, commented on Mr.Tait's forthcoming retirement: 'They should give him a gold watch – one that works.'

Let us consider the similarities in the background of the two officials. Both were Lanarkshire men and came from the two sides of the religious

---

[64] This referee retired very suddenly after having a poor game at Firhill (Thistle–Rangers). During the match, the official booked Paul Gascoigne for his excessive celebrations following a goal, and admitted to feeling 'sickened' by it. He also ordered off a Partick Thistle player for two bookable offences one of which was blessing himself as he left the pitch at half time.

divide in the West of Scotland. Both had started off as young referees and their probable allegiances were assumed and known to the football authorities from the start. Both had made reasonable progress through the ranks, and were recognised as competent officials.

The difference in the treatment accorded the two referees – when they were the subject of controversy or complaint – shows an interesting contrast. O'Donnell was subjected immediately to close scrutiny by the SFA supervisors and, after more than three years as a top-flight referee, was downgraded to the rank of linesman; Tait, on the other hand, was under no form of extra surveillance because of his sympathies and the authorities were quick to leap to his defence, most notably in the controversy over the choice of venue for his final appearance.

It is difficult to escape the conclusion that the accident of a man's religion – a matter which should have no relevance in his ability to perform his job – appears to be of primary importance in some parts of Scotland even at the present time. There are parallels between the cases cited above and those of A.B. Gebbie (Hamilton) and J. Callaghan (Glasgow) already discussed in previous chapters.[65] Unfortunately, it appears clear that the two Catholic officials were treated in a manifestly different manner than their non-Catholic colleagues. O'Donnell was downgraded, and Callaghan was suspended; Gebbie slipped into obscurity and Tait was defended and allowed to retire as planned.

It has been argued by some referees themselves that the recruitment of referees in Scotland has undergone a sea-change in recent decades; at one time the only things required to become a referee were a knowledge of the rules, a degree of personal fitness, enthusiasm for the sport and the application of 'the 18th Law' – common sense. The suspicion has arisen that more and more a certain social cachet is also required: Willie Young is a lawyer, as was Jim Herald. Hugh Dallas is a company director, Andrew Waddell was a pathologist, George Smith a senior civil servant, Bill Mullan a head teacher. Increasingly, there seems little room for such as Jim Callaghan, janitor, or Willie Webb, truant officer.

It raises the issue of the number of Catholic referees in Scotland, and it is a matter best exposed to the light. For decades opportunities were denied Catholics in certain trades and professions and this is beyond dispute: in banking and law, in the newspapers and later in radio and TV, in the police, in the shipyards. Clearly the situation has improved dramatically in the area of job opportunity for any young person of an Irish name and Catholic back-

---

[65] I had finished the chapter on Jim Callaghan before I was informed that he was a Catholic. In fact, the matter of a person's religion is of no importance to me and I remember the surprise on one Celtic supporter's face when I had to admit that I did not know how many Catholics played for Celtic at Lisbon in 1967.

Celtic have also had problems with European referees, as this scene from a European Cup semi-final against Atletico Madrid in 1974 illustrates.

ground. Some of the improvement has been due to a gradual acceptance of Scots with an Irish background into Scottish life, but part is also due to the undoubted fact that economic power no longer resides with native Scots. Multi-nationals based in London, Tokyo and New York are not unduly concerned with a man's religion or racial background, provided he can perform at the required level.

According to the statistics, about sixteen per cent of the population of Scotland is nominally Catholic, and yet the percentage of referees in Scotland who are Catholic is believed to be much lower. Football is still perceived as a working-class sport, and most Catholics would describe themselves as falling into that category. If the above assumptions are correct, why are they under-represented as football referees?

Two reasons have been put forward for this situation: Catholics are not given too much encouragement to enter the ranks of refereeing and, therefore, do not apply. If they do enter and qualify as referees, some feel they cannot rely on the same degree of support as their non-Catholic colleagues.

At first glance the above statements certainly do sound paranoid but, unfortunately, the anecdotal evidence seems to bear out these conclusions. The worst area appears to be in the West of Scotland where sectarianism still holds sway over too many minds, and where a high proportion of the Catholic population lives. It might be expected that the percentage of referees who are Catholic would be correspondingly higher there, but, apparently, this is not the case. One former referee shook his head gloomily, and described the situation as 'the Lanarkshire Mafia' in which Catholics are not welcomed.[66]

In a recent telephone interview with George Smith, now a Referee Supervisor, I was informed that there are just over 2,000 referees in Scotland; 180 Senior Referees, and thirty-six Grade 1 officials. Mr. Smith pointed out with some pride that the application forms sent out by the SFA do not ask any question about the would-be referee's religion – nor does it ask details about his schooling. As a member of the Grading Committee (which is responsible for the promotion or demotion of referees, based on their marks), he assured me that never had he, nor any member, raised the question of a referee's religion as a factor in the evaluation process: 'I literally have no idea if a man is Protestant or Catholic – or even Muslim – and it makes no difference to me in judging him as a referee.'

In a recent book by football journalist Bill Leckie, *Penthouse and Pavement* (Edinburgh, 1999), it was suggested by the author that Rangers and Celtic would always be given preferential treatment by Scottish referees: 'It stands to reason that, if there are thirty on the Grade One books, then maybe twenty will have a leaning towards one of the Old Firm – and will have the same in-built attitudes as everyone in the same boat.'

If the assumption is valid, that Catholics tend to support Celtic rather than other clubs, then it might be difficult to find many Grade 1 referees who have ever had any boyhood feelings for Celtic.[67]

It would be wilfully obtuse to deny that religion does not play a part in Scottish life; unfortunately, too often it exists merely as a badge of identification rather than as a vibrant faith. Take, for example, the practice of blessing oneself, a habit adopted by many footballers world-wide; in Scotland, however, it can be considered 'a bookable offence'.

In one particularly controversial fixture at Firhill in 1996 between Partick Thistle and Rangers, a player for the home side was given a yellow card for blessing himself as he left the field at the interval. The referee struggled to explain his decision: 'Rod McDonald was not booked because he blessed himself. He was booked for ungentlemanly conduct because, in the opinion

---

[66] In recent times the two most prominent Grade 1 referees who are also Catholic would have been W. Mullan (Dalkeith) and G. Smith (Edinburgh). It might be significant that neither official was located in Lanarkshire but were more identified with the East of Scotland.

[67] A doctoral dissertation, *Ethnic and Religious Identity in Modern Scotland*, by J. Bradley of Stirling University indicated the distribution of religious identity as follows: Motherwell had the highest percentage of Church of Scotland members with eighty-seven per cent and Celtic the lowest with one per cent. Celtic led the way among Roman Catholics with ninety-three per cent, followed by Hibernian with thirty-nine per cent, and Dundee United with thirty-two per cent. Hibernian were in first place with regard to 'Other Protestant Religions' with seventeen per cent, followed by Rangers with fifteen per cent. The poll consisted of 443 football fans of nine Premier League clubs.

of my linesman, it was done in such a place and in such a way as to inflame the Rangers support in that area of the ground. I have absolutely no problems with a player crossing himself – as long as it's not provocative.'

The Partick Thistle striker was cautioned later on the pitch for another minor offence and ordered off – to his obvious bewilderment. His manager, Murdo MacLeod, a non-Catholic, was equally shocked, pointing out that the player had been in the habit of blessing himself entering or leaving the field.

Most commentators felt sympathy for this player, performing in a home-fixture who had been punished for a personal religious ritual. Indeed, one of them mused about what would happen if Rangers were drawn against Barcelona in a European Cup tie and the Ibrox support were 'offended' when the visitors took the field, blessing themselves: 'Would they all be booked? Why doesn't the same common sense prevail in this country?'

The actions of the Australian international defender Tony Vidmar must have truly perplexed Rangers followers when he came on as a substitute at Celtic Park on 21 November 1998; upon taking the pitch, he immediately blessed himself! According to the 'reasoning' behind the Firhill referee's decision, he must have been in danger of being booked, and for offending his own team's supporters.

It is a nonsense to state that spectators 'could be inflamed' by a gesture that is universally practised either as a superstitious habit, or as a religious observance. It would not take much action from a club to deal with any of their supporters suffering from such 'inflammation'. For a referee to pay any disciplinary attention to such a gesture – and possibly affect the outcome of the match – is deeply disturbing and it hints at the malaise still extant within some communities in Scotland.[68]

It would be a step forward if Celtic followers, unhappy with a referee's decision-making, would concern themselves only with his competence. Referees, taunted by references to their religion or legitimacy, might understandably feel reluctant to give a doubtful decision to Celtic under those circumstances.

Ideally, a referee is able to put aside his preferences when a football match is in progress, and one Celtic supporter is always amused at the recollection of two League Cup finals. In 1957, with a Church of Scotland elder in charge, Celtic beat Rangers by 7–1, while in 1971, with a devout Roman Catholic officiating, Celtic lost 4–1 to Partick Thistle.

---

[68] Most Celtic supporters were mildly amused at Paul Gascoigne's miming of a flute as he warmed up for an appearance as a substitute at Celtic Park; the indignation was assumed rather than genuine. It should also be pointed out that this particular gesture is not one easily recognisable in most football-playing countries.

CHAPTER ELEVEN

Hugh Dallas

In the immediate aftermath of the Old Firm league match in May 1999, during which the referee, Hugh Dallas (Motherwell) was struck by coins hurled
from the stands, Celtic asked for an independent analysis to assess the extent
to which all those involved might have acted more responsibly. As part of that
review, Christopher Lewis, a behavioural psychologist, conducted an investigation and handed in his findings to Allan MacDonald, Celtic's former Chief
Executive.

In due course MacDonald submitted the two reports to the inevitable
commission of inquiry; he was thanked and commended by that body for
Celtic's willingness to examine the situation objectively and to tackle the
problems. MacDonald explained the reasoning behind the reports: 'I thought
that, bad as it [the situation] was, it could have been much worse. The security
audit concluded that we had done a good job, but made recommendations
about areas in which we could improve and these have been taken on board.
The second report was from a behavioural psychologist to determine how the
people involved could improve themselves.'

It is not known how the actual contents of the reports were made public
as presumably they were meant originally to be confidential, but the information appears to have been leaked deliberately. The tabloid press, eager as
always to sensationalise matters, deliberately highlighted references to Hugh
Dallas in the second report and reported them out of context. Even in the
more sedate press the condemnation of Celtic for commissioning such a
report was widespread, but largely unfounded. Despite the fact that this section constituted only a small part of the report, almost every journalist criticised the fact that a behavioural psychologist had dared to comment on 'the
body language of a FIFA referee'.

It would have been better for all concerned – the clubs, the players, and
the referee – if a decent period of time had elapsed before the conflict
between the Old Firm was renewed. But Celtic and Rangers were due to face
each other in the Scottish Cup final at the new National Stadium on 29 May,
a matter of weeks away, and Hugh Dallas had already been appointed to referee that match. It would have been unprecedented if the referee appointed for
such an occasion had been withdrawn. In fact, it would have been wrong as
the impression might have been given that the official had been remiss in his
handling of the previous encounter. Surprisingly, Richard Gough, a former

Rangers captain, made the recommendation shortly after the match at Celtic Park that the Scottish Cup final should be refereed by an official from another country and suggested England as the most logical choice.

The abiding image of that Parkhead match was the sight of the referee on his knees and obviously dazed with blood streaming from a head wound, the result of being struck by a coin thrown by a Celtic supporter, and the spectacle of three or four Celtic supporters trying to make their way on to the pitch with the intention of harming Mr. Dallas, and being stopped just short of their target by the intervention of Celtic players and subsequent actions by the stewards and police.

The press coverage of the fixture that had shamed Scottish football, and Celtic in particular, was vitriolic in its condemnation of the hooliganism exhibited by Celtic followers and the lapses of discipline shown by some players. Unfortunately, the one aspect that coloured any discussion of that particular Old Firm clash was that the referee had been assaulted and sustained an injury. Rational debate was, therefore, hijacked by the lurid TV images.

Most Celtic supporters recognised that Rangers' winning of the 1998/99 league title was simply a matter of time, but they did not relish the thought of the Ibrox side clinching the championship at Celtic Park. After the match, they agreed that Rangers had thoroughly deserved to win that encounter, and that Celtic's under-strength side, weakened by injury and suspension, had performed poorly.

However, they also remained convinced that Hugh Dallas had displayed questionable decision-making in the first half; the more hysterically disappointed among them, those looking for any excuse, claimed absurdly that the referee's decisions had cost Celtic the league.

Some objective commentators shared the reservations of the majority of Celtic supporters: 'Many thousands who saw the Old Firm game genuinely believe that the referee had a poor match. To describe his performance as 'good' seems to them like citing the San Francisco earthquake as a fine example of urban renewal, or Robert Maxwell as a pillar of pension-fund stability.' (*The Herald*, 3 May 1999) and 'When Dallas awarded a penalty to Rangers for an entirely innocuous collision in the area, it seemed he was either still concussed or was nursing a death-wish' (*The Scotsman*, 3 May 1999). The critical ones – and significantly, most of them were not the usual sports writers – felt that the referee had not handled the situation well, but all commended him for his courage in electing to continue as the match official.

Nothing could disguise the fact that Celtic supporters behaved disgracefully, and that some Celtic players had lost their composure in the heat of battle. Celtic took immediate steps to correct the situation: as already indicated, an outside perspective was essential and this would be provided in the form of the reports. The club apologised to the referee for his shameful treatment – in fact,

Allan MacDonald did so immediately at the end of the game. The two Celtic players (Stephane Mahe and Vidar Riseth) ordered off by Mr. Dallas were ordered to write public letters of apology, and they were fined heavily, Mahe reputedly £12,000 and Riseth £6,000.[69] A telephone hot line was set up to receive information about the hooliganism and those supporters responsible; anybody who had transgressed, either by being arrested by police at the time or through the evidence of CCTV tapes captured on camera, was given a lifetime ban from Celtic Park, in addition to any punishment meted out by the courts. Security measures inside the ground were reviewed and tightened.[70]

This was not enough for some sports writers in the tabloids and the conduct of Stephane Mahe was criticised to an exceptional degree: 'First up, Stephane Mahe was a disgrace. He lost the plot, went totally OTT and deserved to get his marching orders. He has been fined, and may pay the ultimate penalty in the summer when he could find himself being sold' (*Evening Times*, 7 May 1999). The occasion, and its violent and sensational aspects, was a gift seized upon by the newspapers.

Perhaps a more objective review of Mahe's behaviour is required before continuing: early in the match – in fifteen minutes – the Frenchman was booked by the referee for dissent after a foul had been awarded against him in a tussle for the ball with Wallace. Several other Celtic players also protested, and more vigorously than Mahe, about the award, suggesting rightly that Wallace had elbowed Mahe seconds before. In thirty-two minutes Mahe was again fouled, this time tripped by Neil McCann, as he broke into Rangers half of the field; rising to his feet, Mahe gestured furiously to the referee that the Rangers player should be booked, as he was shortly afterwards. Mr. Dallas had little hesitation in pulling out the yellow card for Mahe's gesture and he was ordered off. The actual offence remains unclear. It could hardly have been dissent as the referee did indeed book McCann, which Mahe appeared to be advising; more likely it was for unsportsmanlike conduct in demanding that an opponent be booked.

One sports writer with a longish memory recalled the ordering-off of the Argentinian captain Rattin at Wembley Stadium against England in the 1966 World Cup; it was claimed the referee later said it was for 'the look on his

---

[69] Rangers, apparently, did not fine Wallace (who was also ordered off), but few newspapers made an issue of that.

[70] One fan, already hit with a lifetime ban from Celtic Park for throwing coins at the referee, was later charged and sentenced to three months' imprisonment. During the match at Celtic Park on 27 August 2000, won 6–2 by Celtic, Billy Dodds of Rangers slipped on the track near the corner flag. Before he could regain his feet, a protective cordon of security guards had formed to shield him from any possible harm. It appeared that the recommendations of the security report were being implemented.

face'. Perhaps a similar vehemence in Mahe's expression led to his expulsion at Celtic Park. However, it is difficult to recall any other footballer in Scotland who has been cautioned in similar circumstances – for raising an imaginary card in his hand. It should have been a most unlikely action on the part of a referee conscious that a second caution meant automatic dismissal for the player.

The trouble started at that point: every Celtic player was enraged at the decision, none more so than Mahe who had to be restrained from continuing to argue. Eventually, and only after a considerable delay, Mahe left the field, persuaded to do so by the more composed of his colleagues. At that moment a former Celtic director, perhaps used to the nuances of a Celtic–Rangers battle, turned to his companion and predicted: 'Well, I would wager that a Rangers player will be sent off before this is over – but it won't be till near the end.'

Now, Mahe's conduct, or total loss of composure, was unacceptable for a professional footballer, but it is hard not to sympathise with him to a certain extent. He had been booked twice within fifteen minutes, and on each occasion he had been the victim of foul play. Given the fraught circumstances of an Old Firm clash in which one side has the opportunity to win the championship on the ground of their rivals, it seems that a less draconian response from the match official might have been in order. Referees should have the ability and the coolness to cope with dissent under these circumstances with some degree of flexibility. Mahe's own words, as quoted in the *Evening Times*, are relevant: 'Jozef [Venglos] is not happy with me. He was upset I had been sent off, but he was more angry about my reaction. He also said Mr. MacDonald was very angry. He [Mr. Dallas] must realise players are very motivated and deal with them sensibly especially in the early stages.'

Several newspapers castigated Mahe for his reactions and in terms that might be construed as racist, his Gallic temperament being cited as a contributory factor. In the first Old Firm league fixture at Ibrox in the following season Paul Lambert was injured making a tackle deemed a penalty kick by the match official. While he was being treated, prior to his removal on a stretcher, the Rangers player van Bronckhorst was clearly seen on TV to be asking the referee if Lambert should not have been sent off. The difference in the actions of the two players (Mahe at Celtic Park and van Bronckhorst at Ibrox) lay only in the animation and passion revealed. The intent was the same – an intimation to the referee that an opposing player should be dismissed – but, of course, no caution was administered by that referee (Stuart Dougal) to the Rangers player for his intervention.

I make no apology for having gone into such detail in the incidents involving Mahe (and the encroachment of spectators on to the pitch) because the subsequent coverage in many newspapers distorted those events to an alarming degree. One brief example might suffice: ' ... [Celtic's] pain was compounded after half an hour when Mahe was red-carded. He had committed a foul on McCann, and topped up the order by showing dissent to referee Dallas' (*Evening Times*, 4 May 1999).

However, Celtic supporters, more disappointed than usual at Rangers' title-winning performance at Parkhead, immediately directed their fury on to Hugh Dallas. They pointed out with a certain amount of justification the following: that Mahe had been ordered off harshly; that Rangers' opening goal, a splendid passing move ended by McCann, had started deep in Rangers' half with a handball by Vidmar; that the award of a penalty kick, converted by Albertz, was almost laughable, but that it followed the field invasion and prolonged treatment of Mr. Dallas by Celtic's trainers; that the free-kick which led to the penalty award and taken by van Bronckhorst had been also dubious. All of these incidents took place in a most turbulent first half which ended with Rangers leading by 2–0 and playing against ten men.

What prevented a closer scrutiny of the referee's performance were several things: Mahe's prolonged outburst after the ordering-off; the violent reaction of some Celtic fans; and Mr. Dallas' courage in electing to continue after his injury.[71] As I noted in the introductory chapter of this book, I felt at the time that the referee's decisions were harsh towards Celtic in a dreadful first half; and afterwards, watching the taped match on TV, I had amended my position only slightly.

It was disturbing to find in the following days and weeks that the referee's performance had become the focus of attention, but largely in a revisionist way. Part of this may have been due to the fact that he had been appointed the match official for the Scottish Cup final.

The *Evening Times* of 7 May was quick to point out:

> As for the Celtic fans thinking Dallas is biased against them, I would ask them to cast their minds back to last New Year. This was the ref who denied Rangers a stonewall penalty when Alan Stubbs fouled Brian Laudrup with just seven minutes on the clock. Celtic went on to win that game 2–0, a result that had a huge influence on the destination of the title. He also awarded Celtic a penalty with just two minutes to go a few years ago at Parkhead when they were trailing 1–0, only for Andy Goram to save Pierre van Hooijdonk's kick.

The comments contain more than an element of truth: Stubbs was lucky not to have conceded a penalty kick, but the referee was in perfect position to judge according to the video tape, and Gough clearly pulled down Donnelly to give Celtic a penalty kick, which was saved by Goram. Interestingly, the reporter is exactly correct with the time of the first incident (seven minutes)

---

[71] It has been pointed out to me that, when Kenny Clark (Paisley) ordered off Richard Gough at Ibrox Park on 28 February 1997 for a foul on Neil McCann of Hearts, the time that elapsed between the referee lowering his red card and the player starting to walk towards the pavilion was virtually identical to that taken by Mahe.

but inaccurate with the time of the second (which occurred in eighty-five minutes).

The *Daily Record* on 5 May 1999 produced twenty frames from the TV footage, describing them as 'key decisions in THAT game', and James Traynor, after summarising each, produced a verdict on their correctness. The importance of such an approach depends on three factors: the selection of incident, an objective summary, and the correct interpretation. I would suggest that the journalist made a series of mistakes in all three categories.

First of all, the selection included time-frames (at least fifteen out of the twenty) from the match which showed routine decisions and which nobody had previously considered debatable to the slightest extent. All of these illustrated the undoubted fact that the referee's decisions were correct, but the point remains that almost every decision made by a match official should be correct. Most spectators at the match – and millions of TV viewers – felt that the decision to award Rangers a penalty kick a few minutes before the interval was one of the key moments from the match, certainly as far as the behaviour of the fans was concerned. Astonishingly, this incident was not chosen to illustrate the referee's performance.

Secondly, each frame was accompanied by a text, telling – in the journalist's opinion – what happened. Consider the descriptions: '4 Minutes: Mahe commits his first crime of the match by raising a foot to challenge McCann, who would go on and torment Celtic. Rangers foul – correct.' The use of the emotive word 'crime' seems out of place in the context of a football game, and what other 'crimes' did Mahe commit? And '30 Minutes: McCann fouls Mahe and the Celt gets up and jabs finger at his opponent. He refuses to calm down, and is sent off. Decision – correct but harsh.' As a description of this important incident, the reporter's commentary leaves much to be desired: Mahe was not given a yellow card for 'jabbing a finger at his opponent', nor was he sent off for 'refusing to calm down' as he was given little time by the referee to do so.

Two of the frames were revealing: '14 Minutes: Mahe is booked after reaction to foul given against him while tackling Wallace. Rangers foul – correct. (Wallace should have been penalised in the first place for having used an elbow to keep Mahe at bay. No foul – wrong.)' and '39 Minutes: Porrini is fouled by Wieghorst, although the decision again is harsh but technically sound. Rangers foul – correct.'

These were both critical moments in the course of the contest: the first indicates that Mahe was booked for his 'reaction to foul given against him' without pointing out that it was in the form of a justifiable protest; and the large frame, above the text, shows a relatively calm Stephane Mahe being booked by the referee, and the reporter is accurate in stating that Mahe had been fouled seconds previously. The second frame seems to show Porrini as having rounded Wieghorst – and putting the ball too far in front of him – but off-balance and ready to fall although the Celtic player made little or no contact with him. The referee awarded a free kick for this – despite the fact that his linesman had indicated a goal kick – and this was the specific decision that sparked off the crowd trouble. When the free kick was eventually taken, Mr. Dallas adjudged that Vidmar had been fouled inside the penalty area.

The journalist (James Traynor) offered his overall conclusion:

> ... the evidence in the case of Hugh Dallas versus the Celtic faithful is overwhelming. The referee, while guilty of one or two minor errors, is innocent of wider charges of cheating. Dallas proved he is still the top referee. There was a perception he had made a series of bad calls but the video tape doesn't prove this to have been the case at all. Of course, the majority of Celtic fans still won't believe Dallas' work to have been balanced and will call for him to be dropped from the Tennents Scottish Cup Final. He won't be because he did a good job last Sunday, and the pictures prove as much. (*Daily Record*, 5 May 1999)

'The referee, while guilty of one or two minor errors, is innocent of wider charges of cheating.' The 'one or two minor errors' included sending off a player very harshly after thirty minutes in an Old Firm match, and awarding a highly debatable penalty only nine minutes later. Furthermore, nobody accused the referee of 'cheating' as the criticism levelled by Celtic supporters, while expressed in forceful language, indicated that Hugh Dallas had a poor game, made several wrong decisions, and unfortunately most of those decisions – at least the vital ones – seemed to favour one team.

The journalist's approach – by using stills from the TV footage – was flawed from the outset; a still photograph cannot convey the totality of any incident, and is dependent too much on the specific split-second chosen. However, it gives a false impression of detailed analysis, strict objectivity, and considered judgement – as the text says: 'The pictures don't lie.' Whenever I hear that hackneyed expression, I think of an accountant friend whose operating credo was: 'Figures can't lie, but liars can figure.'

George Cumming's comments set the tone for most of what followed: 'Hugh's performance tonight was magnificent and proved that he is one of the top referees in Europe. He was under tremendous pressure, and he undoubtedly increased his stature in the game.' The SFA's Director of Referee Development has, of course, a vested interest in protecting his officials from unfair criticism but it is also recognised that Cumming and Dallas are close personal friends as well as colleagues. The following day the SFA man expanded his praise:

> Refereeing is very much about man-management and Hugh went through the full range of skills on Sunday. You can always argue about the pushes and the shoves, but generally he made the right decisions – and when you consider he probably made 150 in the game – that is not bad. Hugh is regarded as one of the top ten officials in the world and we get requests from all over the world for him to take charge of potentially difficult matches.

Two points emerge from these comments; nowhere is there any mention of the debatable decisions in this particular match, and the reputation of Hugh Dallas as a referee of world stature is stressed repeatedly. The first is a significant omission, and the second suggests that, rather than the primary task of refereeing a football match at Celtic Park, Hugh Dallas was concerned about proving he was Scotland's top referee. Throughout these sound bites, the official is referred to by his first name – an indication of sympathy, if not outright and unquestioning approval.

There is little useful purpose in automatically defending actions when everybody at the match, and most who watched on television, could judge for themselves. In fact, it reduces such contributions to the order of knee-jerk responses to a situation, and gives the distinct impression of a cover-up.

Predictably, the media reported the party line: 'Amid all the mayhem, Motherwell referee Dallas stood brave and firm and was undoubtedly the best man on the park. No other referee in this country could have controlled such a volatile game with such control and common sense, and be assured that the police and the stewards were relieved that such a resolute man was in charge.' These are the words of Willie Miller, the former Aberdeen captain and manager, in his column for *The Herald* on 3 May.

Similarly, Trevor Steven, the former Rangers midfielder, contributed this thought to the same newspaper: 'It is embarrassing for Scottish football. The game was going well, and Hugh Dallas was having a tremendous game.' In much the same way John MacMillan, the secretary of the Rangers Supporters' Association was given space for his comments: 'It was utterly disgraceful. The treatment of Hugh Dallas was unbelievable. The morons who caused the trouble should be driven out of football for ever. An example has to be made of them.'

Similarly, it was equally disturbing to observe so many members of the press corps clambering into line in order to praise the referee excessively for a below-average performance by his own standards, and to blame the players, particularly Mahe, for starting the crowd trouble.

Regrettably the situation was complicated by another violent incident, when one neighbour late on the night of the controversial match threw a brick or a missile at the windows of Hugh Dallas' house. It would emerge later that this neighbour was under the influence of alcohol at the time, and was also a Celtic season-ticket holder obviously disappointed at the result of the match. He also seems to have had an attitude problem with referees because, as a junior player with Forth Wanderers, he had attacked the official who had ordered him off.

The incident was headlined in all of the tabloids, and featured in the broadsheets. There were several conclusions drawn from this attack, as one writer for *The Herald* stated the next day: ' ... then he has to endure his family being put into a state of alarm by thugs who broke his windows' (4 May

1999). It was an unfortunate incident, coming on top of the referee's bad treatment at the actual match, and not too surprisingly the press coverage was most sympathetic to an official who had behaved with commendable courage in difficult circumstances. However, the immediate assumptions were that it was a number of 'thugs' involved rather than one misguided individual, and that several windows – if not all – were broken, and the accounts stressed that innocent members of his family, his wife Jacqueline, and his sons Stewart (18) and Andrew (16), had been badly affected by this frightening development.

In fact, it seemed as if Hugh Dallas was being cast in the role of the persecuted hero to an absurd level. Consider Archie Macpherson's words – which I hope were very much tongue-in-cheek – in his column for *The Herald*: 'Indeed I would not be inaccurate in claiming that the party now in majority in Edinburgh would have within their ranks a sizeable number prepared to slap a motion of censure on Hugh Dallas if rules of procedure allowed such a thing.'

On the 4 May the *Evening Times* quoted Dallas himself as saying: 'My first reaction was that the spectator was going to get to me because there wasn't anybody between him and myself. All of a sudden I decided I had to stop this guy, and thankfully one or two of the Celtic players appeared from nowhere. It's still blurred in my mind what actually happened. But I saw the Celtic players grab him to the ground and then the security guys got to me.' These words, if they have been reported accurately, suggest that the speaker shortly after the match, and not surprisingly, was still in a state of shock.

In all of this choreographed public relations exercise there were few criticisms of the referee's part in his own misfortunes – not that the treatment meted out to him at Celtic Park, nor at his home, is to be condoned in any way.

It is important to recognise exactly what happened and the order in which these things occurred: the first hooligan managed to get on to the pitch as described by Dallas, and this was before the free kick was taken; Dallas was struck by some small missile, probably a coin, shortly after this disturbance; in the immediate aftermath of the free kick – which was sent too far and beyond all the players – Riseth of Celtic and Vidmar of Rangers became tangled and the Rangers full back threw himself to the ground; Dallas, who had positioned himself surprisingly close to the spot from which the kick was taken, awarded a penalty kick; the second hooligan broke on to the pitch while Celtic players were complaining about the decision; the third intruder appeared seconds after the penalty was converted expertly by Albertz.

There had been a considerable delay while Mr. Dallas received temporary first aid from the Celtic trainer on the pitch. During that time, the referee should have been giving some thought to the unfolding situation if he was capable of doing so. He would have been within his rights in having the game abandoned or, preferably, handed over to the fourth official – another fully qualified referee.

By all accounts, Mr. Dallas is strong, both physically and mentally, and for such an authoritative person to voluntarily surrender an element of control might be difficult. It is a characteristic of those in a state of shock to be able to carry on with some semblance of normality, and the traumatic events of those few minutes – combined with the customary pressure of a vital Old Firm clash – could well have induced such a state. Instead, Mr. Dallas chose to continue, and the *Evening Times* suggested that he had 'feared worse trouble if the game was abandoned.'

The award of a very soft penalty to Rangers, within seconds of the resumption of the match after Dallas' injury, was most unfortunate in its timing. Rightly or wrongly, it gave the impression of vindictiveness. The penalty kick incident took place only a few minutes before the interval and, at that time, the referee received further medical treatment from Celtic's doctor who applied stitches to the wound. Most newspapers, eager to exaggerate, reported that four stitches were required, but reliable information suggests that the number was two, and at the interval some concern was also expressed by Celtic's medical staff about Mr. Dallas' condition.

It was left to the editorial team of *The Herald* (rather than their sports writers) on 4 May to list the ingredients of the hellish brew that had produced a shameful night for Scottish football's prestige:

> A visceral rivalry between two sets of supporters born of age-old blind bigotry; a football match whose result condemned one, Celtic, to the role of humiliated also-rans and handed the league championship to Rangers, the other; a Frenchman playing for Celtic, Stephane Mahe, whose irrational outbursts stoked up a tinder-box atmosphere; *a referee who had seemed to get caught up in that atmosphere before it maliciously and sickeningly turned on him causing him bravely, if wrongly, to continue to officiate the match*; and a SKY-ordained early-evening kick-off that offered far too much drinking time to people who lack the intelligence or common sense to handle alcohol.

The italics in the above excerpt have been provided by the author because I feel they capture an aspect of this match which has been frequently covered up by others in the media. Most sports journalists, who have a vested interest in football's *status quo*, had little difficulty in deciding where to affix the blame for the events. The atmosphere at the match was condemned rightly enough, although the part the media had played in fuelling that ugly mood was largely ignored. The behaviour of the hooligans who invaded the pitch was also condemned as was the behaviour of those who threw coins. The actions of some players were vilified, particularly Mahe's, but the emphasis was on his histrionics *after* the red card was flourished. Rangers players were ticked off for a celebratory huddle at the end of the contest before their own celebrating fans. The performance of the referee was praised excessively, but understandably, in view of his determination to continue.

Within minutes of the conclusion of the match a public relations exercise was being mounted, consciously or unconsciously. The focus was on the referee's bravery: the SFA, through its Director of Referee Development, immediately rushed to praise his official and cited his world-wide reputation, and the media followed suit.

The SFA Chief Executive, David Taylor, shortly afterwards announced provisional plans to open the way for referees to be allowed to explain their decisions publicly: 'Personally, I'm in favour of a limited form of opportunity for referees to explain decisions. Some people claim this takes away the authority of the refs but I think it would do the reverse and enhance the respect.'

Apparently, the SFA did lift its 'ban' on referees talking to the media to allow Hugh Dallas to express his own opinions about the situation, presumably because he was one official unlikely to get flustered in front of cameras or tape-recorders. In all the interviews he was articulate and presentable, but the questions put to him were bland and inoffensive. He was asked by Davie Provan in a television interview if he had given any thought to not taking up the appointment for the forthcoming Scottish Cup final, and he was asked about the effects of the last Old Firm match on his personal life. The answers were utterly predictable: he had never for one moment thought about refusing to accept the honour of officiating at Hampden Park; he would not be cowed into doing so by the actions of such fans who had misbehaved; he condemned the incident at his home, and the effect it had had on his wife and children; in fact, he had received many messages of praise and sympathy from supporters, including Celtic's, in the aftermath of the dramatic match at Parkhead.

The questions, it seemed, had been approved in advance, and the answers prepared. Nobody among the journalists, it is believed, has ever asked the referee if he was satisfied with his performance that day at Celtic Park and, of course, he was not asked to explain some of the more controversial decisions. It was obvious that this unprecedented attention on a Scottish referee was an orchestrated public-relations exercise and Dallas, an articulate and intelligent man, featured personally in the interviews and made a good impression.

It is time to draw a line under that particular Old Firm clash.

Too many Celtic supporters, smarting under the lash of witnessing a humiliating, and deserved, defeat for their team were quick to lay the blame on outside causes: the referee for biased officiating; the media for over-the-top criticism; and the SPL for fining the club for the disorders.

The referee made mistakes, but no evidence exists that he was in any way biased during that match, nor in others involving Celtic; however, for a world-class official, admittedly under stressful conditions, he had a below-average performance – and that is all.

Many in the media did distort the events to make them even more sensational, and largely ignored their own inflammatory articles in the days prior to the event. The coverage after the match suggested that sometimes the relationship between the football authorities and the press can be too comfortable. In particular, the public relations exercise which the press aided and abetted was unacceptable to many fair-minded Celtic supporters who resented the manipulative rewriting of a football match.

The Scottish Premier League eventually fined Celtic £45,000, but the fact remains that the events of 2 May 1999 at Celtic Park were disgraceful and Celtic, apart from a petty huddle by Rangers players in front of their own supporters, were largely to blame. The punishment was warranted, in a sense. While the amount was not excessive, the fact that Rangers, although they were virtually blameless, were allowed to present their case on a separate day and, having objected to the composition of the panel, before a different one, raised some doubts among Parkhead partisans.

The Scottish Cup final between Celtic and Rangers was played at the refurbished Hampden Park on 29 May and won 1–0 by Rangers. The match was refereed by Hugh Dallas and passed without incident, both teams being on their best behaviour and the spectators under the strictest of surveillance. Nobody complained about Dallas' officiating and the frantic claims by Celtic players for a last-minute penalty kick, when a shot was cleared off the goal-line by Amoruso, were recognised as having been turned down correctly by the referee. Some observers felt that the referee had actually learned from the experience at Parkhead, as his customary authoritarian style had been toned down to a noticeable degree. Indeed, since that notorious match in 1999, Hugh Dallas has refereed three Old Firm matches and it is pleasant to record his performances have been exemplary. Both teams have won 1–0 and one match was drawn.

Subsequently, the Scottish Premier League attempted to justify the fine of £45,000 levied on Celtic following the report by its committee of inquiry. In a statement made to explain the grounds for the punishment the committee stated that Celtic's coaching staff had not made it explicitly clear to their players the need for exemplary behaviour for this fixture, and that Mahe's extreme reaction to his being sent off had contributed largely to the subsequent misbehaviour of some fans. Glenn Gibbons, writing in *The Scotsman*, considered the reasons offered as 'not only without precedent but disturbingly close to unjustifiable.' However, Celtic were prepared to pay the fine in order to draw an unsavoury chapter to a close.

The reports submitted by Celtic had been received by the committee and the club was thanked for its contribution to the inquiry. Only the members of that disciplinary committee saw Celtic's report(s); accordingly, some mystery exists as to the later leaking of information contained in it. An objective evaluator might consider that Celtic had acted responsibly in commissioning such an independent report; in fact, Celtic used part of the findings of the psychologist's report to determine the severity of their actions against Stephane Mahe, but there was general ridicule about the club's procedures.[72]

The criticism concentrated unfairly on the brief mention of Hugh Dallas and the comments allegedly made about his performance. Allan MacDonald was eventually forced to repeat his comments on the nature of the report: 'The comments on the refereeing were generalised, and had to do with possible improvements in training and development of referees; they were not specifically about Hugh Dallas although, of course, he was the official on the night. His report embraced many aspects, including a reminder to ourselves that we could improve our players' mental preparations for these occasions.'

It might be well worth considering how the contents of that report might be of some help to the authorities with regard to future procedures: for example, if a referee pulls a muscle during a match and his mobility is affected, the normal procedure is for another official to take over his duties, but had the authorities given any consideration to a head injury which possibly could affect the official's judgement including the critical one of continuing as the match official? A player, semi-concussed after a collision, is not always the best judge of his ability to continue; is a referee a better judge of his own condition after a similar injury?

A few months afterwards, however, Celtic made the point of suggesting that Hugh Dallas not be considered for the last Old Firm league fixture of the Millennium because of his recent experiences at Celtic Park. As one of the top Grade 1 officials, Hugh Dallas might reasonably expect to get the appointment more frequently than most for Old Firm matches, and he was, in fact, duly scheduled for that fixture at Celtic Park on 27 December 1999.

Of course, Celtic were criticised for trying to prevent Dallas from refereeing that particular match, and probably quite rightly. It is not a wise precedent for league clubs to veto the match officials selected for their fixtures; it is certainly not acceptable for clubs to be able to pick and choose referees. However, when clubs and referees have a 'history', sometimes it is better to reach a form of compromise – but in an atmosphere of confidentiality.

The information was leaked to the media before Celtic were officially informed, and this upset MacDonald who was besieged by reporters sensing another sensational development. MacDonald's comments seem reasonable in

---

[72] It is believed that club officials at a high level made efforts after a suitable period of time to communicate with Mahe on a personal and social level; on these occasions the behaviour of the player and the relevant section of the report were discussed in a more relaxed and rational manner. It would appear that, despite provocation by opponents and taunting by rival supporters, Mahe has learned from the traumatic experience. Interestingly, Jim McCluskey (Stewarton) considers Mahe 'a whole-hearted player, but one who occasionally dives in to the tackle. Still, more often than not, he comes out with the ball.'

the context: 'The May match could have been refereed better; that came out in the report. All we wanted to know was whether the people who made that appointment [for the 27 December fixture] had considered that. We understand that they had not been made privy to the information; so, they made the appointment in isolation of the facts.'

During the meeting (or press conference), Allan MacDonald made no specific mention of any Rangers player, although he did make a passing allusion that a gesture by the referee involving a Rangers player had possibly sent a wrong message to the Celtic support. This was reported in a tabloid in an entirely different manner, the newspaper actually putting words into the mouth of Celtic's Chief Executive and claiming to quote him verbatim: 'Was it purely coincidence that, shortly after being seen patting Gio van Bronckhorst, a coin came on the park and struck the referee?'

Some more objective journalists, who did attend the meeting and took notes, have confirmed that Allan MacDonald did not say those words. One problem may have arisen from MacDonald's style of speaking. Celtic's former Chief Executive is an enthusiastic man, animated in conversation, and talkative to a fault. Many have commented on the wide-ranging nature of his discussions and his quick delivery, and have complained about his frequent allusions to the business world, made in the jargon of that milieu.

The apologists for those misquoting MacDonald on the above grounds appear to be unaware of the invention of the tape-recorder. What happened is that the reporters from the offending tabloid(s) have recalled the incident, or checked it with the footage of the match, and attributed words to MacDonald. The tabloids went so far as to suggest that MacDonald (and/or Celtic) might be construed as bringing the game into disrepute (by engaging a behavioural psychologist?) and anticipated dire punishment including the possibility of a record fine. [73]

The main focus of the committee's deliberations on 8 February 2000 centred on MacDonald's alleged comments, the action of Celtic in hiring the services of a psychologist not being considered an offence in any way, except by several newspapers.

However, one disturbing element was emerging from the ongoing controversy:

> Almost certainly contrary to his own wishes, MacDonald has managed to convey to the public at large the idea that Celtic are determined to be rid of Hugh Dallas. The impression of a deliberate and concentrated campaign against the referee over the past nine months has

---

[73] At almost every golf tournament in recent years – especially the Majors – the television commentators have noted the body language of Colin Montgomerie as an indicator of how well he was going to perform. Similarly, the press journalists have frequently analysed his facial expressions in relation to his performance. If these criteria can be employed in golf, why not in other sports?

been impossible to escape. This does not square with reactions from within the club encountered on the night in question. Shortly after the final whistle, I engaged in conversation with a Celtic director and three former players. All were agreed that Celtic lost 3–0 because of their own inadequacies, both in ability and temperament ... in their summary of what had happened, the only mention made of Dallas was a sympathetic one, in relation to the head wound he suffered when hit by a coin. (*The Scotsman*, 1 February 2000)

MacDonald denied the allegation promptly: 'My reason for asking the Scottish Premier League to question the Scottish Football League about Dallas handling the game was nothing personal, but was made purely in the interests of preventing any possible trouble in the light of what had gone before. The Scottish Football League's decision to ignore the report was clearly right; the referee handled the circumstances perfectly. Despite what anybody thinks, I have no problem whatsoever with Hugh Dallas.'[74] As can be gathered from his words, Hugh Dallas did referee that match, the players and the crowd behaved themselves, and the referee completed the fixture (a 1–1 draw) without controversy, a considerable feat in the Old Firm context.

The Scotsman had suggested that it would be a much more serious matter: 'But it was learned yesterday that there is already a feeling inside the SFA that MacDonald's action, with its undertones of distrust and paranoia, is an issue of such gravity that the committee should explore the entire series of events, from the recruitment of Lewis to last weekend's public utterances' (1 February 2000). However, the whole incident seemed to have been resolved amicably enough behind closed doors, the General Purposes Committee apparently accepting MacDonald's explanations without too much difficulty.

There is an interesting twist in the story of the relationship between referee and club. One newspaper printed the news that Dallas applied for the position as Celtic General Manager, but was unsuccessful, the job going to Jock Brown. The reporter, Charles Lavery, assured the author that he stands by his story and is convinced of its accuracy. Neither Celtic nor Dallas have commented officially on the matter, although it is a subject frequently raised in the Celtic fanzines. If the story is true, the suitability of Mr Dallas as a referee for Celtic fixtures might be called into question.

So, in conclusion, in the three Old Firm matches that Hugh Dallas has refereed since the infamous one on 2 May 1999, events on the field have unfolded in a more normal manner without undue controversy. Of course, whenever he is scheduled for an Old Firm clash, the newspapers, broadsheet as well as tabloid, mention the events of May 1999. The suspicion lingers that these newspapers are almost hoping for some sort of repetition of the violence and controversy to occur.

What irritates Celtic supporters, in general, about the media coverage

---

[74] Tommy Burns apparently shares MacDonald's views of Dallas' abilities. In a recent interview with the author, he stated: 'He's probably the best referee we have in Scotland.'

since that fixture is the almost universal praise heaped upon the referee, and the implication that any criticism of him by the Celtic support is mistaken or a consequence of paranoia. This constitutes a highly insulting generalisation of the character of Celtic supporters by those in the media, and seems to suggest that a highly qualified and competent referee cannot simply have a bad day. For example, it was announced in the newspapers almost immediately after the Old Firm match that Hugh Dallas of Motherwell had been appointed to take charge of the 1999 UEFA cup final in Moscow between Parma and Marseilles. He did so, and handled the assignment admirably, with Parma winning comfortably by 3–0. However, the Scottish press prefaced almost every account of the appointment with a reference to the Old Firm clash at Celtic Park, and the implicit message was that Dallas was a world-class official and, therefore, Celtic supporters should stop complaining.

In this context, it is illuminating to compare the media coverage of Hugh Dallas' handling of the 1999 Old Firm league decider and Willie Young's officiating at the 2001 League Cup semi-final. The matches were mirror images of each other and, in my opinion, neither referee was at his best. Dallas was universally praised and Young was roundly criticised. At the risk of being considered paranoid, I should point out that Dallas refereed a match won 3–0 by Rangers and Young a match won 3–1 by Celtic.

I agree that too many Celtic followers are convinced that Scottish referees often exhibit a bias against Celtic – and for sectarian reasons. However, very few Celtic supporters feel that Hugh Dallas is a biased official, and fewer again suggest a sectarian reason.

Paradoxically, this referee's undoubted strength of character might well be his one weakness as an official.

I have often thought, as a Celtic supporter, that I would prefer Dallas to referee an Old Firm match at Ibrox rather than at Celtic Park. Fearless and confident, he always gives the impression of being unmoved by the home support; in fact, he seems to relish having to give an unpopular decision. As the Latin poet Horace says: 'I am vexed when the worthy Homer nods' – and Hugh Dallas cannot be described as a 'homer'. A Hibernian supporter reminds me that the first Celtic match refereed by Dallas after the Old Firm match was at Easter Road on 25 September 1999 and the home supporters in the crowd of 14,734 were outraged by many of his decisions. During the match, a bland, uneventful affair, Dallas ordered off two Hibernian players (Frank Sauzee and Paul Lovering) and booked several more in a match won 2–0 by Celtic, who also had three men booked in a flurry of yellow cards near the end.

During the Euro 2000 competition he awarded a dubious penalty kick to Italy in the closing stages of a match with Turkey, and the incident took place at that end of the ground occupied by Turkish supporters. Once more TV viewers saw some coins being thrown in the direction of the referee, who remained unmoved by the commotion.

Hugh Dallas appears to have started his refereeing career relatively late and was spotted by a Class 1 official when he ran the line at a charity game at Shotts in 1980. Referees are permitted to start their careers under close supervision at the age of sixteen but Dallas was twenty-two years of age at the time, an injured cheekbone having scuppered any chances of a career as a player at the junior level. According to an excerpt in *Scottish Football Quotations* his debut as a referee came two years later: 'On August 16th, 1982 at 3 p.m. precisely, a certain Mr. Hugh Dallas blew his whistle for the first time ever to take charge of Bridgework Amateurs vs. Victoria Amateurs at a local venue in Motherwell and, in the short space of ninety minutes, I never imagined I could upset so many people. But three red cards and six yellow later – and £6 to the good – I had.'

After that prophetic start, Dallas's career followed a steady route. In 1983 he started off as a Junior referee with Glenboig vs. Carluke. In 1986 he graduated as a linesman or assistant referee in senior football. By 1988 he had been promoted to the rank of Class 2 Referee, authorised to officiate in junior football and reserve league fixtures. In 1990, aged thirty-two, he had become a Class 1 referee, and by 1991 was recognised as a FIFA Assistant Referee.

In 1992 he attained the status of a FIFA referee, having made rapid advancement through the ranks of Scottish officials, and in 1993 was given charge of the UEFA Cup tie between Aalborg (Denmark) and Deportivo la Coruna (Spain). In Scotland his progress continued; in 1994 he was given his first Old Firm match and, in 1996, the Scottish Cup final between Rangers and Hearts. Internationally, he was becoming more recognised: in 1996 an appearance in the Olympic Games at Atlanta; in 1998 a France vs. Italy quarter-final in the World Cup; and two years later an appointment for Euro 2000, in which he was one of two referees chosen to establish guidelines for all the officials at the competition.[75]

In his private life, he was also making progress, having founded a successful double-glazing company which was taken over in 1997 in a deal that left Dallas as a commercial director. Today it comprises three factories, employing 120 people, and Hugh Dallas enjoys the trappings of office: a luxurious home and a Jaguar with a personalised number plate. However, he is more easily recognised on the football pitch and, when he, his wife and two children appeared on a TV game-show, *Family Fortunes*, he introduced himself as 'a Scottish football referee'.

His rise to the top has been at a time when changes have been made to the

---

[75] Ironically, Dallas and the other referee involved in the organisation (Pierluigi Collina of Italy) were the ones singled out for media criticism for their handling of matches.

system of rating referees' performances. Not all officials have been happy about the changes in recent years and one well-known referee resigned before the end of the 1993/94 season complaining bitterly: 'Suddenly the time-honoured procedure stopped so no one knows just who is first, second, third etc. in the gradings. Instead, all we are given is percentages for our performances.' This man felt that the standings were being kept secret for sinister reasons:

> The last notification I had put me around 84% which must put me in the top bracket, a position I have held consistently for years. And yet I was ignored for a Scottish Cup quarterfinal, semi, or the final itself. Why? I can only assume it's because I'm not one of their chosen few. I believe the markings are deliberately being kept secret to protect an elite band. And it wouldn't do to embarrass the favoured sons if their markings were lower than the referees who don't have the stamp of approval.

A successful man, by most standards, Hugh Dallas is very conscious of his status in the world of refereeing, and has indicated a determination to maintain that position:

> The public don't realise how competitive refereeing is. If you have any ambition in life at all, you always want to strive to get to the top. Referees aren't any different. [Recognition] is very important to me. It's very important to me now to referee at the top level abroad because it's great to walk on to the field with the Zinedine Zidanes and the Del Pieros and Rivaldos of this world. To be in that position and know that you're at the top, the same as these guys are in their field. You're part of the big picture and I still get a fantastic buzz out of that. (*The Scotsman*, 10 May 2000)

He does not appear to be a man willing to hide his talents under a bushel and, in an age where respect for authority in general has been eroded, Hugh Dallas seems prepared to redefine the role or *persona* of the referee. Strict and authoritative, he stands for no nonsense on the pitch but it could be argued that stubbornness or inflexibility can cause him difficulty in teethy, hectic matches.

It used to be that the highest praise for a referee was his invisibility during the football match but, increasingly, football seems to be becoming part of show business and referees are now part of the act. This can backfire on those who seek attention. Referees who work anonymously should have their occasional errors glossed over without much comment; referees who consciously seek the spotlight should have their mistakes analysed.

CHAPTER TWELVE

Celtic and the Media

Scotland has always had a strong tradition of newspaper reading. In Glasgow during the early pre-television 1950s, it was not uncommon for average households to take more than one morning newspaper as well as an evening one. On Saturday nights most football fans bought, in the cry of the street vendors, *'Times, News – and Citizen!'* This tradition, although eroded by the effects of the electronic media, lingers on and still makes Scotland, particularly the West of Scotland, the most competitive market for newspapers in the U.K. Significantly, the low month for circulation has always been July – and that is the football close season.

A columnist in *The Scotsman* described the changes wrought by time and technology: 'A football match-report [of the past] could be constructed to a simple formula. The first paragraph – which was written last – would make a general statement about the game, perhaps making an observation about the consequences of the result. The telling moment of the match would be described whether it was a goal or a sending-off. Then the report would slip out of order with a long description of the first half. Then it would stop.' Clearly, the emphasis was on the match itself, and the fact that the report terminated abruptly was due to the restraints imposed by space in the newspaper or time.

Alistair McKay continued: 'That approach doesn't work any more. All of the basic information is delivered on TV or radio within seconds of the final whistle. Instead, football reports now tend to rely on quotes from the managers to explain the games, but managers are not allowed to comment on refereeing decisions.'

One journalist, after attending the 1969 Rangers–Celtic cup final, suggested that war correspondents should be sent to cover the fixture; nowadays, it seems, gossip columnists would be more in order. Several similarities come to mind: the emphasis is on the personalities involved, and usually they are depicted in stereotypical fashion; the glib sound bite is faithfully reproduced, perhaps sanitised; the actual contest recedes into the background, while the ramifications are stressed with particular focus on possible sackings or future transfers.

What is missing from so many match reports – with some notable exceptions – is a rational, sequential account of the match lucidly expressed. Perhaps, with the advent of television, this is an inevitable backward step for print journalism, but it remains a matter for regret.

The present-day demands of the media have led to a relatively new type of journalist, a type condemned by arguably the best of all football writers, Hugh McIlvanney:

> As a reporter I have always seen the game through my own eyes. Not so long ago such an assertion would have seemed laughable, since just about every professional in my business could say as much and expect to be believed. In recent years, however, there has emerged a breed of football journalists who appear unable to put pen to paper or fingers to Tandy until some player or manager has interpreted the action for them. They cannot function unless fuelled by quotes. You feel that if they went blind their working efficiency would be unaffected, but if they went deaf they would not have the first idea of what happened on the park. Their method is a plague, and it's spreading. (*McIlvanney On Football*, Edinburgh, 1994)

Another problem – and perhaps a related one – is that certain journalists now give the distinct impression that they believe themselves to be as important to football as the men who play the game or who manage clubs. Perhaps that is an unfair criticism of reporters whose newspapers are primarily responsible for the hyperbole involved in describing their employees. Reading about the journalists makes one wish to consult The Trades Description Act. One recent example (of a highly competent journalist) might suffice: '... the best newspaperman in the business. He's the man with the guts to say what he thinks and the honesty to direct criticism and praise wherever it is due. The *Sunday Mail's* Chief Sports Writer, Hugh Keevins ... his only crime is calling it as he sees it. His views are often hard but always fair and that's why he's the best read columnist in Scotland' (*Sunday Mail,* 7 May 2000).

The columnist might well have been embarrassed by those claims on his behalf, but Keevins' employer felt obliged to describe him in those exaggerated terms on that occasion because the journalist (and the newspaper) was embroiled in an ongoing confrontation with Celtic's Kenny Dalglish. Fortunately, this form of self-praise is still confined mainly to the tabloid press.

Of course, the main purpose of stirring up controversy is to boost circulation figures, and for many in the newspaper trade it is a matter of survival. Martin Clark, the editor of the *Daily Record*, became a notable victim in September 2000, when he was replaced because the circulation figures of his paper, although still the most-read in Scotland, had fallen. Tom Lappin of *The Scotsman* summed up the situation: ' ... when a much-loathed tabloid editor was shown the door. The fact that he had run a viciously reactionary campaign against the abolition of Section 28 was forgotten. The catalyst for his departure was a row over the paper's failure to get the scoop on the Ronald de Boer transfer' (6 September 2000).

To paraphrase a more familiar adage: 'In circulation wars, truth is the first casualty.' In Scotland the struggle for readers (and, therefore, advertisers) is seen most graphically in the case of the war of the tabloids between the *Daily Record* and *The Sun* and, although each has been known to disparage the other's 'foreign' background, interestingly enough, neither newspaper is Scottish-owned.

A most intriguing topic for research would be to examine the football pages of the newspapers particularly during the close-season and calculate the percentage of those suggested transfers that have actually come to fruition. Their scatter-gun approach is one obvious area of criticism, and it seems clear that much of the speculation – reported with cynical certainty – is groundless. However, it does achieve the immediate purpose of creating a headline and, perhaps, persuading football fans to buy that day's edition. Later, of course, if one of the guesses happens to materialise, the newspaper claims full credit for its 'exclusive reporting', ignoring the number of non-stories promoted with equal certainty. Martin O'Neill quipped recently in a television interview: 'Since coming to Celtic two months ago, I have been linked with 210 players. Fair enough, but some of those mentioned I'm not interested in, some I've never heard of ... and two them are dead, I believe.'

Unfortunately, most football fans – and even players – tend to be 'readers' of the tabloids. Tommy Burns shakes his head in some bemusement at the sight of some of his Celtic players studying the back pages of the newspapers: 'They'll tell you that it's rubbish, they know there's no truth in it ... but they read it anyway.' Burns is one who bemoans the lowering of journalistic standards: 'My mother used to send me out for some Ir'n Bru and the *Daily Record*, a Scottish tradition, but nowadays I can't read it.'

Regrettably, football fans seem to have a voracious appetite for every aspect of the game, and the newspapers meet this demand or perhaps create it in a 'chicken-or-the-egg' scenario. Any newspaper which reduces its football coverage in the present climate risks a drop in circulation, but the more cynical journalists will point out that the clubs could not possibly pay for the sheer volume of free publicity willingly provided by the press: information about new signings, complete with photographs, comprehensive articles about individuals associated with the clubs, copious accounts of all games played, and exhaustive previews of fixtures. As far as the clubs are concerned, all these columns have to be laudatory, if not fawning, in tone.

The newspapers – or, more specifically, the tabloids – provide all of this pap cheerfully. Journalists, working for newspapers dependent on increased circulation to survive in a competitive market, have to churn out this sort of mindless material on a daily basis.

When individual journalists fall below this unwritten principle of unstinted praise and adulation, clubs have been known to withdraw privileges from both journalist and newspaper in retaliation. In this regard Celtic do not stand alone: Rangers, in particular, have also let their displeasure at adverse coverage be known and have refused access to players before and after games for interviews. Sadly, other provincial clubs can be just as petty or vindictive. I remember standing behind one of the goals at Tannadice for a Celtic match with Kevin McCarra, and watching him struggle to complete his match report; apparently, Jim McLean, the irascible manager/chairman of Dundee United, had banned his newspaper, *Scotland on Sunday*, from the press-box because he had objected to some minor point that had offended him in a previous edition. Ironically, the particular journalist banned that day had written and supplied the 'Notes on the Visitors' for United's programme – and this service had been provided free of charge!

In Scotland most football coverage is rightly centred around the Old Firm, mainly because supporters of Rangers and Celtic represent the majority of football fans throughout the country. Statistics bear this out: the capacity of Celtic Park is 60,832, of Ibrox Stadium 50,467, and the next largest is Pittodrie with 21,119. Hampden Park, where Queen's Park play before minuscule crowds, is excluded from this list although it has a capacity of 52,046. On a regular basis at Celtic Park and Ibrox the maximum capacity figure is approached, but only on rare occasions are the other grounds in Scotland filled. It has been calculated that, on average, forty-five per cent of all football fans attending a match on a Saturday in Scotland are present at either Celtic Park or Ibrox.

In addition, the newspapers do have a responsibility to report on football at the highest level within the country, and Rangers and Celtic have dominated Scottish football, admittedly to an unhealthy degree. Sports fans want to read about the vital matches, and these almost invariably involve one or the other of the Old Firm. So, it is not surprising that the coverage is concentrated on Rangers and Celtic – and justifiably so, even if provincial clubs feel it is unfair. One English comedian described his version of Hell as 'playing the Empire Theatre in Glasgow on a Saturday night, when both Celtic and Rangers have lost that afternoon.' Newspaper vendors used to report a slump in sales on those relatively rare occasions.

Editors and sports writers are all too aware of how easy it is to alarm Celtic supporters; thus, winding up that support is a regular feature of the tabloids. Columns like 'Sports Hotline' in the *Daily Record* (in which 'fans' phone in comments on recent events and matches) seem to attract the lunatic fringe of football followers. In fact, one is occasionally left with the distinct impression that the excerpts from the alleged telephone calls have been carefully selected only to draw attention to that fact.

The aim is not malice but basically a commercial one. Alarming headlines – the 'Celtic in Crisis' type – do increase sales and Celtic have in the past decade or two provided the basic material for most of these stories with their relative lack of success and off-the-pitch turmoil. It was not the newspapers which created the spectacle of Celtic's frequent managerial changes: Liam Brady, Lou Macari, Tommy Burns, Wim Jansen, Dr. Venglos, John Barnes and Martin O'Neill. The criticism to be levelled at the media is the endless speculation surrounding appointments, and the frequent hinting at trouble in Paradise. John Barnes, for one, blamed the interference of the media for his sacking after only eight months in charge: 'There are hundreds of thousands of fans who can't go to Celtic Park, but they form an opinion from the newspapers, television, and what they read and hear.'

I have stated earlier in this book that almost all football followers are in danger of being labelled paranoid, and it seems almost laughable that relatively uneducated men should pore over the match reports and comments of journalists with such Jesuitical attention, seeking out nuances with an application that scholars and academics would envy.

Celtic have always had uncomfortable relationships with the media, both print and electronic, and this suspicion stems from the conviction that, in general, Celtic will not be treated fairly – and this is worth considering. Certainly, within Scotland for years there was a policy of excluding Catholics from employment with the BBC and, as most Celtic supporters are Catholic, that might very well have been the starting-point of this distrust. Some newspapers, and the *Glasgow Herald* in particular, maintained a similar policy. Ironically, the most famously 'anti-Rangers journalist' of all was Cyril Horne, who worked as Chief Football Correspondent for this newspaper for many years. A highly respected and fearless little man, Cyril Horne's was a lone voice in condemning the Ibrox club's discriminatory employment practices and in speaking out against Rangers' traditionally physical approach. However, it is not too surprising that Celtic were dubious about media integrity when scarcely one word was written in protest about Rangers' practice; Celtic had to conclude that the editors or writers agreed with those policies.

Having completed considerable research for this book, I have to say that much of the traditional suspicion has been misplaced. For most of the past fifty years, Celtic have been given a fair press. In many of the major issues, such as in the Eire Flag debate, the members of the Fourth Estate have been consistently sympathetic to Celtic's position; throughout the Sack the Board campaign, the press was largely on the side of 'the malcontents', who were perceived to be the underdogs at the start, and as winners only at the end of the campaign; during many lean seasons, coverage of Celtic's form was again largely sympathetic, and rarely too critical of the players; Celtic's frequent triumphs have been extolled, sometimes to an exaggerated extent; throughout Jock Stein's tenure as manager, nobody among the press corps dared to whisper a word of criticism, although the signs were there in the 1970s that decay had set in.

In recent times, however, a sea-change in reporting on football has occurred, and Celtic, like many other clubs, have suffered from it. It may be described as a cult of personality, affecting players and managers, and embracing the peripheral extras such as spectators, referees – and journalists.

Television, or perhaps the photo-opportunities now offered by expanded sports pages, have changed football coverage irrevocably. The first Scottish Cup final to be televised live was Celtic vs. Clyde in 1955, and the telecast started at 2:50 p.m. – or ten minutes before the match started. Compare that with the modern coverage of the same event, starting three hours before the kick-off. All too frequently, the commentators, or the 'colour-men', refer back to what was said earlier in terms such as 'As I said at the top of the show.' It would appear that 'the show' (the television production) is more important than the actual game of football.

Astonishingly, spectators become willing participants in the spectacle. Why do the foot soldiers of 'the Tartan Army' dress in such ridiculous ways? Why do so many of them paint their faces? One fascinated observer of the football scene pointed out an interesting phenomenon regarding the behaviour of fans when a goal is scored against their team; most will sit in considerable dejection but others will leap to their feet in outrage, pointing furiously in the direction of the pitch. These spectators, knowing that the television cameras will later pick out the details of the goal, leap up in narcissistic rage to denounce the culprit: a goalkeeper out of position, a defender who failed to pick up a striker. The fact is that these attention-seeking spectators have probably not spotted the critical moment but they give the impression of having done so for the cameras. Similarly, at the end of an important match, why are so many spectators nowadays apparently overcome with such excessive emotion? Look closely, and you can see those so overcome wait patiently for the cameras to pick out their grief.

The day might well come when clubs will pay spectators to attend televised fixtures for them to act as extras in the staged production. At the present time the cameramen have been instructed not to dwell on the empty seats at a televised match because it detracts from the atmosphere.

Celtic supporters have a particular axe to grind with the media in general – the conviction that the affairs of Celtic Football Club are not reported fairly in the newspapers.

The claim bears some investigation and, as part of the research involved in writing this book, I arranged to have lunch with a prominent newspaperman, at which the topic of conversation was the coverage of Celtic by the print media. The perennial question of bias against Celtic in the media was raised, but the editor surprised me with his categorical statement: 'There are no longer as many out-and-out Rangers supporters among the reporters. In fact, most of them are Celtic sympathisers.'

I was genuinely shocked, and asked him to list them for me; he thought for a second or two and then reeled off the following:

We'll start with the ones that you probably know already: Glenn Gibbons of *The Scotsman*, Hugh Keevins with the *Sunday Mail*, Kevin McCarra, who used to be with *Scotland on*

Sunday but now with *The Sunday Times* – all excellent journalists and fairly objective; Gerry McNee with *The News of the World*, Andrew Smith, a former editor of *The Celtic View*, but now with *Scotland on Sunday*, Phil Gordon, Iain McGarry, Ian Paul, Tom Lappin of *The Scotsman* (who is probably more of a Hibs man), Mark Guidi of the *Sunday Mail*. Even some editors like Donald Cowey and Kevin McKenna are 'Celtic-minded' men.

He paused before continuing: 'I could go on and give a few more, but you get the picture. I should say this though. All these men are top-notch journalists and, when they cover a football match, they do so as sports writers not as supporters. They know what they're talking or writing about, and they tell it as objectively as humanly possible. Whenever Celtic – either the team or the club – need to be criticised, it's done professionally.'

He indicated that Celtic can be an editor's dream: a huge club with a passionate following and a penchant for self-destruction.

He also pointed out a distressing aspect: Celtic have been particularly newsworthy since the struggle for control of the club started in the early 1990s, but the internal struggles have not ceased with the emergence of Fergus McCann as the eventual winner. Editors of newspapers are aware that they are being manipulated by 'Celtic-minded individuals' currently out of favour at Celtic Park. Any crisis involving Celtic is guaranteed to produce statements from those still on the outside and the editor described it as 'a free "Rent-a Quote" system. These people are on the phone within minutes of news breaking and, of course, they are messengers of doom.' Editors would be failing in their primary task if they did not pander to this type of coverage, and he pointed out that more frequently it is the sub-editor, rather than the journalist, who comes up with the provocative, eye-catching headline.

Even worse was the deliberate fabrication of news by the disaffected, and he spoke sadly of the hints the newspapers received that Fergus McCann's marriage was in trouble:

> We [the media] suspected that it was an orchestrated campaign, but we had to check out the story. Reporters were sent out to the house, and spoke briefly to Elspeth and she was very upset about that. She had every right to be, of course, but the tabloids had their story for that day. We knew we were being manipulated and used, but we couldn't take the chance of missing a possible story, and letting somebody else get it.[76]

As the same editor indicated, several prominent figures in the media have been clearly identified as having had some Celtic leanings, and this does pose problems for them in establishing beyond doubt the primary attribute of objectivity. The editor indicated that he felt that the Celtic-minded journalists appeared to lean over backwards to be fair, and sometimes were ultra-critical

---

[76] In the aftermath of this unjustifiable intrusion into his private life a public-relations exercise was mounted in the opposite direction. Although a very private person, Fergus McCann was persuaded to pose for pictures with his wife and children at their home and answer questions about their domestic life.

of Celtic as a consequence. On the other hand, he did not feel that Rangers men in the media were as scrupulous in their reporting. It does seem clear, however, that any sports writer, known to be a follower of a certain club or, more infrequently, one who admits his true allegiance, is in danger of having his work scrutinised for any hints of bias.

It is a reasonable conclusion to draw that most football journalists writing in Scotland should be closet followers of either Celtic or Rangers, but not so – apparently. The media, it appears, are populated by Celtic-minded individuals and enthusiastic followers of Airdrie, Hamilton Accies, Hearts, Morton, Motherwell, St Mirren ... and even Shettleston Juniors.[77] If this were a trend characteristic of the entire population, Scottish football would be in a much more equitable financial state.

There has always been a marked reluctance among any football writer in Scotland to be identified as a supporter of Rangers – the country's most consistently successful club, and one regarded as the best supported in the nation. Jim Craig, full back in the Lisbon Lions, tells an amusing story in this regard: he was out of action through an injury and missed the Old Firm fixture but he decided to watch it from the old press-box at Celtic Park. Turning up a few minutes late, he stood for a while at the back watching the action unfold on the pitch. While he was there, Rangers scored and the press-box erupted into celebration with respected journalists – followers of Airdrie, Hamilton, Hearts, Morton, Motherwell, St. Mirren, and Shettleston Juniors – leaping up and punching the air in delight!

One journalist, often identified as a Rangers follower, is TV presenter Jim White. In particular, Celtic followers point to a sycophantic interview with Rangers' star Brian Laudrup, during which White asked: 'Why are you so good?' Nobody could possibly deny that Laudrup was an outstanding player, and an exceptionally sporting one, but the question did indicate a rather uncritical mind. White's denial in March, 1996 of an allegiance to Rangers lacked conviction: 'It just so happens I've got a lot of friends who play for Rangers.'

However, a revealing photograph, taken at the end of the Celtic–St. Johnstone match in 1997 which sealed the championship for Celtic, suggests a different story. It shows the scene at the final whistle with the Celtic bench, manager, trainers, and coaches as well as substitutes, leaping upwards with joy. Behind, Celtic fans in the stands are also starting their celebrations but, amid all the euphoria, one long face reveals clearly an unhappy man!

It would be astonishing if reporters did not have leanings to one particular

---

[77] In his early years as a performer, Billy Connolly's agent used to refer to him as 'a Partick Thistle supporter'; similarly, in the movie *Gregory's Girl*, the hero proclaimed the same allegiance. Clearly, identification with either member of the Old Firm raises too much antagonism to be risked.

club, and such an allegiance does not necessarily mean that the journalist is not qualified, nor is he incapable of being a fair-minded and talented communicator – and he should not be automatically discounted for that loyalty.

In fact, I feel that White is a reasonably talented journalist, and does his job commendably. I would go so far as to state that almost every reporter does have a bias; the fine journalists transcend that in their reporting. Recently, Gordon Smith, a former Rangers player and now an agent, was castigated as being in a conflict-of-interest situation in his role as TV pundit.[78] His reply was refreshingly honest and informative: 'There are numerous people working as journalists and pundits within the game of football. Who knows how many of their opinions are objective and how many are influenced by friendships, club allegiances, the return of favours or even, sadly, religious bigotry? At least I declare an interest by being open about who I represent (as an agent).'

Surprisingly, 'Celtic-minded' journalists are less reluctant to be identified but, according to some Celtic supporters, this is not necessarily a good thing. Apparently, these journalists, described by one editor as 'the Uncle Tims', are actually more derogatory of Celtic than is required; 'Rangers-minded' reporters remain uncritical of their club unselfconsciously.

Some Celtic supporters are incensed at articles critical of the club written by men such as Hugh Keevins or Charlie Nicholas, considering it to be a form of treason. The more cynical among the Celtic following suggest that it is a form of sour grapes. According to this theory, Keevins enjoyed a certain amount of inside knowledge through contacts with previous managers and players but, when Fergus McCann took over, a tightening-up of procedures with the press was ordained and Keevins found himself relegated to the sidelines, and deprived of inside stories. The best 'evidence' for that theory may be found in the journalist's gaffe in proclaiming Artur Jorge as Celtic's new coach in July 1997 only a day before Celtic revealed Wim Jansen as their new man. Keevins was said to be reluctant to run with his educated guess, but had to give in to the insistence of his erstwhile editor at *The Scotsman*, Martin Clark.

Similarly, Charlie Nicholas is equally reviled, it being pointed out that

---

[78] The conflict seems to have emerged in respect of Gordon Smith combining media work which includes television appearances as a pundit as well as a column for a national newspaper, with his role as a player agent, representing such as Craig Burley, Kenny Miller, Paul Lambert. Under these circumstances, Smith's impartiality might well be considered at risk. It could constitute a conflict of interest to represent players when a part-time job gives opportunities for the agent to publicise his players' exploits on the field. Both Burley and Miller have been transferred in the recent past for millions of pounds, and it seems clear to any objective observer that Gordon Smith is in a most awkward position as both agent and pundit.

I know little about his talents as an agent, but he is an exceptional commentator on football matters. Alex McLeish, Hibernian's manager, was the person who first raised the matter in public when he complained of leaks to press about confidential contract negotiations in the case of Kenny Miller, who was eventually transferred to Rangers; Smith repudiated any allegation of wrongdoing on his part.

Nicholas did not last too long at Celtic Park as a player after McCann's arrival. The managing director was reported to be aghast at his salary in view of the player's level of fitness and performance, and he balked at any renewal of his contract. Since then, the critics contend, Nicholas, on TV or in his football column, has been consistently critical of McCann's methods and accomplishments, although his comments on football in general, no matter how ungrammatically expressed, have been perceptive.

Kenny Dalglish, as Celtic's Director of Football, was another obvious target for the journalists. While Dalglish is universally recognised as having been a magnificent footballer, his ability as a manager has been questioned, at Liverpool, Blackburn Rovers and Newcastle United as well as at Celtic. Throughout his managerial career in England, Dalglish was often accused of buying success – and walking out on clubs. This may have been unfair but Dalglish's surly manner in dealing with the media did him no favours. His 'Scottish growl' was a stumbling-block for English interviewers: 'I wonder if the TV sports presenters would consider using subtitles when interviewing Kenny Dalglish,' one letter-writer to the *Evening Standard* complained in 1986.

When he returned to Celtic Park in 1999, both he and John Barnes were viewed as outsiders by the Scottish media, and neither seemed prepared to make much of an effort to improve the situation. Dalglish's suspicions about the press – understandable in the light of his personal experiences at Heysel in 1985 and at Hillsborough in 1989 – were heightened as Celtic struggled through a disappointing season and the criticism mounted.

Journalists have a pack-instinct about sensing vulnerability; it was becoming clear that confusion reigned within the management structure, that dissent was rife within the dressing room as the season was turning into a disaster. Under these circumstances, every manager is economical with the truth in dealing with media questions, and that is perfectly acceptable within limits.[79] For example, it would have been counter-productive to reveal that Celtic were actively looking for a new managerial team, or that Mark Viduka was available for transfer. Understandably, Dalglish retreated into sarcasm in attempting to cope with their increasingly bold questions. The media realised that Dalglish had been a relatively unwilling returnee to the dugout and increased the pressure on him. Everybody assumed that he would be gone by the end of the season, and the type of questioning reflected that.

[79] Glenn Gibbons of *The Scotsman* tells the anecdote about the Celtic player who informed him that Jock Stein would be moving shortly for Dixie Deans, the controversial Motherwell striker, and the story duly appeared in the *Weekly News*, for whom Gibbons was working at the time. Stein was furious about the leak and castigated the journalist: 'I've got players here who are working hard in the belief they're making progress – and now you're telling them I'm going to bring in somebody else!' The moral vigour of Stein's tirade was diluted somewhat when he signed Dixie Deans for Celtic only two weeks later.

In a mistaken form of retaliation, Dalglish took to holding official press conferences in such places as Baird's Bar in the Gallowgate and the Celtic Supporters' Association headquarters on London Road. From his point of view, such an open forum might give 'average punters' the chance to judge for themselves what had been asked (and how it was answered), but the ploy backfired disastrously, the press rightly ridiculing his 'spurious man-of-the-people veneer'. Their near-unanimous ridicule was the clearest indication of how much the relationship between Celtic and the media had deteriorated, and how vulnerable Dalglish's position had become.

However, he was not completely without support for his approach. Eddie Toner, the General Secretary of the Celtic Supporters' Association, agreed with the decision to hold press conferences in public places: 'I believe we get a lot of bad publicity and this is an opportunity to see if what is being said is accurately reflected. I was at last Friday's conference and I was astonished on Sunday when I read some of the papers. I felt it must have taken place somewhere else or I wasn't there.' Alistair McKay, writing in *The Scotsman* on 1 April, 2000 stated: 'In my view, this is a good thing. Kenny Dalglish being passively aggressive with the nation's sportscasters is a more entertaining prospect than all those *Sportscene* interviews. When he is cautious, he is accused of being short of ambition; if he complains about this – and he does – then he is paranoid.'

The situation reached a nadir with the ejection of a prominent journalist from a press conference at the Celtic Supporters' Association headquarters. A few days prior to the confrontation, Hugh Keevins of the *Sunday Mail* had reported on Allan MacDonald's performance at a Celtic Q & A Roadshow session at the Carfin Celtic Supporters' Club, the proceeds of which went to raise funds for a new church at Holytown. The article was highly critical and focused primarily on negative aspects and, without actually stating it, the journalist's column conveyed the impression that he had been physically present at the session. Hugh Keevins is an immediately recognisable figure, quite familiar to Celtic followers, and nobody recalled seeing him there. Thus, there was some hostility towards the journalist, when he arrived for the press conference at London Road.

The trouble started, just before the start, when Keevins was asked to leave the premises by a Finbar O'Brannigan of the Social Club committee, and the tabloid made the most of the situation.[80] The journalist was quoted as saying: 'Being asked to leave an official press conference without being allowed to

---

[80] The *Sunday Mail* front-page headline for 7 May 2000 read 'Bully Bhoy' and the accompanying article started off: 'The thug who barred a *Sunday Mail* writer from a Celtic press conference is exposed today as an armed robber and gang ringleader. Finbar O'Brannigan lies about his past and even his name ...'

put a question to Kenny Dalglish is the ultimate denial of freedom of speech!' In fact, Keevins faxed Dalglish at Celtic Park outlining the questions he claims he would have been asked, had he been allowed to stay. The *Sunday Mail* listed these questions, and the answers the following week:

SM: Have you ever at any time regretted the decision to leave England and return home?
KD: Naw. [sic]
SM: Have you sought consultation with your chief executive in light of Guus Hiddink's appointment as manager?
KD: He hasn't been appointed.
SM: To what extent do you blame the players and not the management for what's happened this season?
KD: We all have equal responsibility.
SM: If you had the opportunity over again, would you still go for John Barnes as your first managerial appointment in your role as director of football?
KD: I've answered that one before. I believe John Barnes will go on to be a good manager.

Some observations might be made about these questions, and answers.

Question 1 invited some soul-searching on Dalglish's part and, as an intensely private individual, he simply refused to play that game and answered curtly. However, if the question-and-answer exercise was carried out by fax as the newspaper claimed, it would have been most unlikely that Dalglish's response would have been in the form 'Naw' as reported.

Questions 3 and 4 clearly invited headline-making responses. As an experienced football man, Dalglish neatly side-stepped the traps contained within the questions and did so with a certain amount of grace and finesse. No respectable executive should blame others for fiascos in the past, and this Dalglish to his credit refused to do.

Question 2 is the most interesting. Keevins had assumed that Guus Hiddink had been appointed as Celtic's new manager/coach, and attempted to embarrass Dalglish with his question. On the other hand, Dalglish simply pointed out that the Dutchman had not been appointed and, of course, he was perfectly accurate in that observation – much more so than the journalist.

The intention of the newspaper was to create headlines and to embarrass the beleaguered Celtic executive but it really was an insignificant incident blown out of all proportion. It was another case of the newspaperman attempting to become the story.

Dalglish was under siege from the media, who sensed his insecurity and who preyed on it; in an earlier age Jock Stein presented another image altogether, and the treatment he received reflected that. It goes without saying that success on the field is an effective shield against criticism, and Stein was the most successful manager in the history of the Scottish game. When he became manager of Celtic in March 1965, Jock Stein was familiar with the milieu in which the Scottish media worked, and his subsequent success changed that dramatically, particularly his relationship with the BBC.

The BBC was another organisation in Scotland that had a restrictive hiring policy within some of its departments, and 'Sports' under Peter Thomson's leadership was an obvious example of this trend. Thomson, particularly on radio, was a most effective broadcaster, but he did not care for Celtic at all, and for many years this antipathy did not adversely affect the Corporation as Celtic struggled. Everything changed with Celtic's astonishing success under Jock Stein, both domestically and in Europe.

Whereas other Celtic officials consistently had been courteous to the members of the media, Jock Stein could be abrasive and rude: when asked to name his favourite comedy, he had answered *Sportsreel* and, on another occasion, when the fledgling television coverage had been particularly inept, Stein had barked at a BBC representative: 'Where did you get your cameras? The Barras?'

Stein made little attempt to hide his contempt for Thomson and his cronies, and they frequently became targets for his biting wit: Thomson was instantly dubbed 'Blue Peter' with unerring accuracy, and another radio man, Richard Park, was referred to frequently as 'Ibrox Park'. This latter journalist may have had some sympathies with Rangers but he was, by all accounts, a fair-minded and well-briefed reporter and did not deserve to be ridiculed by Stein. However, Park's answer to an interview question posed by *Not the View* some years later still leaves the reader in some doubt about his allegiance:

Raith Rovers are my home town team and, in fact, I still remember Stevie Chalmers make his debut [?] for Celtic there. As for the Old Firm, how could I support either Celtic or Rangers when I had friends playing for both teams? It's impossible for supporters to believe it. I'm not saying I didn't care who won, but the Celtic fans thought I was a Rangers supporter and the Rangers fans thought I was a Celtic man. So, I'm still a Raith Rovers fan!

When others within the BBC suggested that relations with Celtic's manager had to be improved, Peter Thomson still tried to veto it: 'No way. I wouldn't approve of that. We'll bide our time. He'll need us before we need him.' Some have considered that Thomson was literally afraid of Jock Stein and his powerful personality. In fact, after Jock Stein's appointment as manager, Peter Thomson was never known to have entered Celtic Park, an incredible state of affairs for an established media personality.

One example of Stein's animosity came at the 1969 Old Firm cup final at which Archie Macpherson was the commentator. Normally, the television crews would be supplied the line-ups by the clubs as a courtesy, and this was vital information in preparing technically for the telecast. Stein simply refused to cooperate with BBC Scotland before the match and supplied neither names nor numbers.

Celtic won that Scottish Cup final by 4–0, a triumph destined to be long remembered by the Celtic support, but Stein was still not appeased after the match, and chased away the BBC manager who tried to detain him on the track. Adding insult to injury, Stein did accept an invitation to speak to David Coleman, hosting *Grandstand* from the London studio. Macpherson had to stand in the background as Celtic's manager, watching a replay of Billy McNeill's headed goal in the second minute, just prior to the actual transmission remarked to Coleman: 'Macpherson sounded sick there.'[81] Stein, undoubtedly a patriotic Scot, was making the point quite forcefully that he preferred to speak to London rather than to Glasgow.

About two years later, with the situation still on a Cold War footing, Archie Macpherson – beginning to establish himself at the BBC – decided to broach the matter with Jock Stein. According to Macpherson's account in his autobiography, the discussion was frank. Stein, apart from his forceful personality and keen mind, possessed another psychological advantage in any discussion about sectarianism. As a Lanarkshire man, and a Protestant, he had a personal knowledge of the subject and was not shy about expressing it. When he asked Macpherson about how many Celtic supporters – or Catholics – worked for the BBC, Macpherson's account in *Action Replays* has an authentic tone to it: 'I gave him the stock answer. "I don't know anybody's religion," I said. That was a mistake. He laughed in disbelief and I remember he turned away and waved at me dismissively. "All right" I added. "I suppose none. At a guess." '

It is pleasant to report that matters did improve gradually between Celtic and the BBC in the wake of that conversation, but the incident does indicate a very unhealthy attitude on both sides of the impasse.

The situation in 2000 as Celtic sought a new manager/coach to replace John Barnes resembled a feeding-frenzy, the pressure being on every newspaper, tabloid or broadsheet alike, to break the news first. Every day a new name was proposed as the most likely possibility, and often the same tabloid would offer up an 'exclusive' on the situation, blithely ignoring the fact that the new information flatly contradicted what it had written previously.

Finally, *The Scotsman* revealed that the appointment was Guus Hiddink. That was a most reasonable supposition as Celtic had already contacted the Dutchman, and reached some form of understanding with him. Indeed, Tommy Burns had travelled to Seville, where Hiddink was coaching Real Betis, and briefed him about the nature of his job.

The *Sunday Mail* of 7 May 2000 later headlined the news: 'Guus Hiddink will arrive at Celtic on Friday.' However, Hugh Keevins' column complained plaintively about the fact that Glenn Gibbons of *The Scotsman* had first broken the story. Keevins suggested that Celtic may have tipped off *The Scotsman's*

---

[81] I remember listening to the FA Cup Final on the BBC World Service in Canada, and hearing David Francey reporting on events at half time from Hampden Park with the score 3–0 for Celtic, and my wife, a Canadian, and totally ignorant of football, asking 'Why is that man crying?'

representative: 'The first leak over Hiddink was bad enough since it practically carried MacDonald's signature,' and he described *The Scotsman* as 'a low circulation newspaper in MacDonald's home town of Edinburgh'.

One irony here is that Keevins had worked as a respected journalist for that newspaper for almost twenty years, and his departure came only one month after a similar crisis at Celtic Park. On that occasion in 1997, under pressure from his editor to name Celtic's new coach, Keevins reported that Artur Jorge was to be unveiled as the successor to Tommy Burns. He revealed all the details: salary, responsibilities, priorities, and provided a complete profile of the man. The press conference was scheduled for the next day (3 July 1997) and, until the meeting started at 3:30, nobody among the assembled media representatives knew with certainty the identity of Celtic's new coach. When Wim Jansen's name was announced, the cynics felt that several among the journalists still did not recognise him.[82]

It might be harsh to blame Keevins for being so wrong-footed as the identity of the new appointment had been a closely guarded secret, with nobody among the journalists being favoured with a hint, including Keevins who had previously enjoyed an inside-track at Celtic Park. His employer, *The Scotsman*, reported Jansen's appointment stoically: 'Scepticism greeted the appointment of Wim Jansen as Celtic's new head coach yesterday' – an embarrassing reversal for the newspaper to have to make.

Once again, as Celtic searched for a new manager, the media were in danger of being thwarted, but *The Scotsman's* coup apparently had prevented that, although the *Daily Record* reminded its readers that it had 'exclusively revealed' Guus Hiddink as the choice but the statement was singularly unconvincing. No doubt that the *Daily Record* had 'revealed' Hiddink's appointment earlier, but hardly exclusively as the same tabloid could have made the same claim about several candidates in the running for the position.

The supreme irony in all the claims asserted by the media lies in the fact that Guus Hiddink did not get the job at Celtic Park.[83] No doubt, some of the same journalists just as promptly pointed out that they had been the first to announce Martin O'Neill's appointment.

Modesty does not appear to be a requisite for being a sports journalist.

In August 2000 BBC Scotland claimed as a scoop the announcement of

---

[82] *The Sun*, for example, when given the information on a Celtic public relations fact sheet that Jansen had coached in Japan, hastily concocted the attention-grabbing headline 'The Second Worst Thing To Hit Hiroshima!'

[83] One has to feel some sympathy for Glenn Gibbons of *The Scotsman*, an excellent sports writer, who had checked all the details of the 'scoop' before submitting them to his editors. It does seem clear that Hiddink was the choice of Allan MacDonald, that negotiations were well advanced, until Martin O'Neill re-entered the contest as a candidate.

'a sensational development in Scottish football', and this would be revealed exclusively on *Friday Sportscene*. The announcement centred on the fact that both Celtic and Rangers would likely be operating within a European League set up involving clubs from Scotland, Holland, Belgium and Portugal within a few years.

It was an exciting development, but scarcely news. On 5 October 1999 at Celtic's AGM, Allan MacDonald, the club's Chief Executive, and Kenny Dalglish, the Director of Football, both spoke enthusiastically of a European-type league within five years; MacDonald attended the meeting in person, Dalglish through a video hook-up. The information was received by the press, noted, mentioned briefly, and largely forgotten until August 2000 – a mere ten months later. And, of course, BBC Scotland took the credit for breaking the news at that time.

Journalists do have one advantage in that they deliver their work on a daily basis, and their medium is a great consumer of material which is forgotten the next day. In recent years Chick Young, on television in one instance and on radio the other, has announced the imminent signing of players for Rangers. One was Eoin Jess of Aberdeen and the information was delivered excitedly; full details were submitted confidently, evaluations made of the role of the player within the Ibrox squad, but Jess continued to play for Aberdeen throughout that season, and continued to do so until a loan transfer to Bradford City in December 2000. The other case was the proposed transfer of Gordon Durie to Rangers from Tottenham Hotspur. Once again authentic-sounding details were given; the specific location of the meeting, the amounts of money involved in the transfer, but the player did not move to Rangers at that time. His transfer, when it was effected, came more than a year later as a result of an entirely different set of circumstances.

I do not recall the journalist ever admitting to his errors, or expressing any regret for transmitting false information. Young's difficulty arose from the fact that he was reporting gossip as news – an increasingly occupational hazard for modern-day journalists.

A most interesting case for a study of the media would involve the treatment of Jock Brown as Celtic's General Manager between June 1997 and November 1998, a total of 510 days.

Certainly, Brown's appointment was not greeted with any great enthusiasm by Celtic supporters in general. The major 'complaint' was that he was not considered 'Celtic-Minded',which he later chose as the title of his book relating the events throughout his tenure. In fact, Brown was eminently qualified for the job: fifty-one years of age; a Scot; Cambridge-educated; a trained lawyer, with several footballers as clients; a recognised sports-commentator; an interest in sport; and a non-Catholic. This latter fact was the stumbling block for many Celtic supporters – although it should not have been a factor.

Unfortunately for Brown, his appointment caught the media by surprise, and several journalists reacted negatively as a result. It has been suggested also that there was a certain amount of jealousy on the part of the media, and this situation was exacerbated with a new policy, strictly enforced, of not leaking information to favoured journalists. Brown, used to confidentiality in his dealings with his legal clients, had no problems with this policy but his former press-colleagues had. As Celtic's General Manager he could have been a gold mine of real information on new signings, players available for transfer; relationships between players and coaches, and, details of salaries. The wish-list was endless, but totally unrequited. Resentment grew very quickly, and Brown's personal manner did not help matters much; journalists, aware that he knew much more than he was revealing, became more and more hostile.

Peter McLean, Celtic's public relations officer, showed him the back page of the *Daily Record* after his first press-conference. It read 'Joke Brown' and McLean's comments were: 'There you are. For fifty-one years you have been subjected to generally positive media comment and your image has not been in question. Now you have joined Celtic; you haven't done anything; you haven't made a decision, but you are now portrayed as a joke. Welcome to the club!'

It proved an impossible situation for Brown. An unpopular choice with the supporters from the start, and the butt of media coverage that can only be described as malicious, he did well to survive for 510 days. I would suggest that, while many among Celtic's support were relieved to see him go, the club owed him a considerable debt of gratitude for a professionally executed tenure. I remember the snide comments made by the media about the appointments of Wim Jansen and Dr. Josef Venglos, and about the signings of Henrik Larsson and Lubomir Moravcik, the quality of the two players being doubted because they cost only £600,000 and £300,000 respectively. I remember the press fury at the departure of Wim Jansen from Celtic Park, and the blame falling on to Jock Brown, unfairly in retrospect. I also remember the tabloids predicting that at least eight out of the title-winning side 'would be leaving very shortly' as a consequence of the manager's resigning. More than that, I remember the winning of the League Cup (for the first time in fifteen seasons) and the annexing of the championship (for the first time in ten seasons), a feat for which the General Manager surely deserves some share of the credit.

The treatment of Brown in the media was vicious, reflecting no credit on the journalists responsible; those journalists sensed Brown's unpopularity with a sizeable percentage of Celtic supporters and played on that fact to the bitter end.

Let us conclude this section on the media with a summary. Celtic have enjoyed a reasonable press-coverage for most of the period covered in this book, and much of what can be construed as a poor press has been caused by the club's lack of success on the field and board room turmoil off it. Like most other clubs in Scotland, Celtic have been subjected to the snipings of the gutter press, anxious to raise circulation. This cheap journalism does not appear to be confined to Celtic but, because Celtic is a prominent club, it attracts more than its share of interest.

CHAPTER THIRTEEN

The Other Side of the Coin

Any objective examination of the coverage of Celtic in the media has to include the *Glasgow Observer's* sports pages. The official newspaper of the Catholic community, this weekly publication covered football almost totally from the Celtic perspective; in fact, its journalists were mere propagandists for the club and none more so than 'Man in the Know'. Over the years a number of different 'journalists' took over this pseudonym but each and every one was a Celtic zealot, almost laughably biased in favour of the club and tilting at the traditional enemies: Rangers, the SFA, referees.

The pseudonym was a cunning one, suggesting that the writer was privy to insider knowledge, and there is no doubt that the club did use his columns to get across its point of view unofficially but effectively.

If Celtic have had reason to suspect the motives of certain sports writers in Scotland, then surely Rangers must have valid reason to complain about the treatment accorded them for decades in the *Glasgow Observer* – that is if they were ever read by any Rangers official, player or supporter.

Consider the calibre of the writing, the depth of feeling – and the content:

> On the terracing at the Dalmarnock end on Saturday there was congregated a gang, thousands strong, including the dregs and scourings of filthy slumdom, unwashed yahoos, jailbirds, night hawks, won't-works, 'burroo' barnacles, and pavement pirates, all, or nearly all, in the scarecrow stage of verminous trampdom. This ragged army of insanitary pests was lavishly provided with orange and blue remnants, and these were flaunted in challenge as the football tide flowed this way and that. Practically without cessation for ninety minutes or more, the vagabond scum kept up a strident howl of the 'Boyne Water' chorus. Nothing so designedly provoking, so maliciously insulting, or so bestially ignorant has ever been witnessed even in the wildest exhibitions of Glasgow Orange bigotry. (1 November 1924)

> Anonymous letters, abusive in tone, are a regular feature and to these I offer no objection so long as the topic is football and nothing else. But a letter, signed 'Ibrox Blue', reaching me this morning, is of a nature so scurrilous and ignorantly bigoted that I can only ascribe its origin to some scummy and slummy skulker of the underworld where bag-snatchers and razor-slashers foregather to devise midnight outrages and curse the Celtic. One has merely to glance at an Ibrox brake-club to see that most of them are only half-witted. So, let us forgive our anonymous assailant who is probably stung to raving madness by his favourites' annual Cup humiliation. (19 March 1927)

The failure of Rangers to win the Scottish Cup between 1903 and 1928, despite periods of league domination was fertile ground for 'Man in the Know's' wit. Describing an Old Firm league fixture at Celtic Park (won 1–0 by Rangers) he pointed out that one Rangers supporter had required medical attention at half time as the Scottish Cup – recently won by Celtic – was being paraded round the track. Bitingly, he attributed the spectator's fainting spell to the unaccustomed sight of Scotland's premier trophy.

He denounced the Rangers following for their behaviour at that particular match in these terms:

> The blue-bedecked crowd at the Dalmarnock end earned fame of a kind by actually pelting with stones and clinkers the collectors, ladies and young boys included, who were carrying round the sheets for the Dalbeth Convent collection.[84] The Blue following have many misdeeds to their credit, but surely this was the dirtiest. Let it never be forgotten that Rangers supporters stoned women and children engaged in a work of charity. The Germans never did anything worse than this, and when the game and the players are merely a shadowy memory this shameful thing will be remembered. (23 April 1927)

Although he could not have known it, 'Man in the Know' was a fanzine subscriber – decades ahead of his time. There is something humorous about his dithyrambic ranting at the injustices heaped upon his favourite team, but he was read widely among a community whose members felt they had reason to be aggrieved. A former Celtic director assured me: 'Everybody bought the *Observer* just to read 'Man in the Know' – and he was trusted and believed by those who read him.'

As I have already suggested, many reporters in the Scottish press were fair and unbiased in their comments about Celtic as a club and as a team. However, one particular journalist deserves individual mention – Cyril Horne, in his days at the *Glasgow Herald*. Unfortunately, Horne appears to be too much identified with the Celtic cause, as a personal friend of Bob Kelly, the chief contributor to the annual Celtic handbook, the ghost-writer of Kelly's autobiography, and a frequent apologist for the club in his columns. Throughout the 1940s and 50s Horne was unusual in that he was very critical of Rangers as an organisation, and frequently for their overly physical approach on the pitch. He seemed to be the only journalist in the popular press who was prepared to raise the issue of Rangers' anti-Catholic policy, or to allude to it. Perhaps the fact that he wrote for a newspaper less dependent than most on its football coverage for circulation gave him a certain licence to be independently minded. But it took considerable personal courage and integrity to do so at a time when Rangers were dominant in Scotland. As a Church of Scotland elder, he objected in principle to the spurious claim that Rangers Football Club represented Scottish thinking on this subject.

The Celtic View was believed to be the first club newspaper, and it was proposed to the Celtic board in 1964 by Jack McGinn, who later became a Celtic director and chairman, and rose to eminence as the president of the SFA. McGinn, who was working in the circulation department of

---

[84] The sheets referred to are the bed sheets carried round the track and into which the spectators were invited to toss in money for the specific charity. I can recall that this appeared to be a common practice especially at Fir Park until at least 1956.

Beaverbrook Papers at the time, claimed to be 'somewhat exasperated at the coverage, or lack of it, about Celtic in those days', and he indicated to the directors that such a newspaper would provide an excellent platform for the club to express its viewpoint – and also provide an invaluable link with the supporters.

McGinn's proposal was accepted and endorsed by the board in March 1965 at the first board meeting attended by the new manager, Jock Stein, who pointed out that the editor should reserve space on the front page of the first issue for a photograph of the 1965 Scottish Cup winners. Considering that the final was still several weeks away, and that Celtic had not won the trophy since 1954, the manager's air of confidence seemed surprising. However, that first issue appeared on 11 August 1965, and the front page featured, as Stein had promised, a team photograph of Celtic with the Scottish Cup.

Mainly due to the surge of adrenaline running through Celtic as an organisation with the astounding success of the team under Jock Stein's leadership, *The Celtic View* also prospered, reaching a circulation figure of 26,000 weekly. This allowed Jack McGinn to repay the £600 loan from the Board, required to set up the new venture.

The newspaper was a critical success as well as a commercial one. The 'Letters to the Editor' section provided a forum for lively and informed debate on current issues, articles were contributed recalling the history of the club, and a page on developments across Europe by Bob McDonald gave the supporters a greater perspective on football. Jock Stein himself played a leading role in educating the fans, praising and criticising them for their behaviour, advising them of his long-range objectives, and giving the occasional insight into the mind of a modern manager.

However, thirty-five years on, the newspaper has changed considerably. It proved to be impossible to sustain the enthusiasm of the early years and, more and more, the tone became defensive. All official publications are conservative by nature, and must reflect the party line on important issues. *The Celtic View* increasingly was perceived to be following this trend, and most Celtic supporters recognised instinctively the paper's shortcomings especially in times of controversy. In fact, one of its past editors (Andrew Smith) felt so guilty about the contents he was 'forced' to print by the Board of Directors prior to 1994 that he described himself as Dr. Goebbels – the infamous master of the Nazi propaganda machine.

Graham Spiers in his former column for *Scotland on Sunday* referred frequently to *The Celtic View* as a source of some amusement.

> The amount of tosh and tripe dug up by these harassed men [the editors] – in impecunious circumstances admittedly – would be enough to make a sitcom. My favourite, I think, remains the 'He Wants to Wear the Hoops' canon of stories in which exclusives ... a Dragan Stoijkovic or a Teofilio Cubillas was dying to play for Celtic, stories of exotic South

Americans wanting to pull on 'the famous hooped shirt' were usually adorned with fantastic detail: players who, when little boys, had grown up in leaking Andean shacks, their fathers normally impoverished drivers of pigs or mules, but the mean walls were plastered with unlikely posters of Charlie Tully or Jimmy McGrory.

Quite often stories which appear in *The Celtic View* reappear in slightly different form in the commercial press a few days later, and usually unacknowledged. The following 'filler' appeared in April 1990 in the sports pages of at least one tabloid:

The stars of AC Milan are on course to capture a world record five major trophies. And TV magnate Silvio Berlusconi revealed yesterday it was the memory of Celtic's Lisbon Lions which inspired him to assemble his multi-million pound side.

Milan already have the Super Cup and World Club championship on display in the boardroom. They lead the league by two points, are in the Italian Cup final, and meet KV Mechelen in the European Cup last eight.

Berlusconi said: 'When I was young, the best team in the world was Celtic. They were absolutely brilliant and were also chasing every honour. I never thought it would be possible to achieve everything. It makes me so proud that the team I have built can do even better than the Celtic team I admired for so long'.

At first glance it appears laudatory towards Celtic (and the Lisbon Lions), and this is highly acceptable to the average Celtic supporter. The distinct impression is conveyed that the reporters of the tabloid are in some form of communication with the owner of AC Milan – an indication of the extensive football coverage offered by the newspaper.

However, the content of this particular filler seemed somewhat familiar. Indeed it had first appeared almost word-for-word in an issue of *The Celtic View* several years earlier. Even worse, the editor of *The Celtic View* – but only after he had left the club's employment to become established as a regular journalist – admitted almost cheerfully that he 'had made up the whole thing to cheer up the supporters'.

Today, *The Celtic View* (priced at £1.95) has an entirely different format: a glossy magazine-type approach, almost exclusively in colour, and with approximately eleven of its forty-eight pages devoted to advertising. Some features remain: a valuable page of statistics for the current season, listing results, scorers, line-ups, attendances, substitute appearances, yellow and red cards distributed, and future fixtures.

With ready access to personal computers, and world-wide linkage through the Internet, it is not surprising that football supporters, despairing of objective or intelligent coverage of their teams, should turn to producing fanzines.

Celtic fans have been in the vanguard of such enterprises. The very first fanzine in British football was probably *The Shamrock*, produced by the Shamrock Celtic Supporters' Club, based in Edinburgh. The publication made its appearance in the early 1960s at the height of the supporters' frustration with the so-called 'youth policy' adopted by the Board of Directors. Significantly it ceased publication about the time of Jock Stein's return to Celtic Park as manager in 1965 – and Celtic's almost immediate success.

Vendors sold *The Shamrock* for sixpence (2.5p) on match days in the approaches to Celtic Park and it did have a certain popularity with the dissatisfied elements among the support because of its radical views on the issues: anti-Board, anti-SFA, anti-Rangers sentiments all vehemently expressed – and its Irish Republican sympathies. Among its extreme views were the following: the SFA should be run by players, and the clubs run by supporters. As an interim measure it proposed that representatives of supporters' clubs should be present at meetings to select Celtic's team.

It did, however, reflect the frustration of those seasons, but at times *The Shamrock* was too highly personal and abusive in its criticism of individuals such as Bob Kelly, the club's chairman, for his intransigence and John Hughes for his inconsistency on the pitch.

At least there was a fierce honesty and directness about its approach, in sharp contrast to the banalities of the popular press in Scotland. Even back in October, 1963 *The Shamrock* was advocating fan-power, as this excerpt from an editorial shows: 'They could call a mass meeting on Glasgow Green and deliver an ultimatum to the Celtic Board to get a real team on the Park, or get out. Otherwise they could boycott the games, and that would certainly make an impression ... after all, the supporters are the only part of the club that cannot be done without. They can replace players, trainers, and even Mr. Kelly, but the support cannot be replaced.'

However, the most successful of all the Celtic fanzines remains *Not the View*, founded in 1987 in a spirit of protest, as its very first editorial comment makes clear:

> It seems to us that any serious criticism of how the team is run at the very top would not be included in the official club newspaper, the *Celtic View* which, apart from its stunning banality and unchanging, conservative format, is becoming more and more like *Pravda*, only putting forward the party line. We aim to print the sort of opinion you hear on the terracing but never see in the 'View'. A group of like-minded supporters who go to the Jungle every Saturday decided that it was time for the views of the ordinary fans to be heard. Over the course of the season we had written many letters to the *Celtic View* but they were never printed. Therefore, in order that we, the ordinary supporters, get a chance to criticise how the team is run we have started this fanzine.

At the conclusion of its first editorial the following paragraph indicated its philosophy: 'You might think once you've finished reading it that it's the biggest load of crap you've ever seen in your life. If so, then send in your articles and opinions and make it better. We'll print anything that's not racist, religiously bigoted, or political.'

In common with most Scottish fanzines, *Not the View* remains uninterested in other clubs – except when engaging in hostility towards them, sporadically in most cases but consistently in the case of Rangers. It did originally set out to be an opposition paper, as its very title suggests. At that time, Celtic were in semi-permanent turmoil with an unpopular board clinging to power, managers tied by financial restraints, and teams often under-performing on the pitch.

Occasionally, *Not the View* ventures into genuinely valuable research: in Issue 11 (March/April 1989) a questionnaire was printed, and the results produced in Issue 13. More than 400 responded to the poll, a quite remarkable figure. This poll was organised in 1989, when opposition to the Board was fragmented but it is significant that, when Fergus McCann took over in 1994, the astute Scots–Canadian businessman availed himself of similar polls to formulate his strategies at Celtic Park. In fact, almost certainly unconsciously, *Not the View* provided a basis for McCann's much-vaunted marketing prowess.

Not the View was able to recognise clearly that it could not change things at Celtic Park, and to its credit it did not disguise that fact.

Some targets remain constant: the former board of directors; the domination of Scottish football by Rangers; the alleged bias of referees; the press coverage of Celtic; the workings of the SFA. At least the constant carping and criticism is accomplished with a sense of humour, and done so while still living up to its original credo of publishing items that are non-racist and non-political.

Frequently *Not the View* is critical of the coverage provided by the newspapers and the established reporters. Their particular animosity is sometimes reserved for those reporters felt to be 'Celtic-minded' but now writing pieces critical of the club and the team's performances. Gerry McNee, who had written several books about the club, is a regular target and in one issue (No.54, March 1995) was virtually accused of plagiarism.

George Murray contributed an article titled 'Filing Copy' and quotes excerpts from two books about Celtic, written some fifteen years apart, and concentrates on the description of the almost legendary goalkeeper John Thomson.[85]

> The ball went to Ernie Hine, the fair-haired Leicester City inside right who stood alone and unmarked twenty yards out. Hine's shot was one of those deliberate, tremendous, gathering-pace-as-they-go majestic shots such as only the great inside forwards seem capable of producing. Thomson was still on his knees as it started on its way. Right from his knees he rose, a gymnast's leap, arms outstretched and body arched. Somehow he got the tips of his fingers to the ball as it sped towards the underside of the bar, and flicked it over. The Villa Park grandstand echoed and trembled to a sustained outburst of applause which went on for minute after minute. (James E. Handley, *The Celtic Story*, London 1960)

---

[85] The actual excerpts were much longer but in the interests of brevity I have produced only one-third of each. However, the larger excerpts reveal much the same unacknowledged borrowing.

Compare

> The ball went clear to Ernie Hine the fair-haired Leicester City inside right who stood alone and unmarked 20 yards out. Hine's shot was one of those deliberate, tremendous, gathering-pace-as-they-go majestic shots such as only great inside forwards seem capable of producing. Thomson was still on his knees as it raged towards him but he rose in a gymnast's leap, arms outstretched and body arched. Somehow he got the tips of his fingers to the ball and pushed it over the bar. The Villa Park grandstand echoed and trembled to a sustained outburst of applause which went on for minute after minute. (Gerald McNee, *The Story of Celtic*, London 1978)

In the earlier book, the author James Handley was scrupulous in acknowledging the source of his material, which he attributed to Bruce Swadel, the former sports editor of the *Scottish Daily Express*. Clearly, the later excerpt owed a great deal to Handley's book (or Swadel's article) but this debt was not acknowledged. It seems that scholars are more appreciative of original research than journalists. Even more interestingly, this was not the first time that McNee had used this same material as it also appears word-for-word in *A Lifetime in Paradise*, the autobiography of Jimmy McGrory, ghost-written by McNee and published in 1975.

Two other fanzines might be mentioned briefly here: *Once a Tim and Bhoyzone*. In November 1990 Matt McGlone became editor of *Once A Tim*, which took a more militant stance than *Not the View* regarding the directors as the financial situation worsened at Celtic Park. For example a regular cartoon feature about the directors was called 'The Board Stiffs'. The fanzine was paid a rather surprising compliment in late 1992, when Michael Kelly suggested to McGlone that his staff 'get the four inside pages [of *The Celtic View*] and do to the media what you do to Celtic'. McGlone, who had had the foresight to tape the meeting with Kelly, was astonished at the offer from Celtic's public relations guru, and eventually declined it.

Once A Tim became very closely identified with two organisations which had sprung up in efforts to effect changes at Celtic Park. The first was Save Our Celts whose inaugural meeting took place at Shettleston Town Hall on 25 February 1991 by invitation only and some 300 attended. The impetus for this initiative probably sprang from the failure of Brian Dempsey to be ratified as a member of the Board of Directors some months earlier. Celts For Change made its appearance in late November 1993 and attracted a crowd of thirty in the Candleriggs as a result of an ad in the *Daily Record* inviting fans to attend 'if they cared about the future of their club'.

A second meeting was held early in December at the same location; this time the attendance was close to 500; only a week later a third meeting was held at Govan Town Hall with 850 present and the talk was now of action including a boycott of Celtic's home matches.

This step – almost unprecedented in Celtic's history – required considerable organisation and the first staged boycott of a Celtic home fixture was scheduled to take place on 26 February 1994, a league match against Kilmarnock. Surprisingly, given that Celtic Park is equipped with undersoil heating, the match had to be called off because of snow but the boycott did take place on 1 March, the rescheduled date. Celtic announced that the official attendance was 10,888, but a market research team had been hired by Celts For Change and their figures were 8,225, of which 1,905 were Kilmarnock supporters.

The writing was on the wall for the Board, and the takeover was effected on 4 March 1994. Shortly afterwards *Once A Tim* decided to cease publication as 'to carry on with the publication and criticise the new owners when they had so much work to do would have been hypocritical'. There has been much speculation among Celtic supporters that *Once A Tim*, after starting off as a typical fanzine, had become more of a front for 'Celts For Change' and a suitable vehicle for the malcontents in the struggle for control of Celtic.

The first issue of *Bhoyzone* appeared in October 1996 and developed from a World Wide Web site on the Internet and its sophisticated appearance suggests a familiarity with the latest technology on the part of the editors. Like *Once A Tim*, the fanzine seemed to cease publication rather abruptly as an independent publication, and now appears as an adjunct to the match programme.

This trend is a touch disconcerting as it gives a slight impression that the legitimate voices of opposition have been silenced or at least muted in their criticism. Its former editor John Cole also writes a column for *The Celtic View*, as does Matt McGlone formerly of *Once A Tim*.

Celtic do have outlets for expressing their points-of-view, as well as in the regular press, and throughout their history have been able to utilise these channels. In recent times, Celtic supporters have been able to outline their grievances about every aspect of football in Scotland, including criticism of their own club.

The once derogatory description of Scottish journalists as 'fans with typewriters' has become a virtual reality.

Conclusions

At various times throughout its history Celtic Football Club have been subjected to unfair treatment from the Scottish football authorities; the SFA, the Scottish League, the Scottish Premier League. This treatment over an extended period of time does appear to have been worse than that accorded most other clubs within Scotland.

The critical question to be answered is this: does this unfair treatment constitute a systemic form of persecution or harassment?

Unfortunately, the question cannot be answered in categorical terms as every football club in Scotland has had occasion in the past to complain about the treatment meted out to it by the SFA and the other authorities.[86] It is perfectly natural that mistakes should have occurred, and these errors should fall within normal parameters. Celtic have suffered, along with other clubs, from these occasional miscarriages of justice, and should have no undue complaint about that sort of human error.

It is also true – and beyond dispute – that certain elements within the SFA have at times treated the club unfairly, and the reason appears to lie in an ingrained prejudice against the Irish/Catholic community with whom Celtic are associated. The problem that exists for many Celtic-minded people is to distinguish clearly between two categories of injustice: honest administrative mistakes and deliberately discriminatory policy. Too often relatively minor incidents have been exaggerated out of all proportion, and motives have been ascribed which bear little resemblance to the facts.

Today in a modern Scotland overt racism and discrimination based on religious (and other grounds) is illegal, but that does not mean it no longer exists.

Private organisations such as social clubs, golf and rugby clubs can and do practise more subtle forms of discrimination, and the SFA can rightly be described as a 'club'. It claims to represent all of Scotland and that claim is reasonably justifiable, but Scotland does have a history of prejudice and hostility towards Catholics (and the Irish). It is quite possible that the SFA does include among its staff and members Scots who still harbour those traditional resentments. While the situation undoubtedly is improving for all minorities,

---

[86] The decision in 1999/2000 by the Scottish League to punish Hamilton Academical certainly appears harsher than any inflicted on Celtic. Hamilton were forced to cancel a fixture when their players 'went on strike' in a dispute over wages: the match was awarded to their opponents, the club was fined £2000, and deducted a further twelve league points. Hamilton, till then safe in the middle of the table, were relegated, with further financial consequences.

anti-Celtic feeling was for a long time the prevailing mood at Carlton Place and later at Park Gardens. George Graham, later knighted for 'services to Association Football', was the leader of this faction throughout the latter half of his long tenure as the SFA's Secretary, and as he was also responsible for recruiting staff as well as carrying out SFA policy the practice continued long after his resignation in 1957.

Celtic were primarily responsible for ousting Graham, but the Secretary had stamped his impression on most aspects of the running of the national association. Subsequent Celtic boards have been suspicious of the motivation of SFA directives ever since Graham's 'rule', perhaps unduly so, but understandably.

Another major problem for Celtic – supporters, officials and players – is the persistent feeling that their greatest rivals have been treated much more leniently for their transgressions. The reason is a historic one:

> What most people seem to have overlooked so far following the Rangers decision to sign non-Protestant players is that the SFA should have taken action years ago. A football club which is religiously bigoted and discriminatory is obviously detrimental to the players, the managers and the supporters, not to mention the reputation of Scottish football abroad. The SFA is made up from the clubs; their directors and representatives form the Scottish Football Association Council which makes most decisions to do with the general welfare of the game. Players, managers, and supporters are not represented. The Council has consistently endorsed the type of religious discrimination in the same way that most sporting bodies condemn South African apartheid. If the SFA had been sincere or willing they could easily have refused registration until Rangers had adopted new policies towards their players and supporters. The real reasons why the SFA have tolerated Rangers for so long are related to the strong emphasis of Protestant lineage in Scottish clubs. Their directors will on Council reflect their own attitudes towards football. (*Banned!*, Strathclyde Student Press, 1976)

In a similar vein, Celtic could complain legitimately that the popular press in Scotland ignored the fact that the country's most successful club was practising a shameful policy of discrimination against a sizeable group within Scotland's population. Only in recent decades – and only when Rangers were suffering a temporary decline in form or status – did any journalist, or newspaper, have the courage to point this out.

As can be seen from even a cursory reading of this book, the vexing problem of refereeing standards has been a recurring one, or perhaps a permanent one. I would have to state that most referees – the overwhelming majority of them – do their best and attempt to be fair. For a variety of reasons it is sometimes difficult to perform at one's best, and an atmosphere of fear and intimidation does not help the situation. Certainly, Celtic have had more than their share of adverse decisions in important matches, and especially in fixtures against Rangers. As far as Celtic supporters are concerned, some referees are depicted as being anti-Celtic consistently. I would suggest that this is a misconception at the present time, but it would be helpful if some administrative mechanism was in place to ensure that errors made by referees were recognised and admitted by the authorities. A cover-up by the SFA, no matter how understandable the motive in protecting its employees, is unhelpful and arouses even more suspicion on the part of the aggrieved club.

Clubs and reporters have a symbiotic relationship: even the most affluent of football clubs welcome the pages of free publicity provided by the media, and the reporters willingly provide this service in order to fill their pages. The relationship remains amicable enough provided the columns produced in the newspapers are filled with admiring and fawning praise. It is only when journalists venture into genuine criticism – or deliberate mischief-making – that friction develops.

One of the more pleasant aspects of writing this book has been the realisation that much of the newspaper coverage of football in Scotland has been both extensive and first-rate – but in recent years circulation-wars have affected football reporting.

Some respectable newspapers have noticeably declined in quality over the years, and now have to be recognised as tabloids – a word that automatically excludes genuine quality. Unfortunately, these newspapers still have large sports desks and employ journalists who have proven in the past that they are capable of producing worthwhile work but, working for a tabloid where the primary concern is with circulation figures, their output has deteriorated to a distressing degree. Too many Celtic supporters have been unduly sensitive to slights in the tabloids, and perhaps are unaware that the reporters are acting under their editors' instructions in bids to increase circulation through controversy.

It does not appear to be a particularly anti-Celtic campaign; in fact, Rangers probably can make similar claims of adverse publicity – one Ibrox wag asserted that five-a-side games at practice-sessions featured 'the back pages versus the front pages'. Gerry McNee, for example, has the distinction of having been assaulted by Billy McNeill and Graeme Souness, the managers of Celtic and Rangers – at different times fortunately. Souness has also berated James Traynor, then with the *Glasgow Herald*, for his reasonably accurate comments after Red Star Belgrade had beaten Rangers in European competition: 'I've been reading your stuff over the last couple of years, and it seems to me that you are just a little Socialist.'

The period covered in this work extends from 1941 to the present day, and until 1970 it appears that the standard of reporting was admirably high, and fair. In almost all of the major issues involving Celtic and the football authorities, the press has consistently come down on Celtic's side when the club has been right. Frequently this sympathy did not affect the outcomes of several matters because the SFA appeared immune to outside criticism. And during this period both the quality press and the tabloids did appear to cover football well. The electronic media (radio and television) were slightly different as there originally existed within them several cliques perceived to be anti-Catholic, and by extension anti-Celtic. The employment practices of the BBC serve as mute examples of this latter trait.

Finally, it has to be recognised that life in Scotland has improved for the descendants of those original Irish immigrations; the opportunities are there in education and employment. Only in pockets, or in individual cases, does outright discrimination occur. Scottish football has been slow to join in this progress, but the situation has improved almost dramatically in recent years.

Celtic supporters can help in that ongoing process.

It is time to put aside an unhealthy preoccupation with past injustices, although they should not be forgotten. It is worthwhile to be aware of the past, and to learn from it, but not to dwell on it. A historical perspective is admirable – but not a hysterical one.

When Celtic were formed in 1887, as an 'alien' club they faced a series of challenges, motivated in part by the undenied fact of the club's Irish and Catholic origins. In order to survive, these obstacles had to be overcome. When Celtic did more than survive – and actually prospered – they had to face other challenges on and off the field. Once more, these challenges were accepted and overcome.

Today, in present-day Scotland and in the world of modern football, different challenges have to be met head-on and, if possible, overcome.

For Celtic-minded people these challenges might mean giving up some long-held perceptions about the club's relationship with the authorities within Scotland, and this could be considered a sacrifice. Children learn to live without a Santa Claus, and Celtic supporters should learn to live without uttering the knee-jerk cries of persecution, comforting as these appeals might be in explaining away reverses.

Prejudice against Catholics and the Irish has been a feature of Scottish life since the Reformation. This is a fact, beyond doubt or argument. In recent years this prejudice has decreased, mainly due to changes in the law of the land and economic pressure although, unfortunately, some visceral remnants might remain. However, a distrust has grown up within 'Irish' or Catholic communities as a direct consequence of blatant discrimination in virtually every aspect of life.

Celtic have always been a flagship for this community's hopes and ambitions and the club – players, officials and supporters – have frequently cited bias on the part of the Scottish game's administrators as a reason for failure. The discrimination against Celtic was real and long-lasting. Thus, the 'paranoia' exhibited by Celtic supporters and officials has been totally understandable and has often been justified, but now it might be outdated.

It might be time to give up this claim in the future, because to continue to blame sinister outside influences for frequent failure on a football pitch is ultimately counter-productive. The Scottish football public has become tired and bored with Celtic supporters' cries of injustice, raised almost automatically at every minor reverse, and some Celtic-minded people share that opinion.

In recent seasons it has been encouraging to note that successive Celtic managers including Wim Jansen, Dr. Venglos, John Barnes and Martin O'Neill have taken the line that 'things even out over a period of time' and this is probably true with refereeing decisions. It would be a great step forward if Celtic followers could accept the lead of their managers in this regard.

However, old habits die hard and memory can be highly selective and too many Celtic followers remember only the injustices. Ritual abuse of referees does not work: any referee worthy to officiate at fixtures of the Scottish Premier League should not be cowed by such unfair treatment and, in fact, his determination not to be bullied or influenced might result in the borderline decisions going against Celtic. It strikes me as obvious that any accredited referee would recoil with indignation at being labelled as incompetent, a much more damning indictment than the automatic allegations of religious bias levelled unfairly at officials.

More and more, match officials find it harder to cover up their mistakes as happened so frequently in the past. Television coverage of fixtures goes far to ensure that football fans actually see what has happened, thus giving them an opportunity to evaluate the performance of the referee. Similarly, print journalists can no longer fudge controversial moments already seen by millions of viewers.

It is another basic tenet of a Celtic supporter's philosophy that the SFA is, and always has been, the enemy. There was at one time a considerable element of truth in this view and I would like to think that the contents of this book have proven that. Again, it might be time to take another tack. Celtic are now recognised as one of the leaders of the modern Scottish game; in general, their opinion is sought and their advice given considerable respect. The basic difference between the stances taken by Bob Kelly and Fergus McCann against the SFA was a vital one: both were incensed at what they considered administrative injustice and fought against it, but Kelly saw anti-Catholic feeling as the primary motivation while McCann saw an anti-business prejudice as the cause. It is an indication of how much the times have changed that both Kelly and McCann were probably correct in their assessments.

Any action taken these days by the SFA against Celtic should be considered strictly on its own merits, and not be discoloured by a century of perceived bias.

Two questions should be asked.

Are Celtic followers capable of breaking away from a tradition of referee baiting?

Are Celtic supporters capable of giving up a tradition of distrust and suspicion?

Nobody can doubt that Celtic have made a massive contribution to the Scottish game, not least of all by winning the European Cup in 1967 (and with a Protestant manager). There still exists a feeling of goodwill for Celtic throughout Scotland, generated by the average Scot's appreciation of the admirable skills exhibited by some Celtic sides and individual players. It is time to tap into that reservoir, but it can be done only by giving up the disreputable habits that have at times disgraced the club and caused rightful hostility from other communities within Scotland.

I would like to think that true Celtic supporters can rise to the twin challenges posed above, but the conduct of many of those who travel to away games continues to be a major stumbling-block to real progress.

The visit of Celtic to a provincial ground these days is too often accompanied by a horde of supporters who seem to take a perverse and outdated delight in depicting themselves as valiant underdogs, defending the downtrodden, and the persecuted – and refusing to bow to the will of the majority. In 2001 this attitude is as false as it is objectionable.

Jock Stein returns to the dugout, having encouraged a section of the Celtic support to stop sectarian chants during a game with Stirling Albion

Consider the following.

Is it any surprise that referees, baited mercilessly by thousands of hostile spectators, might be slow to give too many breaks to the visitors?

Is it any surprise that ordinary, average Scots, there to support their own side, resent the mindless singing of IRA anthems?

Is it any surprise that citizens of smaller Scottish towns should feel alarm and dismay at the invasion of its territory by Celtic legions, many of whom are obviously under the influence of alcohol?